Children's Literature Studies

Children's Literature Studies

Cases and Discussions

Linda C. Salem

LIBRARIES
UNLIMITED

A Member of the Greenwood Publishing Group

Westport, Connecticut • London

Library of Congress Cataloging-in-Publication Data

Salem, Linda C.
    Children's literature studies : cases and discussions / by Linda C. Salem.
        p. cm.
    Includes bibliographical references and index.
    ISBN 1–59158–089–7 (pbk. : alk. paper)
    1. Children—Books and reading—United States.   2. Children's literature—Study and teaching—
United States.   3. Children's literature—Censorship—United States.   4. Education—Curricula—
Censorship—United States.   5. Challenged books—United States.   I. Title.
    Z1037.A1S23   2006
    028.5'50973—dc22   2005028602

British Library Cataloguing in Publication Data is available.

Library of Congress Catalog Card Number: 2005028602
ISBN: 1–59158–089–7

First published in 2006

Libraries Unlimited, 88 Post Road West, Westport, CT 06881
A Member of the Greenwood Publishing Group, Inc.
www.lu.com

Printed in the United States of America

The paper used in this book complies with the
Permanent Paper Standard issued by the National
Information Standards Organization (Z39.48–1984).

10 9 8 7 6 5 4 3 2 1

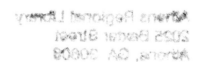

Contents

Acknowledgments vii

Introduction ix

1 Literary Quality 1

2 Are You Ready for a Challenge? 13

3 Religion 23

4 Languages and Books 39

5 Peace and Children's Literature 53

6 Children's Literature and People with Disabilities 69

7 Gender 85

8 Literature with GLBTQ Characters, Themes, and Content 103

Appendix: Book Review Resources 121

Bibliography 123

Index 149

Acknowledgments

I wish to acknowledge the advising, consultation, and expertise offered by J.L. Brown, Evangelina Bustamante Jones, Michael Cart, Robin Clements, Sharon Coatney, Melissa D. Engleman, Doug Fisher, Nancy Hartshorne, Maggie Hawkins, William Huntley, Laurie Smith, and Phillip White.

Introduction

This book is designed for teachers to help them discuss books in ways that inspire collegiality, collaboration, and scholarship in book evaluation and selection. It is specifically designed for preservice teachers, working teachers, and school librarians, enrolled in college-level children's literature courses.

Teachers need the opportunity to discuss multiple viewpoints on children's and young adult literature to enhance their professional discussions with colleagues, students, parents, and community members. This was brought to my attention one day when I was teaching a children's literature course for preservice teachers. Two students approached me quietly and disclosed that someone in their assigned reading group for the class refused to read *Harry Potter and the Sorcerer's Stone* (Rowling 1998) for religious reasons. They explained that this made it difficult for them to complete their group project. Their discussion with me was secretive. While this may have been their attempt not to embarrass the student, it signaled to me their uncertainty about how to discuss this question in order to resolve the problem with their classmates.

This book grew out of the teaching resources I subsequently developed to encourage discussion and problem solving among classmates because of this event. It began with development of a lecture, a case study, and discussion questions about censorship and the *Harry Potter* series. The lecture provided students with information about censorship, book challenges, and the critical literacy approach that relies on dialogue and mutual respect. The study was designed to include many perspectives to present a balanced description of the responses to the J. K. Rowling books in a particular community. Used as a workshop exercise, this allowed for structured discussion time, to encourage honest input and critical analysis, and encouraged students to build on their knowledge about the case with their own research.

Each chapter in this book begins with a bibliographic essay that introduces the topic of the chapter to the reader and points out some of the most interesting and important developments since the 1970s. The bibliographic essay is not exhaustive but is designed as a starting point for discussion and further research.

One or two studies follow the essay, depending on the chapter. Not all of the studies in the book are scenarios surrounding books and schools. Resource review studies are also used.

A list of references for each chapter is provided at the end of the chapter. These references represent sources that teachers can use to conduct further research to find multiple perspectives about books. In this way, teachers can continue to follow the social and literary history of literature as it unfolds.

Overview of Studies

The study presented in Chapter 1 on literary quality concerns the story of the expansion of a California state reading list. Chapter 2 on book challenges includes a study that describes a parents' organization that is mobilizing to identify "bad books." A second study in Chapter 2 concerns the reconsideration of the use of Maya Angelou's book *I Know Why the Caged Bird Sings* (1970) in curriculum. Chapter 3 on religion includes a case that describes how J. K. Rowling's *Harry Potter* series was banned in a community. This chapter also includes a study that recounts how religion played a role in a recent Texas textbook adoption process. In Chapter 4, the chapter on languages, one study very briefly introduces readers to a debate about Ebonics in Oakland. This is perhaps the least developed of the studies but refers students to a book on the debate that does explore it in depth. The other study in the chapter on languages is an invitation to students to explore resources for finding books for youth published in many different languages. Chapter 5, describes a case in which objections were raised and students became involved in a debate about the use of Luis J. Rodriguez's book *Always Running: La Vida Loca, Gang Days in L.A.* (1993). The study in Chapter 6, the chapter about children's literature and people with disabilities, revisits an older title, *The Summer of the Swans* (Byars 1970), and invites students to examine various interpretations of the depiction of characters in the story. In Chapter 7, the chapter on gender, the study asks students to review and analyze the uses of gender-based reader's resources on the Web and invites students to try "reading against the grain" together. Finally, Chapter 8 is about GLBTQ (gay, lesbian, bisexual, transgendered, questioning)-themed literature for youth. The case included in this chapter describes a request for reconsideration of the use of *Rainbow Boys* (Sanchez 2001) at a school and provides various perspectives on the book from reviewers and from the book's author Alex Sanchez.

Method for Developing Cases Based on Real Events

In the *Handbook of Research on Teaching the English Language Arts*, a *case study* is defined as "an empirical study that investigates a contemporary phenomenon within its real-life context when the boundaries between phenomenon and context are not clearly evident and when multiple sources of evidence are used" (Birnbaum, Emig, and Fisher 2003, 192). Other examples of the case approach used in the field of language arts include James Moffett's book *Storm in the Mountains: A Case Study of Censorship, Conflict, and Consciousness* (1988). *Meeting Censorship in the School: A Series of Case Studies* (1967) by Dennis J. Hannan and published by the National Council of Teachers of English, is another example.

The studies provided in this book are meant to help teachers explore multiple perceptions about books, and the stories that surround books, as told by teachers, parents, students, politicians, administrators, reviewers, publishers, reporters, authors, and librarians. The cases are written using excerpts from print, Internet, and interview resources. The cases do not tell the complete story, and they may not tell the story well, depending on the resources. They reflect the bias, spin, and interpretation of reporters and others who quote and are quoted to recount the story. To focus students on the events and not the individuals involved, in many cases, the names of those who were quoted in news and other sources are omitted. This is especially true when the news source or account seemed subjective. Other names are included usually if the individual's point of view seemed clear. Resources are referenced that were used to develop a description of a case. The studies in this book are not meant to provide a complete treatment of the views on any work or about any particular case.

Cases are intended to stimulate discussion and analysis of multiple perspectives. The case descriptions are an attempt to sketch out basic events and describe clearly articulated opinions. The studies are meant to provide a "measure of vicarious experience because case study presents a holistic and lifelike description, like those readers normally encounter in their experience of the world" (Birnbaum, Emig, and Fisher 2003, 192). Some cases tell a story of a community's response to literature based on the contents of newspaper articles, wire service items, and newsletter articles. Other cases describe literary perspectives of books based on book reviews from different publications and from different years. Resources consulted included scholarly journal articles and books, book reviews, opinions from Web sites, and personal interviews.

Readers are encouraged to analyze, with the help of the background essay for each chapter, what might have contributed to changes in the reception of a book. The cases invite analysis and discussion and are not meant to judge perspectives.

This book is designed to excite teachers about continuing to research stories that surround books and to encourage them to teach about the cultural resonance of books. This resonance may involve the relationship of one case to other cases, or it may be a result of those who create information about the case (192). It may relate to "historical background, physical setting, economic, political, legal or aesthetic" concerns (193).

The studies will be the most effective if students read the books described in the cases. While cases may be examined without this background, discussions are more interesting and critical when students bring their opinions about books to bear upon the views expressed in the cases.

The topics discussed in this book were selected based on the lack of resources in these areas available to me as an instructor for teaching preservice teachers about children's literature. The topics reflect those areas of bibliography for which I found myself creating resource lists and activities to supplement course materials.

References

Angelou, Maya. 1970. *I know why the caged bird sings.* New York: Random House.

Birnbaum, June, Janet Emig, and Douglas Fisher. 2003. Case studies: Placing literacy phenomena within their actual context. In *Handbook of research on teaching the English language arts,* 2nd ed., eds. James Flood, Diane Lapp, James R. Squire, and Julie M. Jensen, 192–200. Mahwah, NJ: L. Erlbaum Associates.

Byars, Betsy. 1970. *The summer of the swans.* New York: Viking Press.

Hannan, Dennis J. 1967. *Meeting censorship in the school: A series of case studies.* Champaign, IL: National Council of Teachers of English.

Moffett, James. 1988. *Storm in the mountains: A case study of censorship, conflict, and consciousness.* Carbondale: Southern Illinois University Press.

Rodriguez, Luis J. 1993. *Always running: La vida loca, gang days in L.A.* Willimantic, CT: Curbstone Press.

Rowling, J. K. 1998. *Harry Potter and the sorcerer's stone.* New York: A. A. Levine Books.

Sanchez, Alex. 2001. *Rainbow boys.* New York: Simon and Schuster.

1

Literary Quality

Children's and young adult books are evaluated for quality from both sociological and literary perspectives. Many groups weigh in on books. Scholarly judgments about books are expressed through the identification of a canon, through critical book reviews, and through articles and books on literary analysis and criticism. Literary critics debate the parameters of literary quality by applying different forms of analysis. Instruction in the analysis of literature typically includes the application of "various approaches, literary and social, to the process of critical interpretation and evaluation" (Rosenblatt 2003, 72).

Teachers and librarians express judgments about books through the creation of booklists, bibliographies, and awards and through book reviews. Literary quality is the most important selection guideline to teachers and librarians. The definition of *literary quality* has been layered and qualified by teachers and librarians in fluid and interesting ways, and this is in evidence through a retrospective review of the professional literature since the 1970s. Many different selection guidelines and evaluation criteria have been designed to be used for different types of books. These guidelines incorporate the principles of reader response theory and formal literary analysis, but they also reflect attention to trends in pedagogy, like whole language learning, genre studies, and most recently, critical literacy.

Parents and other community members express their views about books but do so through less formal but more direct venues. Their voices are often heard in meetings with teachers, in newspaper editorials, on Web sites, through organized groups, and at school board meetings.

Educational community tension around the use of literature in schools involves the tension created between those who want literature to transmit values, those who want an emphasis on classic, standard, Western literature, and those who "seek to change the canon to reflect the diverse minority groups in our society" (Rosenblatt 2003, 71).

Critical Literacy

Some educators think that literature for young people can teach social responsibility. For example, many teachers and librarians think it is important to alert "children to the ways in which literature may convey prejudice" (Pinsent 1997, 3). They support limiting the influence of "negative stereotypes and prejudiced language" found in books (3). To this end, numerous sets of evaluation guidelines and criteria have been written to raise awareness about prejudice reflected in literature for youth (Pinsent 1997, 5; Briggs 1996, 24).

The critical literacy approach to using books with young people asks readers "to think about what effect" readings have on "different groups of people" in the service of social justice. It asks readers to be aware of "what other people's writing does to us" (Fox 2001, 110). Readers should consider multiple viewpoints and examine sociopolitical issues (Lewison et al. 2002, 382). Critical literacy is based on teaching students "that texts are culturally, socially, politically, and historically constructed and situated" (390). It relies on teachers' willingness to challenge, examine, and possibly revise their own "long-held beliefs" (390).

The premise of critical literacy is a sociological one. Joel Taxel explains the importance of a sociological approach to the study of children's literature. It is "impossible to understand the evolution and development of children's literature without situating the books of a given era in the sociocultural and political milieu of that period" (Taxel 1995, 160–161).

Appreciation of Fiction

Others think that "literature cannot and should not be expected to teach" social responsibility (Babbitt 1996, 34). Students come to school having already learned social responsibility, and fiction should be used to teach the "appreciation of fiction" (34). According to the Children's Literature Association, literature programs should emphasize "theory of literature," not "cultural, political, religious, or social indoctrination" (May 1995, 12). Author Virginia Hamilton writes that she writes "fictions and not sociology" (Hamilton 2001, 23).

Political Correctness

Mem Fox credits critical literacy with raising awareness but worries that it can turn children into "tiresome little thought-police allowing no texts at all to pass muster without groans of Puritan self-righteousness and finger-pointing" (Fox 2001, 110). This reputation for hyper-vigilance has led some to criticize approaches that emphasize the importance of including multiple and diverse voices in fiction collections. The criticism is that this approach leads to selecting books based on political correctness first, then literary quality.

Fox recognizes how her words affect readers. She examines her own writing to limit "stereotyping," marginalizing, and doing "social, economic, or emotional harm" (109). Author Katherine Paterson writes that it causes her anguish to think that she has written something offensive to one of her readers. But, she admits, the books she writes will never be politically correct because she cannot avoid bias. Paterson cannot eliminate herself entirely from her writing, and her books may always offend someone (Paterson 1996, 344). Paterson creates characters who "will never be blameless role models for today's children and youth" and whose stories "invite disappointment or even disapproval from left, right, and centre—in short, from any reader who looks to fiction to support a point of view rather than to mirror human experience" (349).

But in his literature review on the topic, Joel Taxel (1995) traces how the use of the term *political correctness* has been a strategy for attacking multiculturalism and for ending discussions about diverse communities. The history of this conflict resides in James Banks's description of multiculturalists and Western traditionalists. Banks explains that multiculturalists seek curriculum reform to "more accurately reflect the histories and cultures of ethnic groups and women" (Banks 1993, 7). Western traditionalists fear that feminist scholars, ethnic minority scholars, and others threaten "western history, literature, and culture" (4). The term *PC* (politically correct) has also been used to criticize the use of inclusive language (Pinsent 1997, 2).

The value remains preeminent that book selectors must place literary quality ahead of selecting books that do not include offensive content (Harris 1995, 279). Teachers have argued that these are not mutually exclusive goals. Literary scholarship extends beyond formalist definitions of literary quality. Many approaches to literary analysis are conceptually designed to consider the meaning of offensive content within a determination of literary quality.

Analysis of Literature

The importance of consulting literary criticism for teachers has long been acknowledged by the National Council of Teachers of English, by the Children's Literature Association, and by the International Reading Association (Stott 1981, 40; Rosenblatt 1991, 62; 2003, 72). Many readings succinctly describe the devotion of the New Critics between the 1930s and the 1960s to the one "right" interpretation of a work based on formalist analysis by literary experts and how this approach influenced classroom teaching practices (Rosenblatt 1991, 58; May 1995, 22; Parker 1991, 23). The civil unrest of the late 1960s and 1970s set the tone for reader response theory to validate multiple "aesthetic" interpretations of works based upon the reader's personal identification with a reading or the psychological or sociopolitical interpretations made by readers of a work (Rosenblatt 1991, 59; Zipes 1996, 366).

In the 1970s, the structuralism movement invited critics to apply linguistic concepts in literary analysis. Then the deconstructionists challenged the signification of words themselves and challenged critics to decenter works of literature in order to locate other meanings or emphases (Rosenblatt 1991, 59; May 1995, 23). For example, Beverly Naidoo deconstructs racism in literature and positions it as a form of violence. Naidoo asserts that educators "have a responsibility for developing this type of critical awareness in young readers" (1995, 36). She writes that children "need to learn how to deconstruct racist imagery and to understand the processes by which people have been, and are, denied their humanity" (36).

Some argue that the influences of approaches to literary analysis since the 1970s have reverberated through the publishing world, as views of "feminist critics, Marxist scholars, [and] minority critics" have influenced what books have been published for children (May 1995, 23).

Sources to Consult for Multiple Viewpoints

Canon

The history of literary analysis relates to some controversy over the Children's Literature Association's attempt to identify a canon of children's literature called for by John C. Stott in his 1978 presidential address to the organization (May 1995, 29). Hershel Parker gives a traditional argument in favor of canon setting. He argues that without instilling in students "some knowledge of an (ever-varying) core of American classics," we give up "the idea of having any communal knowledge of American literature," and the society "will be poorer if we lose the aesthetic and richly socializing experience of internalizing a set of national classics" (Parker 1991, 22).

Contemporary scholars argue that literary analysis has moved past one "right" interpretation and that reader response theory, feminist analysis, cultural analysis, psychological/mythological analysis, new historicism, and other approaches to literature have opened interpretation to multiple perspectives. For example, Peter Hunt writes about the "idea that 'literature' is the writing authorized and prioritized by a powerful minority" and that "the concept of a 'canon'" or adhering to it means "prioritizing one group" and "alienating the rest" (Hunt 1996, 10).

Perry Nodelman thinks *canon* suggests "regulation and representation" and "universally binding standards" (1980, 3). Nodelman has argued that the Children's Literature Association (ChLA) did not want to create "a binding list of teachable titles" but a list of "admirable books," if only to "define what is admirable in children's literature" (May 1995, 30). A canon could be "a list of children's books" that we all "agree are particularly important (because they are controversial, or innovative, or popular) or particularly admirable" or historically significant. A canon lists the books that anyone "interested in children's literature should know, including . . . literate children" (Nodelman 1980, 8). Nodelman developed a tentative list of books everyone interested in children's literature should know, drawing on the consensus reflected in survey results from the readership of the *Children's Literature Association Quarterly*. This list is not a canon but is meant to be a subject of argument (5). The ChLA effort to identify a canon resulted in a three-volume publication titled *Touchstones: Reflections on the Best in Children's Literature* (1985). This work includes descriptions of books accompanied by essays explaining why "a particular book might be considered a touchstone" for excellence (Nodelman 1985, v, 30). Volume 1 includes fiction books; volume 2 addresses folk literature, poetry, myths, and legends; and volume 3 is about picture books.

Booklists

Those in the teaching and library professions create many best books lists. They distinguish books with awards and honors. These resources help guide others in book selection (May 1995, 29). The process of list making and bibliography creation among teachers and librarians is one they see as ongoing and creative, and one booklist is never viewed as the last word on book recommendations. As the professionals who make the purchasing decisions that influence the book market, they use lists to communicate about which books are best for different purposes (29). Listing is usually governed by literary merit.

The National Council of Teachers of English (NCTE) regularly publishes booklists to address the needs of different grades. There is *Adventuring with Books: A Booklist for Pre-K–Grade-6* (NCTE 2002), *Kaleidoscope: A Multicultural Booklist for Grades K–8* (Hansen-Krening 2003), *Your Reading: An Annotated Booklist for Middle School and Junior High* (Brown and Stephens 2003), and *Books for You: An Annotated Booklist for Senior High* (Beers and Lesesne 2001). These lists help "teachers, librarians, parents, and students connect with good recently published books" (Brown and Stephens 2003, xvii).

In addition to teachers and librarians, young readers create best books lists. For example, the International Reading Association and the Children's Book Council sponsor Children's Choices at http://www.reading.org/resources/tools/choices_childrens.html. They also sponsor Young Adults' Choices at http://www.reading.org/resources/tools/choices_young_adults.html. The Childrens' Choices list appears in the October issue of *The Reading Teacher*. The Young Adults' Choices list appears in the November issue of *The Journal of Adolescent & Adult Literacy*.

Awards, Honors, and Notables

Many booklists and awards select books based on literary excellence. The Caldecott Medal, the Newbery Award, and the Pura Belpré Award are sponsored by the American Library Association's Association for Library Services to Children (ALA/ALSC). Every year the ALA/ALSC also creates a list called Children's Notable Books. The Coretta Scott King Award is sponsored by the ALA's Ethnic and Multicultural Information Exchange Round Table (EMIERT). The ALA's Young Adult Library Services Association (YALSA) sponsors the Michael L. Printz Award for Excellence in Young Adult Literature. Other awards made based on literary merit include the Americas Book Award; the *Boston Globe–Horn Book* Awards for Excellence in Children's Literature; the Children's Literature Association's Phoenix Award; the Josette Frank Award of the Bank Street College of Education; the Michael L. Printz Award for Excellence in Young Adult Literature; the National Book Award for Children's Books (U.S.); the Scott O'Dell Award for Historical Fiction; the Sydney Taylor Book Award; and the Tomas Rivera Mexican-American Children's Book Award. Many other book awards exist, but these are some of the best known.

Book Review Sources

Book review sources help teachers, librarians, scholars, parents, and young readers choose what they need from the growing number of books published for young readers. Many of these sources offer an online source to consult for finding book reviews. For a list of book review resources that are written from many perspectives, see Appendix A. This list of review resources is also online at http://infodome.sdsu.edu/research/guides/clreviews.shtml.

Databases

The role of the book awards, booklists, and book reviews as tools for selection has been transformed by book databases. For example, the subscription-based *Children's Literature Comprehensive Database* at http://clcd.odyssi.com includes nearly 900,000 records, including 130,000 critical reviews of thousands of children's books. About 1,500 new reviews are added each month. The database lists the book awards, booklists, and reviews for many titles. The database is searchable by fiction, nonfiction, grade level, age, genre, subject, author, title, review, reviewer, best books lists, and awards. In this resource, the criticism and praise from scholars, teachers, and librarians are gathered together in one record for a book. Searchers can read book reviews from a variety of sources. They can find out the awards books have won and lists on which they have been included.

Full-text databases of children's books are also available at no charge to searchers. For example, *Literature for Children* at http://palmm.fcla.edu/juv is a full-text archive of historical children's literature intended for scholars to use for research. *The International Children's Digital Library* at http://www.icdlbooks.org offers teachers an extensive full-text collection of books published all over the world and in many languages.

Case: Expansion of Reading Lists in California

The input of many voices plays a role in list making, as in the case of the expansion of the California Department of Education's *Recommended Literature: Kindergarten through Grade Twelve*.

In 1998, two members of the San Francisco School Board, Steve Phillips and Keith Jackson, proposed that 40 percent of required reading for "high school students come from nonwhite authors" (Asimov 1998e). Nanette Asimov of the *San Francisco Chronicle* wrote a series of articles following the story and recording many opinions about the case. The description of this story is drawn primarily from her reports but presents the basic story.

In 1998, San Francisco high school students were required to read Mark Twain's *Huckleberry Finn*, Chaucer's *Canterbury Tales*, and *Romeo and Juliet* by William Shakespeare. The board members' proposal required ten books per year, seven of which would come from a required reading list that would include four books by authors who are not Caucasian (Asimov 1998e).

Steve Phillips, one of the board members proposing the plan, argued that black children from the projects learn differently because of the impact of their environment. In particular, the existing requirement to read *Huckleberry Finn* was offensive because of the repeated use of the word *nigger* in the book. At the time of the proposal, the board mostly supported the plan, although one board member pointed out that a "required" reading list did not limit teachers from using the books they wanted to use in classes (Asimov 1998e).

Yvonne Larsen, president of the State Board of Education, called the proposal "literary affirmative action" and opposed it, calling for literature selection according to excellence and for "scholarly reasons." Board member Phillips, who had been an English major at Stanford University, argued that "great literature transcends" ethnicity and culture but also that it comes from all cultures, and he argued against requiring literature from only one culture (Asimov 1998e).

National and state response to the proposal came quickly. The U.S. Department of Education, under Education Secretary Richard Riley, stated that it did not endorse curriculum percentages based on ethnicity. Delaine Eastin, the California State Superintendent, said she opposed "racial quotas" in book selection and recommended encouraging children to read much more to expose them to literature from diverse perspectives. Ward Connerly, the University of California regent, well known for leading the "effort to eliminate affirmative action in state hiring, contracting and public education," argued that great writers will rise to the top of best book lists because of literary excellence and that other requirements for adding books to lists made the quality of the books on the lists "suspect" (Asimov 1998d). San Francisco Mayor Willie Brown did not endorse the proposal, citing lack of information about it, but supported increasing diversity and providing many "different quality sources to students" (Asimov 1998d). School Superintendent Bill Rojas opposed the proposal, arguing that no research supported the approach, but he supported providing more "diversity in the reading selection" (Asimov 1998d).

Hundreds of San Franciscans, including parents, students, teachers, and business owners, attended the meeting when the board was to vote on the proposal. In a meeting lasting five hours, community members "demanded more literature by nonwhite authors," and protestors' signs read "Every Ethnicity Has Classics" and "Ethnic literature is American literature" (Asimov 1998b). A teacher argued that the current list was "race-based," and a bookstore owner questioned the relevance of works in Middle English by Chaucer to students. Students argued that gaining admission to a black college was harder when only one book by an African American author was taught in high school. Board members argued that they wanted to include literature from many perspectives and to ensure that students graduated with "knowledge of the classical canon of literature" (Asimov 1998b).

The result was that the board did not set quotas but did unanimously adopt a resolution to diversify the required reading list according to "race, ethnicity and sexual orientation" (Asimov 1998b). The final resolution also required the required reading list to include works "referenced on the SAT" (Asimov 1998a).

The controversy called attention to the lack of diversity in California's recommended reading list. Carol Jago, regional director of the California Reading & Literature Project at the University of California at Los Angeles (UCLA), called for the inclusion of quality literature by a wide range of writers such as Amy Tan, Gloria Naylor, Laura Esquivel, Cynthia Kadohata, and Itabari Njeri (Asimov 1998c). The California Association of Teachers of English, the California Reading Association, and the California Department of Education supported expanding the list (Asimov 1998c).

The resulting expanded list of 2,700 titles was developed into a searchable database, now located at http://www.cde.ca.gov/ci/rl/ll. The list was expanded by a team of library media teachers, teachers, curriculum planners, administrators, and parents (http://www.cde.ca.gov/ci/rl/ll/litrlacknowledge.asp).

Debby Lott was the consultant for the Reading Language Arts Leadership Office of the California Department of Education and content specialist for the expansion of the list. Lott said the objectives for the new list were to update it with contemporary works; to provide a resource to meet the new language arts standards; to have books where every child in California could see themselves; and to represent the six most used languages in California. She said that teams from across the state tallied how books matched various categories of grade-level span, culture, language, genre, and curricular connections (Debby Lott, personal communication).

Consultants who helped to revise the list call it a "work in progress" because books will be added and deleted in coming years. The database format will make this process easier.

Critics have wondered whether the list's lack of clearly identifiable literary standards reflects poorly on California teachers' ability to agree upon what the classics are and to teach them (Rutten 2001). Some teachers have argued to have classics that were dropped from the list restored (Groves 2001). Some believe that a "core, mandatory reading list" made up of classics is the key to "transmitting at least the basics of a common literary culture" (Rutten 2001). Others argue that California is "such a diverse state" that a "single set of books is too narrowing" (Rutten 2001).

Discussion Questions

1. How did the concept of "classic literary canon" influence this case?

2. How did various approaches to literary analysis and criticism play a role in this case?

3. What role did critical literacy play?

4. How was the revision of the booklists influenced by multiple perspectives?

5. What views about the proposal were represented by national, state, and local officials?

6. What views were represented and what issues were raised by the local community? How did these differ from other views about the case?

7. How and why did the school board's decision consider concerns of traditionalists and multiculturalists?

8. How did local, state, and national officials respond to the idea of requiring more books by authors based on ethnicity?

9. How was the concept of literary quality debated?

10. Did the school board make the right decision? Discuss why or why not.

11. Why did the San Francisco case influence the eventual major redesign of the state recommended reading list?

12. What differences do you think changes to required reading lists made?

13. How does the database format of the recommended list change how it is used?

References

Asimov, Nanette. 1998a. S.F. high schools to get diverse authors list. *San Francisco Chronicle*, March 21.

———. 1998b. School board strikes deal on books. Resolution stresses diversity, not quotas. *San Francisco Chronicle*, March 20.

——— 1998c. State's teachers agree—Book list too white. *San Francisco Chronicle*, March 14.

———. 1998d. New foe of race-based book lists. San Francisco proposal wrong, school chief says. *San Francisco Chronicle*, March 12.

———. 1998e. San Francisco weighs race-based reading list. 40% by nonwhites proposed in schools. *San Francisco Chronicle,* March 11.

Babbitt, Natalie. 1996. Protecting children's literature. In *Only connect: Readings on children's literature*, 3rd ed., ed. Sheila Egoff, Gordon Stubbs, Ralph Ashley, and Wendy Sutton, 32–38. New York: Oxford University Press.

Banks, James A. 1993. The canon debate, knowledge construction, and multicultural education. *Educational Researcher* (June–July): 4–14.

Barton, D. 1998. Schools pushed to have more works by minority writers on reading lists. *Rocky Mountain News,* April 5.

Beers, G. Kylene, and Teri S. Lesesne, eds. 2001. *Books for you: An annotated booklist for senior high.* 14th ed. Urbana, IL: National Council of Teachers of English.

Briggs, Julia. 1996. Critical opinion: Reading children's books. In *Only connect: Readings on children's literature*, 3rd ed., ed. Sheila Egoff, Gordon Stubbs, Ralph Ashley, and Wendy Sutton, 18–31. New York: Oxford University Press.

Brown, Jean E., and Elaine C. Stephens, eds. 2003. *Your reading: An annotated booklist for middle school and junior high.* 11th ed. Urbana, IL: National Council of Teachers of English.

California Department of Education. 2002– . *Recommended literature: Kindergarten through grade twelve.* Sacramento, CA: California Department of Education. http://www.cde.ca.gov/ci/rl/ll.

Day, B. 1993. State refuses to take book off school reading list. *Los Angeles Times*, April 16.

Fox, Mem. 2001. Have we lost our way? *Language Arts* 79(2): 105–113.

Fractor, Jann Sorrell, Marjorie Ciruti Woodruff, Miriam G. Martinez, and William H. Teale. 1993. Let's not miss opportunities to promote voluntary reading: Classroom libraries in the elementary school. *Reading Teacher* 46(6): 476–484.

Galda, Lee, and Bernice E. Cullinan. 2003. Literature for literacy: What research says about the benefits of using trade books in the classroom. In *Handbook of research on teaching the English language arts*, 2nd ed., ed. James Flood, Diane Lapp, James R. Squire, and Julie M. Jensen, 640–647. Mahwah, NJ: Lawrence Erlbaum Associates.

Groves, Martha. 2001. The state education department vastly widens best books list. *Los Angeles Times*, June 29.

Hamilton, Virginia. 2001. Author profile. In *Beauty, brains, and brawn: The construction of gender in children's literature*, ed. Susan Lehr, 21–23. Portsmouth, NH: Heinemann.

Hansen-Krening, Nancy, ed. 2003. *Kaleidoscope: A multicultural booklist for grades K–8*. Urbana, IL: National Council of Teachers of English.

Harris, Violet J. 1995. "May I read this book?" Controversies, dilemmas, and delights in children's literature. In *Battling dragons: Issues and controversy in children's literature*, ed. Susan Lehr, 275–283. Portsmouth, NH: Heinemann.

Hunt, Peter. 1996. Defining children's literature. In *Only connect: Readings on children's literature*, 3rd ed., ed. Sheila Egoff, Gordon Stubbs, Ralph Ashley, and Wendy Sutton, 3–17. New York: Oxford University Press.

Levy, P. 1992. Reading lists diversify, but complaints continue. *Minneapolis Star Tribune*, September 21.

Lewison, Mitzi, Amy Seely Flint, Katie Van Sluys, and Roxanne Henkin. 2002. Taking on critical literacy: The journey of newcomers and novices. *Language Arts* 79(5): 382–392.

Los Angeles Times. 2001a. A reading list must appeal to students to be teachable. July 23.

Los Angeles Times. 2001b. State education department vastly widens best books list. June 29.

May, Jill P. 1995. *Children's literature and critical theory: Reading and writing for understanding*. New York: Oxford University Press.

Naidoo, Beverly. 1995. Undesirable publication: A journey to Jo'burg. In *Battling dragons: Issues and controversy in children's literature*, ed. Susan Lehr, 31–38. Portsmouth, NH: Heinemann.

National Council of Teachers of English. 2002. *Adventuring with books: A booklist for pre-K–grade 6*. Urbana, IL: National Council of Teachers of English.

New York Times. 1989. Education. School reading lists shun women and black authors. June 21.

Nilsen, Alleen Pace. 1991. Speaking loudly for good books: Promoting the wheat & winnowing the chaff. *School Library Journal* 37(9): 180–183.

Nodelman, Perry. 1985. *Touchstones: Reflections on the best in children's literature*. 3 vols. West Lafayette, IN: Children's Literature Association.

———, ed. 1981. Children's literature & literary theory. *Children's Literature Association Quarterly* (Spring): 9–40.

———. 1980. Grand canon suite. *Children's Literature Association Quarterly* (Summer): 1, 3–8.

Parker, Hershel. 1991. The price of diversity: An ambivalent minority report on the American literary canon. *College Literature* 18(3): 15–30.

Paterson, Katherine. 1996. Cultural politics from a writer's point of view. In *Only connect: Readings on children's literature*, 3rd ed., ed. Sheila Egoff, Gordon Stubbs, Ralph Ashley, and Wendy Sutton, 343–349. New York: Oxford University Press.

Pinsent, Pat. 1997. *Children's literature and the politics of equality*. New York: Teacher's College Press.

Rosenblatt, Louise M. 2003. Literary theory. In *Handbook of research on teaching the English language arts*, 2nd ed., ed. James Flood, Diane Lapp, James R. Squire, and Julie M. Jensen, 67–73. Mahwah, NJ: Lawrence Erlbaum Associates.

————. 1991. Literary theory. In *Handbook of research on teaching the English language arts*, ed. James Flood, Julie M. Jensen, Diane Lapp, and James R. Squire, 57–62. New York: Macmillan.

Rutten, Tim. 2001. Weighing the classics. Whitman and Cervantes are out, but educators say California's new reading list is a serious blueprint for compromise in the culture war. *Los Angeles Times*, July 15.

Stott, John C. 1981. Literary criticism and teaching children. *Children's Literature Association Quarterly* 1: 39–40.

Taxel, Joel. 1995. Cultural politics and writing for young people. In *Battling dragons: Issues and controversy in children's literature*, ed. Susan Lehr, 155–169. Portsmouth, NH: Heinemann.

Walsh, D. 1998. San Francisco proposal is more extreme than others. *San Francisco Examiner*, March 13.

Washington Post. 1995. Deciding what to read. April 28.

Zipes, Jack. 1996. Taking political stock: New theoretical and critical approaches to Anglo-American children's literature in the 1980s. In *Only connect: Readings on children's literature*, 3rd ed., ed. Sheila Egoff, Gordon Stubbs, Ralph Ashley, and Wendy Sutton, 365–376. New York: Oxford University Press.

2

Are You Ready for a Challenge?

In 1967, a committee of the National Council of Teachers of English sponsored a study to collect information about how teachers reacted to book challenges. The result was *Meeting Censorship in the Schools: A Series of Case Studies* (1967). This resource provides "illustrations . . . for future teachers of English of what the English teacher might do when confronted with attempts to curtail the student's right to read" (Hove and NCTE 1967, viii). In it, case studies showed instances of teachers defending books and instances of teachers censoring books.

As a teacher or librarian, how would you react to a book challenge? Since the NCTE study, many scholars and organizations have created resources for teachers to use to understand book challenges and to come up with democratic and creative options for enlightened responses to them.

These resources include history, statistics on challenges, professional guidelines for selection and reconsideration of books, essays in defense of particular books, and updates on the law and recent challenges to books and banned books.

Increased access to ideas stimulates more discussion and debate. In *Battle of the Books: Literary Censorship in the Public Schools, 1950–1985* (1989), Lee Burress explains how paperback book access in the 1950s increased realistic literature in schools. Burress describes how the 1950's Gathings Committee was "established because of the belief that cheap paperback books . . . were a serious moral threat to the republic" (1). The committee proposed a federal censorship board to restrict the movement of books.

In *Censored Books: Critical Viewpoints* (1993a), Karolides, Burress, and Kean continue to explain influences on the response to books. As affordable paperback books increased access to American literature in schools, the democratic values of self-reliance and the equal worth of all persons became more prominent in the curriculum. Debates about these ideas became debates about using particular books. The authors explain that increasing attendance and diversity in schools in the second half of the twentieth century created more tax-paying readers with diverse opinions about books used in public schools (Karolides, Burress, and Kean 1993b, xiv).

In *Censorship and Selection: Issues and Answers for Schools* (2001), Henry Reichman provides an overview of legal issues and statistics on censorship reported by the American Library Association, the National Council of Teachers of English, and the People for the American Way. Reichman concludes that contemporary society debates surround the use of library materials, classroom materials, school libraries, student press, extracurricular materials, and the Internet. Challenges are based on a variety of topics, including gay and lesbian themes, profanity, religion, and violence. By examining these challenges and developing responses to them, educators debate and reflect upon the meaning of academic freedom, the purpose of education, and the definition of censorship (Reichman 2001, 5–10).

Definitions of Censorship

For every resource about censorship, there is a definition of censorship. Reichman defines censorship as "the removal, suppression or restricted circulation of literary, artistic, or educational materials—of images, ideas, and information—on the grounds that these are morally or otherwise objectionable in light of standards applied by the censor" (2001, 2).

Burress (1989) provides definitions and concepts of censorship and selection from many sources. Censorship has been defined as "the attempt to influence teacher decisions on the selection and use of literature . . . using other than purely professional criteria" (Peterson 1975, 4). The act of censorship includes suppressing use of information, removing books from the library or classroom, limiting access to library and instructional materials, and limiting or restricting a student's right to read, to learn, or to be informed and the teacher's right to academic freedom (Bryson and Detty 1982, 49).

Censorship is a negative process and is different from criticism that is a form of discourse and communication about a book. Censorship may be an act of omission. For example, librarians practice self-censorship when they avoid the use of controversial materials (Tremmel 2002, 1).

Intellectual Freedom and the Freedom to Read

The Office for Intellectual Freedom (OIF) of the American Library Association (ALA) defines censorship as the "suppression of ideas and information that certain persons—individuals, groups or government officials—find objectionable or dangerous" (Office for Intellectual Freedom 2005). It defines intellectual freedom as "the right of every individual to both seek and receive information from all points of view without restriction," providing for "free access to all expressions of ideas through which any and all sides of a question, cause or movement may be explored." "The Freedom to Read Statement" adopted by the ALA in 1953 is today endorsed by the National Council of Teachers of English and many other organizations. Affirming the freedom to read as a democratic right guaranteed in the Constitution, it states that "parents and teachers have a responsibility to prepare the young to meet the diversity of experiences in life to which they will be exposed, as they have a responsibility to help them learn to think critically for themselves." It goes on to state that this responsibility cannot "be discharged simply by preventing them from reading works for which they are not yet prepared." Finally, it states that "in these matters values differ, and values cannot be legislated; nor can machinery be devised that will suit the demands of one group without limiting the freedom of others."

Dealing with Challenges

The literature suggests that the teaching and library professions agree that a request for a book's reconsideration is a democratic process. To make this process as transparent and fair as possible, many schools and libraries develop policies and procedures that govern both the selection of books and the process for reconsidering a book. The OIF Web pages also offer teachers many resources for dealing with challenges to books (http://www.ala.org/ala/oif/challenge support/dealing/Default1208.htm). These resources include the *Workbook for Selection Policy Writing* (OIF 1998).

Selection Policies and Principles

Background information about any former complaints about a book in an educational setting or about common criticism of particular books is helpful to know. Teachers can investigate locally to learn about any concerns that have been expressed about the use of particular books in the local setting. In addition, it is useful to find out about any policies or procedures governing who select books, the criteria that should be used, and the content of reading lists. It is also helpful to learn the process a particular school uses for hearing and responding to requests for reconsideration of materials. Such policies and procedures may or may not exist. They may be out of date. They may be detailed and specific or very vague. They may be enforced or ignored. Relationships between teachers, parents, students, administrators, and school board members may also have influenced how discussions about books unfolded.

The *Workbook for Selection Policy Writing* (1998) includes an example of a school district's selection policy, a selection policy statement, selection criteria, and guidelines for dealing with a book challenge and handling the reconsideration of challenged materials.

Book selection is a positive, "democratic process that credits the reader with intelligence and protects their right to read" (Asheim 1953, 67). Book selection is a process of adding materials to enhance the curriculum, to supplement textbooks, and to provide books for readers' enjoyment. In this process of adding to a collection, selectors consider literary quality; appropriateness for reader's level; excellent treatment of controversial issues; the ability to stimulate intellectual and social development; authenticity; appropriateness; interest; content; importance of a book; and the context of use (OIF 1998). Selectors also consider the match of a book to a collection, the balance of popular books and quality literature, and books that offer a variety of diverse experiences and perspectives in which readers can find themselves and others. Selectors also bring their personal philosophy of book selection to the process.

Sources for Finding a History of Concerns About Books

Another way to learn about the background of a book's history of censorship, controversy, or praise is to consult the many print resources that report about the common concerns and opinions expressed about particular books. The first source to consult is the book itself. Reading and evaluating the book in question is essential. By consulting book reviews, a researcher can learn about how a book has been evaluated. (See Appendix for book review sources.)

SLATE Support for the Learning and Teaching of English is an advocacy newsletter from the National Council of Teachers of English that keeps track of and reports on cases of book challenges and censorship in the United States (Suhor 1999, 2000a, 2000b, 2001, 2002). *SLATE* representatives across the United States assist in tracking cases and become involved at the local level as advocates for the freedom to read.

Celebrating Censored Books (Karolides and Burress 1985), *Censored Books: Critical Viewpoints* (Karolides, Burress, and Kean 1993a), and *Censored Books II: Critical Viewpoints, 1985–2000* (Karolides 2002) are two books written specifically to help teachers prepare to defend book choices that may be controversial. These works offer essays that provide rationales for using particular books. The essays are contributed by authors, teachers, librarians, and curriculum specialists in defense of frequently challenged books. Each essayist explains why to read and why to recommend a book. They describe their impressions and interpretations. They describe the concepts in a book and the emotions a book might elicit. They discuss how the book meets curriculum goals and how it relates to the skills, abilities, and interests of students. Essays describe why a book is important in light of the concerns expressed about it. For example, essays describe ways in which literary and popular culture influence a book. These sources include information about how frequently a book is used, reviews to consult about the book, and any awards it has won.

In *Caught Off Guard: Teachers Rethinking Censorship and Controversy* (1999), Ellen Henson Brinkley suggests that teachers consider the subtle distinction between the terms *complaint*, *protest*, *challenge*, and *censorship*. By doing so, teachers may be better able to analyze the specific concerns in controversies they encounter. In turn, this helps teachers determine a measured response (11). Brinkley recommends that teachers prepare to expertly defend their curriculum so that they feel confident when taking the risks inherent in sharing their experiences and political views (13–20).

Case: Parents against Bad Books (PABBIS)

In Fairfax County, Virginia, a parents organization was started called Parents against Bad Books (PABBIS). The pabbis.com Web site reports on books that "parents find objectionable" (Honawar 2001a). At the pabbis.com Web site is the statement that public schools do not have "a mandate for a teacher to use any material they want or personally deem appropriate" (http://www.pabbis.com). The pabbis.com Web site calls attention to references to sex, violence, profanity, and racially insulting quotes in books used in schools by listing the quotes at the site. The organization does not question the literary quality of books included on the list (Seymour 2001).

The goal of PABBIS is to ensure that parents are informed of "how material used and discussed in school is selected" and to make schools document the "rationale for selection" of books (http://www.pabbis.com). One PABBIS idea is that teachers would send home parental-consent forms before "assigning any book that has sexually explicit or anti-religious material" in it (Honawar 2001c). PABBIS collected hundreds of signatures on a petition asking for "a set of specific standards as to what is appropriate reading material for children of different age groups" (Seymour 2001).

Teachers express concern that having to send out such notes could inhibit or intimidate as they make reading selections. Many of the book reviewing sources teachers consult specify appropriate age range next to each review, designating this as "Gr. 9–12" or "Gr. 5–9" and so on.

Parents associated with PABBIS have actively filed numerous book challenges to "draw attention" to a systemic problem that involved parents are not informed of the mature literature available to children in school (Seymour 2002a).

The pabbis.com Web site coaches parents on challenging books, cautioning that they may be labeled a censor or a right-wing lunatic and may be challenged by the American Civil Liberties Union (ACLU) and the ALA. It advises that for individual book challenges parents should ask what the course/library objectives are; if any alternative materials were considered to meet the objectives; what sources were consulted to identify alternative sources; why this book was selected and others rejected; why less controversial books were rejected; and the name and position of the individual who approved the book for use (http://pabbis.com/whattodo.html).

In one example of a challenge from the organizers of PABBIS, a parent in Virginia filed a formal challenge to the inclusion of *Druids* (1991) by Morgan Llywelyn on a suggested reading list and a challenge to the presence of the book in local school libraries. The objection was that the book explicitly referred to oral sex and desire to rape (Honawar 2001a). The school board voted to restrict the book to high school libraries, as suggested by the school superintendent (Cho 2001). Even so, the school superintendent sent a note to school board members to advise them that one of the schools decided to remove the book from the collection and another school had lost their copy and would not replace it. *Druids* was also taken off the suggested reading list.

One school board member said that "schools have a 'moral obligation' to fulfill parents' expectations that schools are safe for their children" (Honawar 2001b). Related to this challenge, another school board member asked a school staff committee to create guidelines for selecting reading materials for English assignments, reading lists, and library materials (Honawar 2001a). The committee recommended notifying parents of readings assigned to students through a syllabus or list. In addition, it recommended a school-based review panel inside each school including the principal and two teachers "to review print materials used in classroom instruction for "culbtural and ethnic differences, language or word choice, religion, disabilities, violence and implied or explicit sexual situations" but not to review age appropriateness (Honawar 2001a).

Patrick Welsh, English teacher at T.C. Williams High School in Alexandria, Virginia, writes that he often "feels in the middle of culture wars" and argues that some, like the Right to Read Coalition fighting PABBIS, would "elevate academic freedom over everything, including good taste and common sense," while others, like PABBIS, "not only underestimate the savvy of kids but exaggerate the power of literature or film to corrupt them" (Welsh 2002). Welsh points out that it is his job as a teacher to give students "material that will mean something to them" in order to "instill a love of literature" (2002).

Discussion Questions

1. Is censorship involved in this case? Why or why not?

2. Do the parents' proposals and challenges infringe upon the right to read or the intellectual freedom of students? Why or why not?

3. What selection policy, procedures, or criteria might help the teachers and the school when interacting with a parents' organization like PABBIS?

4. Discuss your thoughts about the parental role in determining what books should be used in the curriculum.

5. Discuss the approach you would use to select books and readings for your classroom library and for reading assignments.

6. What issues does securing parental consent for each reading that includes controversial content raise for teachers?

7. To what extent does this case reflect open dialogue about the way that books are used? What else might have happened to encourage dialogue about the books in question?

8. Look at the pabbis.com Web site. Discuss the tone of the site. Does it contribute to open dialogue with teachers about books? Does it inhibit dialogue?

9. Discuss you thoughts in general about this case and what it means for professionalism.

Case: *I Know Why the Caged Bird Sings*

In 1988, several parents in the Vista Unified School District in San Diego County complained about the use of the book *I Know Why the Caged Bird Sings* by Maya Angelou. Teachers were using the book with ninety-three ninth-grade honor students. The parents were concerned the sexual violence in the book would negatively affect students who had had a similar traumatic experience (Yasuda 1988b). One parent asked about the effects of the rape scene in the book on a child in class who may have been molested or raped. The parent wondered if the teacher would be prepared to offer crisis intervention in such a case (Yasuda 1988a). To end the controversy, the teacher teaching the book deleted the rape and molestation scenes from the reading assignment (*Los Angeles Times* 1988). The teacher said the book was chosen for "literary merit, but also to teach students about racism and coming obstacles" (1988).

The parents requested the school remove the book from the required ninth-grade reading list. Commenting on the professional role of teachers in selecting materials, one parent involved with the case asserted the belief that "the responsibility of educating our children is a partnership of the community, the teacher and parents" (Yasuda 1988b). This parent said she was not a "book-burning woman" but wondered if thirteen- and fourteen-year-olds should be required to read the book (Yasuda 1988c). One teacher commented that teaching only positive content did not prepare students for the real world.

The matter was turned over to the Language Arts Committee made up of teachers who met to discuss it. They denied the parents' request to cease using the book in a 19-to-3 vote and recommended to the school board that the book stay on the list. Teachers asserted that this book was used to explore the qualities of courage, dignity, and perseverance. The teachers offered the solution that children could be given an alternative reading assignment and that no student would be required to read the controversial passages. The board accepted this recommendation (*Los Angeles Times* 1988).

The group of parents appealed this decision to the school board, saying that other books could be used to explore qualities of courage, dignity, and perseverance without involving the issue of sex. The board supported the parents' views and removed the book from the list. The board said it would reevaluate the book for required use with the eleventh grade, where it might be more appropriate. The board said this was not restricting anyone's reading of the book but just not requiring that it be read by ninth graders (Yasuda 1988b). *I Know Why the Caged Bird Sings* has been on the California K–12 Recommended Reading List since 1995.

Discussion Questions

1. Who are the decision makers in this process at different points in the process?

2. Who are the ultimate decision makers in this scenario?

3. Was this a case of censorship? Why or why not?

4. Does the term *censorship* apply when restricting materials from a required reading list for young people? Why or why not?

5. Were the students' rights to reading restricted? Are students still free to read the book?

6. How could the Language Arts Committee have responded differently to this situation?

7. Could the Language Arts Committee have changed this outcome?

8. Reflect on the comments of parents and teachers. With which of these comments do you agree? Why?

9. How would you have responded as a board member to this scenario? How else could the board have responded?

10. Did the school board reverse the Language Arts Committee's recommendation? Did they take the parents' side? Why do you think this was their decision?

References

Angelou, Maya. 1970. *I know why the caged bird sings*. New York: Random House.

Asheim, Lester. 1983. Selection and censorship: A reappraisal. *Wilson Library Bulletin* 58: 180–184. (Quoted in Burress 1989, 10)

———. 1953. Not censorship but selection. *Wilson Library Bulletin* 28: 67. (Quoted in Burress 1989, 10)

Brinkley, Ellen Henson. 1999. *Caught off guard: Teachers rethinking censorship and controversy*. Boston: Allyn and Bacon.

Bryson, Joseph E., and Elizabeth W. Detty. 1982. *Censorship of public school library and instructional material*. Charlottesville, VA: Michie Company. (Quoted in Burress 1989, 9)

Burress, Lee. 1989. *Battle of the books: Literary censorship in the public schools, 1950–1985*. Metuchen, NJ: Scarecrow Press.

Cho, David. 2001. Fairfax school board limits access to book. Parents want *Druids* banned. *Washington Post*, February 14.

Honawar, Vaishali. 2001a. Book decency rules weak, parents say. *Washington Times*, October 22.

———. 2001b. Fairfax board OKs keeping explicit book. *Washington Times*, February 14.

———. 2001c. Is it vital reading or vile reading? Fairfax parents want veto power over additions to class book lists. *Washington Times*, February 12.

Hove, John, and NCTE. 1967. *Meeting censorship in the schools: A series of case studies*. Champaign, IL: National Council of Teachers of English.

Karolides, Nicholas J. 2002. *Censored books II: Critical viewpoints, 1985–2000*. Lanham, MD: Scarecrow Press.

Karolides, Nicholas J., and Lee Burress. 1985. *Celebrating censored books*. Racine, WI: Wisconsin Council of Teachers of English.

Karolides, Nicholas J., Lee Burress, and John M. Kean, eds. 1993a. *Censored books: Critical viewpoints*. Lanham, MD: Scarecrow Press.

———. 1993b. Introduction. In *Censored books: Critical viewpoints*, ed. Nicholas J. Karolides, Lee Burress, and John M. Kean, xiii–xxii. Lanham, MD: Scarecrow Press.

Knowles, Elizabeth, and Martha Smith. 1999. *More reading connections: Bringing parents, teachers, and librarians together*. Englewood, CO: Libraries Unlimited.

Llywelyn, Morgan. 1991. *Druids*. New York: William Morrow.

Los Angeles Times. 1988. "Caged bird": Let it sing. November 13.

Office for Intellectual Freedom. 2005. *Intellectual freedom and censorship Q & A*. Chicago: American Library Association. http://www.ala.org/ala/oif/basics/intellectual.htm.

———. 1998. *Workbook for selection policy writing*. Chicago: American Library Association. http://www.ala.org/Template.cfm?Section=dealing&Template=/ContentManagement/ContentDisplay.cfm&ContentID=77103.

Peterson, Carolyn. 1975. A study of censorship affecting the secondary school English literature teachers. Ed.D. diss., Temple University. (Quoted in Burress 1989, 10)

Reichman, H. 2001. *Censorship and selection: Issues and answers for schools*. Chicago: American Library Association.

Seymour, Liz. 2002a. Couple asks schools to get rid of nine books. *Washington Post*, December 1.

———. 2002b. Fairfax couple challenges schools' books; district to reconsider multi-layered system after examining list of 23 works. *Washington Post*, December 1.

———. 2001. A novel effort to ban books in Va.; Fairfax parents' group uses Web to push for school standards. *Washington Post*, June 17.

Suhor, Charles. 2002. From the front line. Fewer calls, more book bannings—Why? *SLATE Support for the Learning and Teaching of English Newsletter* 27(3): 1, 6.

———. 2001. From the front line. No shortage of censorship calls. *SLATE Support for the Learning and Teaching of English Newsletter* 27(1): 1, 8.

———. 2000a. From the front line. Censorship cases up, way up. *SLATE Support for the Learning and Teaching of English Newsletter* 25(3): 1–3.

———. 2000b. From the front line. Recent *SLATE* anti-censorship actions. *SLATE Support for the Learning and Teaching of English Newsletter* 26(1): 1–3.

———. 1999. From the front line. Recent *SLATE* Anti-censorship actions. *SLATE Support for the Learning and Teaching of English Newsletter* 25(1): 1–4.

Tremmel, M. 2002. Censoring ourselves: Another side to book challenges. *SLATE Support for the Learning and Teaching of English Newsletter* 27(3): 1, 6.

Welsh, Patrick. 2002. Why I teach "bad books." *Pittsburgh Post Gazette*, September 1.

West, M. 1997. *Trust your children. Voices against censorship in children's literature.* New York: Neal-Schuman Publishers.

Yasuda, Gene. 1988a. Teacher panel resists censorship call, wants book to stay on required reading list. *Los Angeles Times*, December 18.

———. 1988b. Controversial autobiography book is cut from list at Vista schools. *Los Angeles Times*, November 18.

———. 1988c. Angelou book's listing in curriculum attacked. *Los Angeles Times*, October 17.

3

Religion

The religions of ancient Greece and Rome are extinct. The so-called divinities of Olympus have not a single worshipper among living men. They belong now not to the department of theology, but to those of literature and taste.

(Bulfinch 1979, 13)

The attacks of September 11, 2001, left Americans speechless to talk about how these events were related to religion. As crimes against Muslims escalated during this period, Americans looked to the protection of religious freedom guaranteed in the First Amendment more than ever. As the nation continues to debate the meaning of religious freedom post 9-11, it is possible that the constitutional mandate to protect religious freedom in the Establishment Clause is misunderstood, unclear, and possibly in jeopardy. Americans understand very little about one another's religious beliefs and less about how to discuss them as a protected freedom. A poll conducted by the First Amendment Center in 2003 showed that 22 percent of respondents were aware that freedom of religion was a right guaranteed by the First Amendment. Some 42 percent of those polled "strongly agreed" that the First Amendment goes too far in the rights it guarantees; 66 percent believed Americans have the right amount of religious freedom. When asked if "people should be allowed to say things in public that might be offensive to religious groups," 49 percent agreed, while 50 percent disagreed (Mumford 2003, 19–26). These responses explain why the debate about religion and schools is more contentious than ever.

Perhaps this is why educational philosophers are recommending that educators treat the freedom to believe as part of the "multicultural agenda" (Fraser 1999, 5). James Fraser clarifies the approach, writing:

> The point of a school approach to religion in which everyone learns from every-one else is not a dilution of belief or a slow movement toward a common faith. The goal is rather a common democratic culture in which a diversity of citizens, each holding their own creed with passion and wisdom, respects other citizens who hold other creeds, or no creed, with equal passion and—it is hoped—equal wisdom. (7)

Because beliefs are often not obvious when people meet, preservice teachers studying the topics of education and children's literature together often experience surprise at classmates' reactions to books where religion is concerned. When surprising reactions occur, there are important opportunities for students to discuss and explore belief systems together. These reactions are important to talk about because they are the same variety of responses that children and parents may also have to a book. This chapter provides a context for holding discussions about reactions to books based on belief. It also provides a starting point for researching how it is that American education, children's literature, and schoolbooks have together been shaped by religion, science, and humanism. Finally, a discussion of this topic would be incomplete without considering the influence of religion on both works of fiction and textbooks. Both types of work have been affected by religion.

Since the seventeenth century, the nature of science, humans, and God has shaped Western and American children's fiction. Early on, the purpose of writing for children was to provide religious and moral instruction. In fiction, however, this purpose gave way to including humanism, science fiction, fantasy, myth, and occult themes to entertain, enlighten, comfort, and challenge young readers.

Fantasy

During the 1860s and 1870s, modern fantasy emerged as "creative and critical minds increasingly turned to the imagination as a source of inspiration and sustenance in an age of anguished religious doubt" (Moss 1987, 66). George MacDonald "established the conventions of modern British fantasy" as entertainment informed by his religious background. MacDonald was influenced by innovative Romantic thought that tends to "diminish, and at the extreme to eliminate the role of God" (Abrams 1971, 91). MacDonald "constructed a divine order of his own" and embodied "his most deeply and profoundly felt convictions about the place of the divine spirit in the material world and the relationship between adult and child, creature and creator, the imagination and spiritual growth" (Moss 1987, 68).

Lewis Carroll also created an imaginary world in *Alice's Adventures in Wonderland* (1865). He portrayed an entertaining, funny, child-centered, chaotic world that made fun of religious instructional traditions and freed Alice from God reliance for her destiny (Moss 1987, 71–72). Carroll celebrates the "play of the intelligence and imagination," including the "pleasures and terrors of fantasy," in a world that "puts the child in control" (Moss 1987, 71).

Humanism

Beginning in the 1880s, literature began to incorporate humanistic worldviews about the nature of God and of humans. Books were published whose stories and characters did not assume that God existed and in which humans were in charge of their own destiny and not always driven by seeking redemption (Milner and Milner 1987, ix). Critics of this humanistic worldview in literature included Edmund Fuller, who wrote that this view "provides a corrupted and debased image of man . . . not in keeping with Judeo-Christian tradition" (Milner and Milner 1987, ix). Secular humanism became a cause for book challenges against those authors whose characters were self-reliant and self-confident and changed the world instead of relying on a higher power to change it (McGovern 1995, 55).

The National Council of Teachers of English website offers a SLATE Starter Sheet that excerpts the 1980 SLATE Newsletter article, "The Attack on Humanism." It states that the "Humanist movement was founded in 1933 by educator/philosopher John Dewey, along with R. Lester Mondale" and others (http://www.ncte.org/about/issues/slate/sheets/108544.htm; *SLATE* 1980, 1). It offers the following description of the function of humanism:

> Humanism's function has been to provide concerned human beings with an acceptable alternative to the traditional religious imperatives which are rooted in supernaturalism, mysticism, and miraculism. Humanism offers the reasoned view that human beings alone shape their own destinies, leaving to scientific inquiry the probing of nature's unknowns in the endless search for truth, knowledge, and facts. (*SLATE* 1980, 1)

Writers with a humanist worldview have often stood against

> bigotry, formalized religion, and the notion of a supernatural deity . . . and . . . have called on their audiences to think independently and to take responsibility for their actions . . . (and) have stressed the commonality of human experience and lauded moral excellence achieved not by following the dictates of any sect, but through recognition of the human potential. (McGovern 1995, 55)

Science Fiction

Mary Shelley's *Frankenstein* (1818) was "one of the earliest attempts to present transcendent power in scientific form" (Marsalek 1995, 39). In the late nineteenth century, science fiction began encroaching upon the transcendental territory in literature that once was the domain of religion and the supernatural in seventeenth-century works like John Milton's *Paradise Lost* (1668) about heaven and hell. Kenneth Marsalek (1995, 39) compares transcendence in science fiction to transcendence in religious literature.

> [T]he transcendent powers of science fiction are scientific rather than magical. . . . [S]cience fiction is populated by aliens, androids, and mutants from other

planets and dimensions rather than by spirits and demons from heaven and hell. . . . [Science fiction] . . . does not purport to present reality, it broadens our perspective, it prepares us for the future, it inspires humans to achieve not only technological wonders but the improved social conditions portrayed . . . compared to religious or occult literature that prepares us to understand the powers of good and evil and warns against dangers.

Religion in children's books was less frequently included between the 1930s and the 1950s (Adams 1989, 5). In 1950, C. S. Lewis published *The Lion, the Witch and the Wardrobe*, the first in a series of Christian allegorical fantasy books for children. In the 1960s and 1970s, Ursula LeGuin and Madeleine L'Engle each began writing science fiction and fantasy stories about imaginary supernatural worlds that incorporated themes of good and evil. Finding solutions meant a battle with evil, in LeGuin's case, a Jungian shadow self, and in L'Engle's case, a spiritual, external power.

During the 1970s, "the new realism" and the "born-again" phenomenon began to change how belief was presented in children's literature (Adams 1989, 5). Stories that include "realistic religion," in which a major theme is the criticism of organized religion, are among contemporary children's books. M. E. Kerr, Katherine Paterson, and Cynthia Rylant all write stories based on their personal experiences with religion. Kerr's message is that all religions include hypocrisy and sincerity. Paterson hopes to offer readers a place of rest for their souls in her stories. Rylant writes stories that include confrontation with fundamentalist religions that trick and frighten people into believing in salvation and loving God through threats of hell (Adams 1989, 9).

Harry Potter

The digital communications revolution and hyperconsumer culture of the 1990s changed how information reached young people. Wicca was introduced to young people through television programs like *Buffy, the Vampire Slayer*. J. K. Rowling's Harry Potter series became popular because the accessible writing depicted a supernatural world in which the science of magic that students learned at Hogwarts closely resembled the science of digital science in readers' lives. The series' popularity exploded when people began banning it, burning it, and challenging it for religious reasons.

The series threatened biblical literalists because of depictions of children learning magical practices prohibited in the Bible like witchcraft, wizardry, and premonition and prompted calls for schools that are "serious about diversity . . . to honor the concerns of [parents] who see Harry Potter as a direct assault on Christian values" (Manzo 2001, 2). Responses ranged from a book burning in Alamagordo, New Mexico, to a federal court ruling to allow access to the book in an Arkansas school (Ishizuka 2002, 27; *School Law News* 2003, 3). Parents and church officials have demanded that the books be removed or access restricted and allowed only with permission slips. Protests from community members have led to cancellation of Potter events at libraries. Pat Robertson, along with other Religious Right spokespeople, has condemned the books for including Celtic, druidic, satanic, and pagan religious imagery; for training children in Wicca practices; and for offering an attractive presentation of witchcraft to children in a children's format (Boston 2002, 8–12). Not limited to the United States, or to conflicts with Christianity, the Harry Potter books have also been banned from schools in the United Arab Emirates because they conflict with the teachings of Islamic religion (*Houston Chronicle* 2002).

Even so, there were many in the Christian religious community who co-opted the popularity of the series for religious instruction. Harry Potter books helped students "develop the quality of spiritual discernment" (Zaleski 2001, 72). Parents now use the books to teach Bible lessons and to show what forbidden practices are in the series, and one church school even decorated its church like Hogwarts for its Bible school to reframe the story in religious terms (Dancy 2001). This type of response from Christian religious groups echoes early religious response to evolution. Thus, the entertaining Potter books are used to enhance dry religious teachings, and this is reminiscent of the use of scientific discovery to make more exciting literature to teach religious lessons. Christians have written articles to non-Christians about Harry Potter. For example, Christian librarian Kimbra Wilder Gish explains how passages in the books offend and threaten those reading from a biblical standpoint and who may interpret the imagery as real (Wilder Gish 2000).

Influence of Philip Pullman

Philip Pullman's imaginary worlds incorporates his own beliefs, in his case, atheism, or broad agnosticism. In response to what Pullman calls the Christian propaganda of C. S. Lewis's Narnia books, Pullman calls the His Dark Materials series, "Paradise Lost, in three volumes, for teens" which retells Milton's *Paradise Lost* (Wagner, 2000). In American editions of this series, the quotations from *Paradise Lost* that appear at the beginning of each chapter have been removed. Humanists have traditionally called supernaturalism and mysticism the domain of religion (Milner and Milner 1987, 1). J. K. Rowling's Potter fantasy series reclaims the religious territory of supernaturalism and mysticism in the same way science did in the eighteenth and nineteenth centuries. Pullman's fantasy series overtly incorporates an imaginary world whose inhabitants can create 'republic of heaven' (Wagner 2000).

This convergence of themes that directly question religious beliefs in popular contemporary children's literature is a compelling argument for approaching belief systems as part of the multicultural agenda.

Books Challenged

During the second half of the twentieth century, examples of challenges to books on religious grounds have included those in the Harry Potter series by J. K. Rowling; *Bridge to Terabithia* (1972) by Katherine Paterson; *The Martian Chronicles* (1958) by Ray Bradbury; *Macbeth* (1623) by William Shakespeare; *The Chocolate War* (1974) by Robert Cormier; *The Merchant of Venice* (1600) by William Shakespeare; *Brave New World* (1932) by Aldous Huxley; *Firestarter* (1980) by Stephen King; *Forever* (1957) by Judy Blume; *Franny & Zooey* (1955) by J. D. Salinger; *The Genetic Code* (1962) by Isaac Asimov; *The Grapes of Wrath* (1939) by John Steinbeck; *Inherit the Wind* (1955) by Jerome Lawrence and Robert Lee; *Catcher in the*

Rye (1951) by J. D. Salinger; *East of Eden* (1952) by John Steinbeck; and *Elmer Gantry* (1927) by Sinclair Lewis.

Textbooks

A nonsectarian approach to instructional books in schools emerged in the late 1800s. Horace Mann intended that the common school would give children "informed and free choice regarding which form of religion, if any, might be appropriate" (Fraser 1999, 30). Even so, Mann's school libraries were controversial for the Unitarian books they included that reflected Mann's own faith (Fraser 1999, 30).

Religious influence on textbook content goes back many years. The didactic tradition of using religious content to teach subjects in a moral way was seen in the 1700s New England primer that taught the alphabet using religious rhyme (Ford 1962, 4). Other alphabets published after 1850 were both religious and secular and included *The New ABC* (c. 1855), *Grandpapa Easy's New Scripture Historical Alphabet* (c. 1870), and *The Sunday ABC* (c. 1875) (Demers 1993, 76–77).

In the 1700s, religion lessons were also part of teaching science, using characters who would appeal to children, as in John Newbery's *Newtonian System of Philosophy* featuring the imaginative and entertaining young character Tom Telescope (Telescope, Goldsmith, and Newbery 1761). The religious view of "scientific inquiry as a virtue" continued through the publication of Walter Kingsley's classic *The Water-Babies* in 1863 and Arabella Buckley's *The Fairyland of Science* (c. 1800–1899?) (Rauch 1989, 13, 16–17).

As the institution of the common school became widespread, it created a lucrative textbook market for publishers who modified textbook content based on belief systems of the people in the market. The publishing firm of Truman & Smith published the *McGuffey Eclectic Readers* to offer the Ohio, Kentucky, and Indiana markets a Protestant schoolbook, that is, a "handbook of common morality" (Fraser 1999, 40; Lindberg 1976, xv, xix). Editions published of this title between 1836 and 1920 sold 122 million copies and had an influence "second only to the Bible over millions" of people (Lindberg 1976, xxii). Moralistic and didactic, the *McGuffey Readers* were written for "a white, Protestant, middle-class audience" and presented a wide range of literature (xvi).

Science Textbooks

In the late 1800s, science textbooks like Asa Gray's *Elements of Botany* described discoveries in evolutionary biology and in the geological sciences as part of the intelligent design of God (Fraser 1999, 118). Often these books credited God with science or disclaimed that science contradicted Christianity.

By the 1920s, the changing views of the nature of God made textbook content a battleground for religious beliefs and freedom. Charles Lyell's geological timeline that the creation of the earth happened over millions of years contradicted biblical timelines. Charles Darwin's theory of evolutionary biology encroached on the territory of creationism. The instruction in these theories in schools to growing audiences threatened the authority of Christian religious leaders and upset fundamentalists. Fundamentalism emerged in the 1890s as a theological school of thought characterized by militant dedication to antimodernism and a literal interpretation of the Bible, although originally *The Fundamentals*—the set of books on which fundamentalism was founded—referred to evolution as a "new name for creation" (Fraser 1999, 119).

By the 1920s, writers in both the scientific community and the educational community were in favor of teaching evolutionary biology to provide students with the correct scientific ideas. The growing high school population that went from 20,000 students in 1890 to almost 2 million by 1920 spurred on the national debate. Between 1901 and 1929, creationists "introduced antievolutionary bills in thirty-seven state legislatures," and Tennessee, Mississippi, and Arkansas made the bills law (Davis 1999, 666–667).

When Tennessee teacher John Thomas Scopes used George William Hunter's textbook *A Civic Biology,* he was convicted of teaching evolution, a theory that denied "the story of the divine creation of man as taught in the Bible" (*Scopes v. State* 1926). The case drew national attention that embarrassed the fundamentalist movement and marked it with a reputation for being antiscience and antiintellectual (Fraser 1999, 125). Textbook publishers backed off from including emphasis on Darwin or evolution in textbooks.

After 1950, "In God We Trust" was added to U.S. currency, and "Under God" was added to the Pledge of Allegiance. In 1962, the Supreme Court defended a student's right not to recite prayer in schools (*Engel et al. v. Vitale et al.* 1962). Creationists argued that they had a right to protection of religious freedom through "balanced treatment" laws that would make it necessary to give creationism treatment equal to that of evolution in teaching in Arkansas and Louisiana. The Supreme Court found balanced treatment laws unconstitutional (Davis 1999, 669). In 1999 the state of Kansas allowed that teaching of evolution in schools become optional. In 2004, the State Schools Superintendent in Georgia unsuccessfully proposed replacing the word *evolution* with the term *biological changes over time* (*Associated Press State & Local Wire* 2004).

Meanwhile, commercial competition among publishers for the textbook market has created an ongoing rhetorical contest. The definition of *truth* is loudly debated in front of school boards and to publishers to influence the presentation of facts in textbooks.

Since the 1990s, increasing parochial home schooling has continued to create a market for instructional religious books. As contemporary science proceeds into the genetic and cybernetic age, discoveries will be increasingly counter to many religious faiths' literal understanding of the world. These discoveries will be reflected in children's fiction and instructional materials. However, the truth will be able to be customized for niche market audiences as digital technology has made on-demand customized textbook services a cost-effective and efficient way of producing instructional materials that are increasingly Web based.

Advocacy Groups and Watchdogs

Interested groups participate in debates about the portrayal and character of belief in fiction and instructional nonfiction for children. Some of these include the American Library Association, the Association of American Publishers, the American Booksellers Foundation for Free Expression, the Association of Booksellers for Children, the Children's Book Council, the Freedom to Read Foundation, Americans United for Separation of Church and State, the National Coalition against Censorship, People for the American Way, and the PEN American Center. These organizations document, report, and fight censorship including restriction of access to materials based on belief systems. Organizations like Americans for a Sound Economy, the Christian Coalition, the ProFamily Forum, and the Eagle Forum have in the past challenged or attempted to succeed in restricting the use of books that express a humanist worldview and scientific explanations of creation. According to Phyllis Schlaffely of the Eagle Forum, her concerns include "depriving children of their free exercise of religious rights" and imposing "profane or immoral fiction," "new age practices," or "anti-Biblical materials" on them (Fraser 1999, 190–191).

World Religions

This chapter has focused on attention on the Judeo-Christian community and on humanists. Bibliographies like *Children's Books about Religion* (1999) by Patricia Pearl Dole provide broader coverage. Describing books for preschoolers through young adults, Dole lists information about over 700 creation stories, songbooks, prayer books, mysteries, and biographies relevant to Judeo-Christian, Buddhism, Hinduism, Native American religions, and a variety of other faiths (Burgess 1999). Bibliographic articles are also published that provide critical and historical treatment of children's books (Saxena 1999; *Hindu* 1998). Books like *Twenty Jataka Tales* (1985) by Noor Inayat Khan; *Muslim Child: Understanding Islam through Stories and Poems* (2002) by Rukhsana Khan and Patty Gallinger; *The Broken Tusk: Stories of the Hindu God Ganesha* (1996) by Uma Krishnaswami; and *The Mishomis Book: Voice of the Ojibway* (1988) by Edward Benton-Banai are examples of religious content books for children.

Nel Noddings writes that the "best teachers will . . . present . . . the full spectrum of belief . . . but also the variety of plausible ways in which people have tried to reconcile their religious and scientific beliefs" (Noddings 1993, 144). This approach to multicultural education leads to mutual respect and understanding but does not promote any religion.

As multicultural education and globalization raise awareness about diversity of belief, inclusion of non-American books in classrooms can enlighten readers about the different perspectives of God and belief in countries where children grow up with war, genocide, oppression, and non-Western religious beliefs. The International Board on Books for Young People (IBBY), the journal *Book Bird*, and the International Youth Library all promote international understanding through children's books. A free full-text database called *The International Children's Digital Library* at http://www.icdlbooks.org provides digital reproductions of books from many countries in many languages.

Case: Adoption of History and Social Sciences Textbooks in Texas in 2002

Texas is one of twenty-two states in the country using a textbook adoption process. Books are adopted for use in public schools and open-enrolled charter schools. One goal of the process is to create a list of materials from which districts may select items to buy using state funds. Another goal of the process is to reject any materials that contain "factual errors," do not meet physical specifications, and do not include at least 50 percent of the essential knowledge and skills of the subject and grade level.

The Textbook Administration Division of the Texas Education Agency (TEA) coordinates the process. The Commissioner of Education heads the agency and—along with the State Board of Education (SBOE)—selects textbooks for adoption. The SBOE has fifteen-elected members (http://www.tea.state.tx.us/sboe). Instructional materials are adopted every eight years according to an adoption cycle.

To complete the job of reviewing textbooks submitted by publishers, the commissioner appoints state textbook review panels. Recommendations for the panels are made by the State Board of Education, educational professionals, parents, and members of the private sector. Any Texas resident can recommend panel members, but publishers and their affiliates may not recommend members.

The review panels review the books publishers have submitted for consideration for adoption for a particular subject. Review panel members spend time evaluating textbooks to determine if a book includes at least 50 percent of the elements of the knowledge and skills of the subject and grade level, to list any factual errors they find, and to verify physical specifications are met. To complete this process, panel members meet with publishers to ask questions. The panel members "submit evaluations to the commissioner of education. Based on these evaluations" and based on "information provided by publishers, and staff recommendations, the commissioner prepares a preliminary report recommending that instructional materials be placed on the conforming list, be placed on the nonconforming list, or rejected" (http://www.tea.state.tx.us/textbooks/adoptprocess/overview.html). This report is submitted to the SBOE along with a report detailing any factual errors to be corrected in instructional materials.

The Texas Education Agency provides twenty Regional Education Service Centers throughout the state where textbooks may be reviewed by the public. Texas residents may file written comments regarding instructional materials submitted for adoption.

At least one public hearing is held before the SBOE approximately two months before the scheduled vote on adoption. The SBOE, by a majority vote, decides which books will be adopted or rejected. Local districts that select books that are not adopted only receive 70 percent of the price limit funding for that book.

The SBOE may reject a book that contains "factual errors," does not meet physical specifications, and does not include at least 50 percent of the essential knowledge and skills of the subject and grade level. The SBOE may negotiate for changes based on these criteria.

Texas textbook adoption influences textbook content nationwide. Texas is the second largest market in the country. California is the largest. Changes that publishers make to Texas textbooks show up in other states' textbooks.

The Texas social sciences and history textbook adoption for 2003–2004 represented $230 million in sales for publishers. During this adoption process, the board membership was made up of ten Republicans and five Democrats. In 2002, 250 social studies and history textbooks were reviewed, including topics on government, geography, economics, sociology, and psychology (Manzo 2002a, 11).

After the Commissioner of Education submitted a list of books to the SBOE, three public hearings were held between July and September. Hundreds of people and many groups voiced opinions (Manzo 2002a, 11). The Texas Freedom Network, established to combat the influence of the Religious Right, organized a postcard campaign to lobby for "factually accurate books free from promoting religious beliefs or political agendas." The Texas Public Policy Foundation, a research agency that promotes limited government, sponsored a $100,000 study that produced a list of 533 alleged mistakes (Manzo 2002a, 11). Other groups speaking out included Americans United for the Separation of Church and State, the Texas Public Policy Foundation, the Texas Chapter of Citizens for a Sound Economy, and the Texas Eagle Forum.

In response to the opinions at hearings, and also in response to groups contacting them, publishers began making changes to textbooks under review before the SBOE requested any changes. The SBOE had to request an updated list of all of the changes that publishers made before they could vote. Because many of the changes were made external to the SBOE request for changes, they reflected the agenda of interest groups lobbying publishers.

The interpretation of "factual error" was also a subject of debate as board members argued that "factual error" could refer to "partial information on a topic that could lead to inaccurate interpretation—or facts that are presented with an inherent bias" (Manzo 2002a, 11). It was on this interpretation of "factual error" that the SBOE was able to request an increase in the inclusion of Hispanic heroes in Texas history in texts.

The following list includes the changes that were lobbied for by groups and that were requested by the SBOE and that may have origins in religion or belief (Manzo 2002b, 17).

Remove passages promoting positive aspects of socialism and communism.

Include more prominent role of Christianity in nation's history and include how the United States was founded as a Christian nation.

Do not depict the United States as a Christian nation because the nation was founded on a principle of religious freedom expressed in the Constitution and the First Amendment.

In *Environmental Science: Creating a Sustainable Future* present all sides of debatable issues instead of stating absolutes about how global warming and acid rain negatively affect the environment.

Include only "factually accurate books free from promoting religious beliefs or political agendas."

Include a religiously correct timeline for glacial movement, using "over time" instead of "millions of years" to "eliminate references to 'fossil fuels being formed millions of years ago.'"

Deleted a passage that explained that Osama bin Laden's orders to his followers to kill Americans are counter to Muslim teachings and that "no idea could be further from Muslim teachings." Critics said the book was too kind in describing Muslim beliefs.

Objections to statements that the Quran encourages honesty, giving, and love led to the publisher deleting the passage.

Reject the book *Out of Many: A History of the American People*—objection to paragraphs on prostitution, birth control, and gay rights in the early West.

Overemphasis on the women's rights movement.

Overstatement of the discrimination against a black woman.

Failure to explain the American republic and founding principles.

Increase content from the Hispanic perspective and Latino heroes.

Gilbert T. Sewall, the president of the American Textbook Council, a New York City–based organization that reviews history and social studies texts, said "the selection process forces publishers to sanitize content and avoid words or concepts that offend people" (Manzo 2002b, 17). The publishing industry views the 4.2 million public schools students in Texas as a way to get a bestseller if you can win an adoption (Lord 2002, 46). Former Oxford University Press president Byron Hollingshead said the process leads to "a lot of self-censorship among publishers" (Manzo 2002b, 17).

The following year, the biology textbook adoption came up in Texas, and the school board adopted eleven biology textbooks that included Charles Darwin's theory of evolution. In this case, the scientific community overwhelmed the State Board of Education with a letter signed by 550 Texas scientists to stop an effort to lessen the importance of evolution in textbooks. The goal of the scientist lobby was also to prevent the success of the Discovery Institute, an organization promoting intelligent design theory in which a higher power is responsible for creation in science. The Discovery Institute hoped to convince the SBOE to request changes that would detail the weaknesses in the theory of evolution. Some images in the microevolution section pointed out the connection between humans and animals. These were removed from texts (Castro 2003; Dawson 2003, 36).

Discussion Questions

1. How does one determine a factual error in materials from a perspective of belief?

2. Search on the Web for some of the organizations mentioned in the case. Do they have a religious orientation? What is the mission or purpose of each of the organizations?

3. How would you evaluate a textbook on the basis of belief?

4. A student comes to you after class and tells you that they cannot read a particular book that has been assigned to them for religious reasons. What would be your approach to this situation?

5. Parents asks for their child to be excused from reading and activities for a particular book based on their belief system. How would you proceed?

6. Students in a class are discussing a student who is excused from participation in a book discussion for religious reasons. Two students in class are questioning and criticizing the student's culture for limiting the student's participation in reading the

books the class is reading. How would you approach this? What if the discussion you heard was among teaching colleagues or other school personnel?

Case: Reception of Harry Potter Series in Zeeland, Michigan

By 2001, there had been complaints about J. K. Rowling's Harry Potter books from over twenty-seven states, according to Beverly Becker, associate director of the American Library Association's Office of Intellectual Freedom in Chicago (Elizabeth 2001). Most complaints were made on the grounds that the series promotes "Satanism and the occult" and come from fundamentalist and conservative Christians (Elizabeth 2001). Judith Krug, director of ALA's Office of Intellectual Freedom, says that the books "explore the classic theme of good vs. evil, not Satanism" (Elizabeth 2001). Christian journalist Richard Abanes argues that although the books should be accessible in libraries, they do "contain real-world occult practices" including references to "numerology, astrology, crystal-gazing and communicating with the dead" (Elizabeth 2001).

In 1999, a parent in Zeeland, Michigan, complained about the use of Harry Potter books in the 4,500 student school district for reasons of witchcraft and violence (Suhor 2000a). The school superintendent instructed staff to remove the books from the school libraries and make them only accessible with a parent's written permission (Reinstadler 2000a). The superintendent ordered that because the books were controversial they should not be read aloud in class, and he halted the purchase of future Potter books. The superintendent ignored the district's policy for reviewing controversial materials (Reinstadler 2000b). The school board voted to support the restrictions to ban the books.

Mary Dana, an eighth-grade teacher, argued the process "went around prescribed board policy concerning books that are challenged . . . and that requiring permission immediately put a chilling effect on their access. Those books didn't receive fair hearing until months after the restrictions were put in place" (Boston 2002, 10). Dana encouraged students to petition and protest and to form the group Muggles for Harry Potter (10).

The group grew into a national organization to fight efforts to restrict access to J. K. Rowling's books in the United States. Muggles for Harry Potter sponsorship soon included the NCTE, the Freedom to Read Foundation, the Association of American Publishers, the Children's Book Council, the Association of Booksellers for Children, the National Coalition against Censorship, the American Booksellers Foundation for Free Expression, and PEN American Center ("Muggles" 2000, 81).

Charles Suhor, representative of SLATE/NCTE, supported parents, students, and teachers by writing to the Zeeland paper and to Tom Bock, president of the Board of Education for the Zeeland Public Schools. Suhor argued that in NCTE experience "few instructional materials do not include something that is offensive to someone" and urged the district to follow its policy for reviewing materials (NCTE 2000).

The board appointed an advisory committee to review the case, and the committee recommended lifting the restrictions. In May 2000, the superintendent lifted all restrictions, except for a ban on classroom readings in K–5 classrooms (Suhor 2000). The *Grand Rapids Press* reported that school board president Mr. Bock tried to have Mary Dana removed from her position as mentor to new teachers (Reinstadler 2002). This was unsuccessful. Bock stepped down as school board president (*Associated Press State & Local Wire* 2002). Dana and Nancy Zennie, the volunteer reading tutor who worked with her to defeat the ban, were honored at the Library of Congress for their work in this situation (Reinstadler 2002). Most cases of challenge to the Harry Potter books are for reasons of witchcraft, wizardry, and supernatural content in the books.

Discussion Questions

1. What selection process is played out in this case?

2. Who are the decision makers?

3. Who was left out of the process?

4. Speculate about a different outcome beginning at the point when the parent complained.

5. Discuss the roles played by the superintendent, Suhor, and Dana in this case. How were each of these players effective or ineffective?

6. What difference did each one make?

7. What could they have done differently?

8. Why did the school board initially support the superintendent?

9. What do you believe was instrumental in reversing the restrictions after two years? And why?

10. Who or what influenced the outcome of this case?

References

Abrams, M. H. 1971. *Natural supernaturalism, tradition and revolution in romantic literature*. New York: W. W. Norton, Inc.

Adams, Karen I. 1989. The "born-again" phenomenon and children's books. *Children's Literature Association Quarterly* 14(1): 5–9.

Associated Press State & Local Wire. 2004. Superintendent proposes dropping reference to evolution. January 29.

———. 2002. School board president reportedly resigns over Harry Potter controversy. January 4.

Benton-Banai, Edward. 1988. *The Mishomis book: Voice of the Ojibway*. Saint Paul, MN: Red School House.

Boston, Rob. 2002. Witch hunt. *Church & State* 55(3): 8–12.

Brinkley, Ellen Henson. 1999. *Caught off guard: Teachers rethinking censorship and controversy*. Boston: Allyn and Bacon.

Buckley, Arabella B. c. 1800–1899? *The fairyland of science*. Philadelphia: Henry Altemus Co.

Bulfinch, Thomas. 1979. *Bulfinch's mythology*. New York: Viking Penguin.

Burgess, Sue. 1999. Professional reading. *School Library Journal* 45(12): 168.

Cassidy, L. 2002. Challenge to a summer reading list. *SLATE Support for the Learning and Teaching of English Newsletter* 27(3): 3–4.

Castro, April. 2003. Board votes to keep evolution in Texas textbooks. *Columbian* (Vancouver, WA), November 8, sec. A.

Christopher, Kevin. 2003. Evolution battle in Texas textbooks. *Skeptical Inquirer* 27(6): 7.

Dancy, Shelvia. 2001. Finding the spiritual power of Harry Potter. *Washington Post*, June 30, sec. B.

Davis, Derek. 1999. Kansas schools challenge Darwinism: The history and future of the creationism-evolution controversy in American public education. *Journal of Church & State* 41(4): 661–676.

Dawson, Jim. 2003. Antievolutionists lose critical fight in Texas textbook decision. *Physics Today* 56(12): 36–38.

Demers, Patricia. 1993. *Heaven upon earth: The form of moral and religious children's literature, to 1850.* Knoxville: University of Tennessee Press.

Dole, Patricia Pearl. 1999. *Children's books about religion.* Englewood, CO: Libraries Unlimited.

Elizabeth, Jane. 2001. Like magic, Harry Potter draws a record number of complaints. *Pittsburgh Post-Gazette*, November 17.

Engel et al. v. Vitale et al. 1962. 370 U.S. 421.

Ford, Paul Leicester, ed. 1962. *The New England primer: A history of its origin and development.* New York: Teachers College, Columbia University.

Fraser, James W. 1999. *Between church and state: Religion and public education in a multicultural America.* New York: St. Martin's Press.

Galley, Michelle. 2003. Texas adopts biology texts, evolution included. *Education Week* 23(12): 5.

Goldsborough, James O. 2004. Another attempt to deny evolution. *Copley News Service*, February 12.

Hindu. 1998. The sweet serenity of books. September 6.

Holden, Constance. Texas resolves war over biology texts. *Science* 302(5648): 1130.

Hood, Lucy. 2002. Textbooks await nod from the state this week: Chairwoman thinks board will OK list. *San Antonio Express-News* (Metro/South Texas ed.), November 14.

Houston Chronicle. 2002. Book banning spans the globe. October 3.

Ishizuka, Kathy. 2002. Harry Potter book burning draws fire. *School Library Journal* 48(2): 27.

Johnston, Robert C. 2002. State journal: Politics and prose. *Education Week* 22(2): 18.

Karolides, N. J. 2002. *Censored books II: Critical viewpoints, 1985–2000.* Lanham, MD: Scarecrow Press.

Khan, Noor Inayat. 1985. *Twenty Jakata tales.* New York: Inner Traditions International.

Khan, Rukhsana, and Patty Gallinger. 2002. *Muslim child: Understanding Islam through stories and poems.* Morton Grove, IL: Albert Whitman.

Kingsley, Charles. 1863. *The water-babies: A fairytale for a land-baby.* New York: T. Nelson.

Krishnaswami, Uma. 1996. *The broken tusk: Stories of the Hindu god Ganesha.* North Haven, CT: Linnet Books.

Larson, Edward J. 1997. *Summer for the gods: The Scopes trial and America's continuing debate over science and religion.* New York: Basic Books.

Learning the lonestar way. 2002. *Ecologist* 32(9): 6.

Lindberg, Stanley W. 1976. Introduction. In *The annotated McGuffey: Selections from the McGuffey eclectic readers 1936–1920.* New York: Van Nostrand Reinhold.

Lord, Mary. 2002. Remaking history: The latest skirmish in the Texas textbooks wars could decide what kids will read across the nation. *U.S. News and World Report* 133(20): 46.

Mabin, Connie. 2002. Groups spar over what goes in social studies books. *Abiline Reporter News Online,* November 12. http://www.texnews.com/1998/2002/texas/texas_Groups_sp1112.html.

Manzo, Kathleen Kennedy. 2002a. History repeats itself in Texas for textbook-review process. *Education Week* 21(43): 11.

———. 2002b. Texas board adopts scores of new textbooks. *Education Week* 22(13): 17.

———. 2001. Charmed and Challenged. *Education Week* 21(11): 1–4.

Marsalek, Kevin. 1995. Humanism, science fiction, and fairy tales. *Free Inquiry* 15(3): 39–44.

McGovern, Edythe. 1995. Secular humanism in literature. *Free Inquiry* 15(3): 49–55.

Milner, Joseph O'Beirne, and Lucy Floyd Moorcock Milner, eds. 1987. *Webs and wardrobes: Humanist and religious world views in children's literature.* Lanham, MD: University Press of America.

Moss, Anita. 1987. Sacred and secular visions of imagination and reality in nineteenth century British fantasy for children. In *Webs and wardrobes: Humanist and religious worldviews in children's literature,* eds. Joseph O'Beirne Milner and Lucy Floyd Moorcock Milner. Lanham, MD: University Press of America.

Muggles for Harry Potter. 2002. *SLATE Support for the Learning and Teaching of English Newsletter* 25(3): 4.

"Muggles for Harry Potter" coalition fights censorship. 2000. *Journal of Adolescent & Adult Literacy* 44(1): 81.

Mumford Jurding, Christy, ed. 2003. *State of the First Amendment.* Nashville, TN: First Amendment Center. http://www.ncte.org/news/muggles2000March13.shtml.

National Council of Teachers of English. 2000. NCTE pledges anti-censorship support to "Muggles for Harry Potter" coalition. http://www.ncte.org/news/muggles2000March13.shtml (accessed July 18, 2002).

Neal, Connie. 2001. *What's a Christian to do with Harry Potter?* Colorado Springs: Waterbrook Press.

Noddings, Nel. 1993. Humanism and unbelief. In *Educating for intelligent belief or unbelief.* New York: Teachers College Press.

Rauch, Alan. 1989. A world of faith on a foundation of science: Science and religion in British children's literature: 1761–1878. *Children's Literature Association Quarterly* 14(1): 13–19.

Reinstadler, Kym. 2002. Potter book fight brews discord. *Grand Rapids Press*, January 4.

———. 2000a. Harry Potter backers push to get rid of ban. *Grand Rapids Press*, February 18.

———. 2000b. Harry Potter backers will confront school board over ban. *Grand Rapids Press*, February 18.

Religious Right groups join forces to select Texas textbooks. 2002.*Church & State* 55(9): 17–19.

Saxena, Ira. 1999. Indian children's stories through the centuries. *Bookbird* 37(2): 56–61.

School Law News. May 2003. Court orders Harry Potter books back in Arkansas Schools. 31(5): 3.

Scopes v. State. 1926. 54 Tenn. 105 (Tenn. S. Ct.).

SLATE Support for the Learning and Teaching of English Newsletter. 1980. The attack on humanism. 5(9): np. http://www.ncte.org/about/issues/slate/sheets/108544.htm (accessed August 26, 2005).

Suhor, Charles. 2000a. From the front line. Censorship cases up, way up. *SLATE Support for the Learning and Teaching of English Newsletter* 25(3): 1–3.

———. 2000b. From the front line. Recent *SLATE* anti-censorhsip actions. *SLATE Support for the Learning and Teaching of English Newsletter* 26(1): 1–3.

Susswein, Gary. 2002. Conservatives want to strip textbooks of facts, critics say. *Austin American Statesman*, November 13.

Telescope, Tom, Oliver Goldsmith, and John Newbery. 1761. *The Newtonian system of philosophy: Adapted to the capacities of young gentlemen and ladies, and familiarized and made entertaining by objects with which they are intimately acquainted: Being the substance of six lectures read to the Lilliputian Society.* London: John Newbery.

Torrey, Ruben Archer, and Amzi Clarence Dixon. 1910. *The fundamentals: A testimony to the truth.* Chicago: Testimony Publishing Company.

Wagner, Erica. 2000. Divinely inspired. *The Times* (London), October 19.

Wilder Gish, Kimbra. 2000. Hunting down Harry Potter: An exploration of religious concerns about children's literature. *Horn Book Magazine* 76(3): 262–272.

Zaleski, Jeff. 2001. Religion notes. *Publisher's Weekly* 248(15): 72.

4

Languages and Books

New teachers in linguistically diverse classrooms think about how to use children's literature to best serve their students. Many experienced teachers have written about the approaches they use (Truscott and Watts-Taffe 2003, 187). They use dual-language books; books originally written in various languages; dialect books; literary classics and traditional literature from other countries in translation; easy reader second-language books for older language learners; stories about the experiences of linguistically diverse children; and stories embedded in cultural contexts. They frequently develop methods based upon what researchers are learning about bilingual education. It is enlightening and exciting for educators and librarians when they become aware of children's and young adult literature written in many languages, from many different countries, that they might access and share with students.

Changes to Federal Language Education Policy

The Bilingual Education Act, or Title VII of the Elementary and Secondary Education Act (ESEA), became law in 1968 (Lessow-Hurley 2000, 8). In 1974, the Supreme Court in *Lau v. Nichols* (1974) held that "children must receive equal access to education regardless of their inability to speak English" (8). This eventually led to many states adopting bilingual education requirements, and by 1980, all fifty states permitted and nine required it (Ovando and Collier 1985).

In the 1990s and 2000s, "English for the Children" (http://www.onenation.org) organizers successfully campaigned to passed English-only laws for education in Arizona, California, Texas, and Massachusetts. These laws allow English learners one year of instruction in their home language and then require them to enter mainstream monolingual classrooms so students will develop language as quickly as possible.

When the ESEA was not reauthorized by Congress and the No Child Left Behind (NCLB) Act became the education policy for the United States in 2002, the term of the Bilingual Education Act was over. Under NCLB, federal funds continued to support the education of English-language learners. The Office of Bilingual Education and Minority Language Affairs, or OBEMLA, was officially designated the Office of English Language Acquisition, Language Enhancement, and Academic Achievement for Limited English Proficient Students (OELA). In the new law, "federal grants for improving the instruction of English language learners are addressed under Title III, Language Instruction for Limited English Proficient and Immigrant Students" (Crawford 2003; Dicker 2000, 63; http://www.ncela.gwu.edu/oela/obemla). The new policy supported developing English-language proficiency in students to prepare them for all-English instruction. Previously, the policy had supported instructional programs that included attention to the preservation of native-language skills.

Bilingual Education Research

Convincing numbers of studies have given credence to some assumptions of bilingual education. First, teaching in the English-language learners' home language does not interfere with English learning, provided that students are also taught in English (Cummins 1994, 38). Second, a common underlying proficiency (CUP) in one language supports a learner's acquisition of proficiency in a second language (38). The transfer of the conceptual base of knowledge about the first language aids proficiency development in the second language (Freeman 1998, 25). Destroying the conceptual base of knowledge in the first language, or subtractive bilingualism, has negative effects on the learner. Third, it has been observed that conversational proficiency in a second language develops in about three years of education in both the home language and the second language. Academic proficiency in the second language has been observed to take six years of education in both languages (Dicker 2000, 63; Cummins 1994, 34; Hudelson and Rigg 1994–1995, 5). Forcing students into all-English classes too soon may hinder development in subject areas. For example, second-language learners, proficient in math, benefit from receiving math instruction in their home language to build on their existing proficiency (Gutierrez 2002, 1047).

These concepts contribute to development of criteria for selecting books to use with bilingual learners.

Criteria for Book Selection

The term *bilingual education* does not encompass the use of bilingual books in the classroom. Bilingual educators usually prefer using books written in the students' first language, particularly in lower grades. In upper grades, teachers appreciate having the same book titles in both English and Spanish, or in students' first languages, provided translations are excellent. This is desirable and always preferable to using bilingual books, which may be confusing and not the most effective for supporting linguistic transfer. Some teachers report they are looking for books in which the students' first language is presented in a natural way and not books that are written in "Spanglish" (Torres-Zayas 2004). Bilingual education teachers and scholars recommend looking for certain elements of culture, translation, language, design, and story when selecting books to promote language development (Freeman 1998; Hudelson et al. 1994; Smallwood et al. 1993, 46). They recommend using children's literature of high literary quality. In particular, Yvonne S. Freeman has identified detailed criteria for book selection (Freeman 1998, 23). It is also critical to consider for whom and for what purpose a book was written because this may change the way in which the language is crafted. That is, authors write some books to help people learn to read and to stimulate linguistic transfer. They also write books to celebrate variety in linguistic forms, but reading these may confuse young readers who are learning languages.

Language(s), Language Form, and Dialect

Language development and linguistic transfer are stimulated by books that include repetition; alliteration; rhythm; rhyming; and vocabulary that encourage phonological and phonemic awareness (Freeman 1998, 31; Smallwood et al. 1993; Smallwood 1991, 56). Many of the most used bilingual books are books of poetry.

Bilingualism in literature implies the presence of two languages in a work. *Bilingual literature*, far less common, refers to works in which two languages appear with "equal or at least comparable weight, format or scope" (Rudin 1996, 10). *Literary bilingualism* refers to "the use of secondary language elements in monolingual literature" and occurs frequently (10). Comprehension, literary quality, understanding of second-language development, and the difference between identification and stereotyping appear to be central issues of concern for teachers who have thought about the use of books that incorporate literary bilingualism. Determining whether the literary bilingualism improves "the literary merit of the story and makes it comprehensible and appealing" to all readers is important (Barrera, Quiroa, and Valdivia 2003, 149). For beginning readers, books with too much nonstandard language might interfere with their reading (Smallwood 1991, 14). For more advanced readers, literary bilingualism promotes their exploration of language variety and "gives them a better understanding of what language entails"(Rosberg 1995, 10). It can "demonstrate the cultural variety and richness" of a language (Hudelson et al. 1994, 169). According to the National Council of Teachers of English (NCTE), all students have a right to this exposure. In 2003, NCTE passed a resolution encouraging educators to affirm a "student's right to their own patterns and varieties of language . . . or whatever dialects in which they find their own identity and style" (NCTE 2003; Larson 1974, i).

However, here is a divergence into two important concerns. The first concern is the evidence that supports that second-language development and linguistic transfer are enhanced by development in the first language. The second concern is the issue of cultural identification and connection with texts as opposed to stereotyping. The issue of Ebonics in the Oakland school system has resulted in the entanglement and confusion of these two concerns.

For older readers, literary bilingualism has been seen as a useful way to develop the cultural authenticity and realism of a book for readers who can better identify with characters and settings. On the other hand, when this serves to perpetuate a stereotypical social background for a group, incorporation of dialect has caused objections (Hudelson et al. 1994, 169).

What teachers do, including book selection, "is strongly influenced by how they define language proficiency and their understanding of second-language development" (Truscott and Watts-Taffe 2003, 193). For example, linguistic minority children have at times been wrongly assigned to special education classrooms for this reason (Morales 2001, 17). For another example, Aileen Moffitt teaches first grade in the Oakland school system, where teachers are trained to recognize the patterns of Ebonics, contemporary African American speech. She created a booklet highlighting African American authors because she believes that "the reading books in America have left African-Americans out" and that teachers must "put them back in" (Chiles 1998). The Ebonics debate and the Oakland, California, case are explored in depth in *The Real Ebonics Debate: Power, Language, and the Eduation of African-American Children* (Perry and Delpit 1998).

When teachers become aware of and explore their personal feelings about accents, dialects, language forms, and languages, they develop a new level of critical sophistication in the book evaluation process. When using books that include dialects, accents, or variant forms of languages, it is important to discuss these elements with readers. Readers can explore their own perceptions of nonstandard language (Freeman 1998, 33). They can also gauge the variety of student feelings expressed about nonstandard language, dialect, and accent, should this occur in class, and respond (27).

Translation

Authentic texts, originally written in the home language, are preferable to English titles that have been translated into the home language (Hudelson et al. 1994, 166). Literary heritage exposes readers to other cultures and raises their awareness of language forms associated with their home language (Rosberg 1995, 9). When using books translated from English into the home language, stories should include those that are relevant to readers, translated well, and of high literary quality like *Tuck Everlasting/Tuck para siempre* (Freeman 1998, 33; Hudelson et al. 1994, 164). Authenticity and perspective in translation are influenced by the translator's background in the region or culture described in the work and rely also on the background of the reader (Rudin 1996, 91). Overtranslation and overly literal translation can lead to " 'unreal' rather than authentic language patterns" in translated works (Barrera, Quiroa, and Valdivia 2003, 162).

Translation recreates a story "by remaining true to the tone, style, plot, characterization, and the emotion the author originally expressed." Translated text should be checked for accurate translation of "concepts, language, and meaning" by someone from the language group (Singh and Lu 2003, 2). Attention to translation can offer insight about any language form or dialect content in a book (Hudelson et al. 1994, 168).

When using a book that may present an unfamiliar culture, it is important to determine whether or not second-language learners are engaging "the real meaning of a text" (Lessow-Hurley 2000, 88).

At a 2004 workshop on *Current Issues: Books in Spanish for Young Readers*, Isabel Schon said that the effect of poorly translated books is that students will not enjoy or read them. The workshop offers attendees a list titled "Caveat Emptor/Inferior Translations" to inform attendees of books that have been poorly translated into Spanish.

Schon and workshop instructor Adalin Torres-Zayas recommended using books that were originally published in Spanish as opposed to books that were published in English and translated into Spanish. When a translation of an English book is desired in Spanish, she recommends seeking out "exquisite renditions." In her article "*El gato garabato* (The Cat in the Hat)," Schon features annotated bibliographic entries for "high-quality original works written by Spanish-speaking authors," "exquisite renditions of English-language titles," and books published in Spanish-speaking countries (2005, 1208).

Design Elements

In monolingual picture books, the illustrations must communicate the story. By using picture books to communicate abstract concepts, teachers can contribute to linguistic transfer between two languages when the linguistic concept base is not yet developed. Determining the effectiveness of the context cues found in illustrations is a recommended criterion for evaluation. That is, books are most effective that include illustrations sophisticated enough to communicate abstract concepts like democracy (Freeman 1998, 31; Lessow-Hurley 2000, 56). When two languages are present, compare the placement and presentation of the text to evaluate the value of the languages, that is, whether one dominates or appears more important than the other. When a story is primarily communicated through the text, typeface should be clear and legible.

Literary Quality

Literary quality encourages bilingual learners to "engage in smart talk, create deep understandings . . . become lifelong readers and thinkers" (Hudelson et al. 1994, 164). It evokes aesthetic responses and inspires the expressive and creative use of language (Smallwood et al. 1993, 46). It also invites readers to enjoy a beautiful or fun book in their first language. Schon says that there is "no magic formula" but that excellent books in a child's first language are those that "spark the joy of reading" in them (Torres-Zayas 2004). Effective use of narrative voice, development of complex characters, interesting plots, relevant settings, human themes, rich language, and cultural context all contribute to a book's literary quality.

Engaging Stories

Engaging stories that are predictable and have repetitive incidents are recommended for promoting language development. They should include stories of cultural heritage, human experience, and the human condition. They should be complex enough to stimulate learners to try out multiple interpretations. Picture books that tell good stories in engaging ways are encouraged regardless of the language of the book (Torres-Zayas 2004). Identifiable stories, with realistic settings and characters, stimulate students to share similar stories from their own lives (Bauer 2003, 25). Students' stories can include talking about places they have lived, their families, their neighbors, the seasons, music, and cars (McKay 1992, 35).

Instructional Design

Teachers encourage using children's literature in a variety of ways to develop language skills. They encourage eliciting personal stories, encouraging informal talk, and designing thematic instruction to develop the language concept base of students and to motivate "spontaneous" conversation (Lessow-Hurley 2000, 59; Smallwood 2002).

Gail Weinstein-Shr encourages teachers to put aside the book they are reading to a group and get students talking about the story being read and to share their own similar stories (McKay 1992, 35–36). In *Stories to Tell Our Children* (1992) she includes pieces written by language minority students, reaction exercises, dictations, and exercises to get students to talk about stories in relation to their own personal stories (35–36).

Researchers recommend strategies that allow time for students to "read texts at their own levels" and that "acknowledge student's native cultures and languages" (Truscott and Watts-Taffe 2003, 197). Miriam Rosendo's approach, Book Browse, allows students time to casually discuss books together in their home language. Rosendo's goal is to stimulate the use of expressive language in both the home language and in English (2000, 35). In Rosendo's observations of Book Browse, she reports that students read, tell, demonstrate, and retell each other stories. They discuss illustrations and text. They listen, express opinions, and connect with other books (33). They memorize stories, pretend to read, and mimic readers' expressions in the retelling. They explore the "rhythm, sounds, vocabulary, and structures" of their home language (33–37). They exhibit code-switching to English, a demonstration of "linguistic creativity and sophistication" (Lessow-Hurley 2000, 62).

Thematic book grouping extends beyond grouping books by theme, to book grouping by author, illustrator, story versions, genre, culture, and age. Using thematic instruction encourages the use of "oral language, reading, writing, and critical thinking for learning and sharing ideas" (Peregoy and Boyle 1993, 40). Reading books together that are connected in some way stimulates discussion and allows students to relate their own stories to each other (Freeman 1998, 34; Hudelson and Rigg 1994–1995, 5). In a modified literature circle approach, four to six copies each of several different, thematically related books are provided, and among these are books that second-language learners will be able to read (Coelho 1998, 222).

Criticism of Bilingual Books and Recommendations

In her article, "Bilingual Books: Celebration vs. Confusion," Isabel Schon writes that the publishing industry continues to publish many bilingual books regardless of concerns of researchers and bilingual educators (2004d, 136). Many bilingual educators choose not to use bilingual books in the classroom (Torres-Zayas 2004). They believe it is best for "children to master their native language first" and not to confuse new readers by expecting them to handle two languages simultaneously (Schon 2004d, 136). Bilingual books seem like a good idea to parents who think the books teach two languages. Often reviewers of the books do not have the needed background to perceive "mangled grammar, inappropriate expressions, and literal interpretations that make no sense." Schon urges educators to "select only those bilingual books that are faithful to the spirit, rhythm, and symmetry of both languages, and books that reflect all linguistic differences, colloquialisms, and popular expressions that add charm to the work" (136).

Self-Confidence and Language Learners

Teachers have the opportunity to create a comfort zone of respect for students' home languages through children's literature. English-only settings can lead children to "lose contact with their native language," associate it with "shame and humiliation," and remove children from "their everyday cultural realities" (Morales 2001, 17). Negative attitudes toward a language lower the language's status. Students are aware of such attitudes and may let negative attitudes influence their self-concept and their respect for their primary language (Lessow-Hurley 2000, 69).

Students' confidence may influence their willingness to make errors in front of others that learning a language requires (48). Teachers raise the status of home languages by using children's literature in ways that support, recognize, value, and respect bilingual students. Using children's literature to affirm culture and language is one way to support, recognize, value, and respect bilingual students and their cultures.

Books at Home and in Libraries

Students might increase their comfort level and confidence by taking books used in class home to practice independent reading and reading with their families. Helping students and their parents or guardians contact with local public librarians contributes to language and cultural development and to community participation. Public children's librarians have supported development of and access to special collections of bilingual books for community children based on parents' group requests. Public librarians provide bilingual collections to support their communities.

Linguistically Diverse Children's Literature Resources

The Internet has helped build communities of teachers, librarians, academics, parents, and organizations committed to providing better access to books that affirm and celebrate students' identities through language.

Started in 1997, and observed every April 30 nationwide, El Día de los Niños/El Día de los Libros celebrates libraries' and teachers' commitment to connecting children, books, languages, and cultures, to honor home languages and cultures, and to promote bilingual and multilingual literacy (http://www.texasdia.org/history.html).

In 2002, the California Department of Education enhanced the *Recommended Literature: Kindergarten through Grade Twelve* (http://www.cde.ca.gov/ci/rl/ll) database to include books in Chinese, Chinese/English, Filipino, Filipino/English, Hmong, Hmong/English, Spanish, Spanish/English, Vietnamese, and Vietnamese/English and is searchable by these languages.

In 2002, the *International Children's Digital Library* at http://www.icdlbooks.org was launched by the University of Maryland College Park to "create a collection of more than 10,000 books in 100 different languages," freely available full-text in digital format. So far, the database offers digitized versions of books in 392 different languages.

Dr. Isabel Schon directs the Barahona Center for the Study of Books in Spanish for Children and Adolescents at California State University, San Marcos. She is well known for her popular and invaluable bibliographies. These include *Recommended Books in Spanish for Children and Young Adults: 2000 through 2004* (2004), *Recommended Books in Spanish for Children and Young Adults, 1996 through 1999* (2000b), and the series *Books in Spanish for Children and Young Adults: An Annotated Guide* (1993).

In addition to these bibliographies, Schon has contributed by demonstrating a wide range of thematic bibliographies. These have been published in journals and include supernatural tales; science books; books for young adults classics, realistic fiction, fantasy, and historical fiction; history books; Newbery winners; poetry; works published in Mexico, Spain, Argentina, Chile, Bogotá, and Venezuela; and books about Latino children and families in the United States (Schon 2003a, 2003b, 2003c, 2003d, 2004a, 2004b, 2004c).

These and other titles were the basis for the creation of the database *Books in Spanish for Children and Adolescents*, created through the Barahona Center. The database includes information on 6,000 titles and book review information (http://www.csusm.edu/csb). The Web site also includes many educators' resources including lists of recommended translations of award-winning titles and Web sites of interest. The Center offers the workshop "Books and Reading Strategies for Bilingual Students in Grades K–8" that focuses on book selection, cultural reading style, using literature to teach reading through strategies such as reader's theater, reciprocal teaching, SSQ3R (the reading technique of survey, question, read, recite/retell, review), vocabulary strategies, and directed reading/thinking activities.

The Center Web site recommends other Web sites about books in Spanish for children, including Mundo Latino at http://www.mundolatino.org/rinconcito.

Other reviewing sources for books in Spanish include Críticas. An English Speaker's Guide to the Latest Spanish-Language Titles at http://www.criticasmagazine.com.

The Galludet Press catalog at http://gupress.gallaudet.edu/catalog.html is a source for children's books in signed English.

Other professional resources include NABE, or the National Association for Bilingual Education, found on the Web at http://www.nabe.org. This organization provides resources on research and practice.

Professional journals that frequently publish articles and bibliographies on the topic include *Language Arts*, *The New Advocate*, *The Reading Teacher*, *The Bulletin of the Center for Children's Books*, *The Hornbook*, *School Library Journal*, and *TESOL Journal*. For example, the *Journal of Youth Services in Libraries* published the annotated bibliography "Bilingual Books for Children" that includes translations of books originally written in Chinese, Hopi, Inktitut, Japanese, Khmer, Korean, Multilingual books, Russian, Swahili, Thai, Tibetan, Vietnamese, and Spanish (Association for Library Services to Children 2001).

Case: Ebonics

In 1996, the Oakland School Board passed a resolution to expand an existing program in which district teachers are trained to recognize the nonstandard speech patterns of Ebonics, contemporary African American speech, in order to help students to speak Standard English (Chiles 1998). After three years of this approach, results for Prescott Elementary School students on the California Test of Basic Skills rose by as much as 15 percent. Aileen Moffitt, a first-grade teacher in the system, created a booklet highlighting African American authors because she believes that "the reading books in America have left African-Americans out" and teachers must "put them back in" (Chiles 1998). Theresa Perry and Lisa Delpit have discussed this case in depth in *The Real Ebonics Debate: Power, Language, and the Education of African-American Children* (1998).

Discussion Questions

1. Search for articles about the Oakland Ebonics case and review Perry and Delpit's book and discuss your views of the case.

2. When and how would you share books that are written in or that include non-Standard English, dialects, or accents as part of the text and story?

3. How would you design booklists based on languages?

4. What criteria would you use for selecting books in other languages for your classroom library?

5. Would you include bilingual books and/or books that included bilingualism in your classroom library? Discuss reasons for including or not including each type of book.

Resource Study: Study of the *International Children's Digital Library* and Sources of Books in Spanish

To begin to appreciate the range of books for children originally written in languages that are not English, it is useful to review full-text books offered through the *International Children's Digital Library* at http://www.icdlbooks.org.

In addition, to begin to think in terms of publishers, distributors, and book sellers (other than those in the United States), it may be useful to review some of the Web sites for them around the world that produce books for children written in Spanish.

Argentina—Librería García Cambeiro—http://www.latbook.com

Central America—Vientos Tropicales—http://www.vientos.com

Cinco Puntos—http://cincopuntos.com

Colombia—Editorial Norma—http://www.norma.com

Costa Rica—Editorial Costa Rica—http://www.editorialcostarica.com

Mexico—Librerias Gandhi para Niños y Jóvenes—http://www.ghandi.com.mx

Spain/Europe—http://www.casadellibro.com

Uruguay—Librería Linardi y Risso—http://www.chasque.apc.org/lyrbooks

Venezuela—Ediciones Ekare—http://www.ekare.com

United States sources include:

Continental Book Company—http://www.continentalbook.com

Lectorum Publications, Inc.—http://www.lectorum.com

Mariuccie Iaconi Book Imports, Inc.—http://www.mibibook.com

Santillana USA—http://www.santillanausa.com

In addition to publishers of books written in Spanish not in the United States, the *ICDL* provides a list of links to "Contributing Publishers" of the books represented in the *ICDL* database at http://www.icdlbooks.org/links/publisherslink.shtml.

Discussion Questions

1. Explore the publishers' Web sites for books in Spanish and compare these. How do they differ?

2. Explore the publishers' Web sites at the *ICDL* publishers' link to examine the organizations producing children's books around the world. Discuss your observations about these publishers from their Web sites.

3. Discuss the value and possible classroom uses of the *ICDL* Web site.

References

Alfaro, Cristina. 2004. Cross linguistic transfer: What must highly qualified teachers know? Lecture presented at San Diego State University, San Diego, Spring.

Association for Library Services to Children. International Relations Committee. 2001. Bilingual books for children. *Journal of Youth Services in Libraries* 14(2): 32–37.

Baker, Colin. 1993. *Foundations of bilingual education and bilingualism.* Bristol, PA: Multilingual Matters, Ltd.

Barrera, Rosalinda B., Ruth E. Quiroa, and Rebeca Valdivia. 2003. Spanish in Latino picture storybooks in English: Its use and textual effects. In *Multicultural issues in literacy research and practice,* ed. Arlette Ingram Willis, Georgia Earnest Garcia, Rosalinda B. Barrera, and Violet J. Harris, 145–165. Mahwah, NJ: L. Erlbaum Associates.

Bauer, Eurydice Bouchereau. 2003. Finding Esmerelda's shoes: A case study of a young bilingual child's response to literature. In *Multicultural issues in literacy research and practice,* ed. Arlette Ingram Willis, Georgia Earnest Garcia, Rosalinda B. Barrera, and Violet J. Harris, 11–27. Mahwah, NJ: L. Erlbaum Associates.

Chiles, Nick. 1998. Talk of success with Ebonics: Class posts higher test scores. *Austin American-Statesman* (Texas), June 14, sec. Insight.

Coelho, Elizabeth. 1998. *Teaching and learning in multicultural schools: An integrated approach.* Bilingual Education and Bilingualism. Philadelphia, PA: Multilingual Matters, Ltd.

Connor, Steve. 1997. World's languages dying at alarming rate: Shrinking linguistic diversity mourned; state's native tongues especially hard hit. In *The New Press guide to multicultural resources for young readers*, ed. Daphne Muse, 464. New York: The New Press.

Crawford, James. 2003. A few things Ron Unz would prefer you didn't know about English learners in California. http://ourworld.compuserve.com/homepages/JWCRAWFORD/castats.htm.

———. 2002. The bilingual education act, 1968–2002. Obituary. *Rethinking Schools Online* 16(4). http://www.rethinkingschools.org/archive/16_04/Bil164.shtml.

Cummins, Jim. 1994. Primary language instruction and the education of language minority students. In *Schooling and language minority students: A theoretical framework*, 2nd ed., 3–46. Los Angeles: Evaluation, Dissemination and Assessment Center, California State University.

Dicker, Susan J. 2000. Official English and bilingual education. In *Sociopolitics of English teaching*, ed. Joan Kelly Hall and William G. Eggington, 45–66. Tonawanda, NY: Multilingual Matters, Ltd.

Evans, Carol. 1994. Monstruos, pesadillas, and other frights: A thematic unit. *Reading Teacher* 47 (February): 428–430.

Freeman, Yvonne S. 1998. Providing quality children's literature in Spanish. *New Advocate* 11 (Winter): 23–38.

Gutierrez, Rochelle. 2002. Beyond essentialism: The complexity of language in teaching mathematics to Latina/o students. *American Educational Research Journal* 39(4): 1047–1088.

Hudelson, Sarah, Julia Fournier, Cecilia Espinosa, and Renee Bachman. 1994. Chasing windmills: Confronting the obstacles to literature-based programs in Spanish. *Language Arts* 71 (March): 164–171.

Hudelson, Sarah, and Pat Rigg. 1994–1995. My *abuela* can fly: Children's books about old people in English and Spanish. *TESOL Journal* 3 (Winter): 5–10.

International Relations Committees 1998–99 and 1999–2000. 2001. Bilingual books for children. *Journal of Youth Services* 14 (Winter): 32–37.

Larson, Richard L. 1974. To the readers of CCC: Resolution on language. Students' right to their own language. *College Composition and Communication* 25(3): i.

Lau v. Nichols. 1974. 414 U.S. 563.

Leistyna, Pepi, Magaly Lavadenz, and Thomas Nelson. 2004. Introduction—Critical pedagogy: Revitalizing and democratizing teacher education. *Teacher Education Quarterly* 31 (Winter): 3–15.

Lessow-Hurley, Judith. 2000. *The foundations of dual language instruction*. 3rd ed. New York: Addison Wesley Longman.

McKay, Sandra Lee. 1992. Stories to tell our children. *TESOL Journal* 1 (Spring): 35–36.

Morales, Candace A. 2001. Our own voice: The necessity of Chicano literature in mainstream curriculum. *Multicultural Education* 9 (Winter): 16–20.

Moran, Carol E., and Kenji Hakuta. 2001. Bilingual education: Broadening research perspectives. In *Handbook of research on multicultural education,* ed., James A. Banks and Cherry McGee Banks, 445–462. San Francisco: Jossey-Bass.

Movers & Shakers. 2002. The people who are shaping the future of libraries. *Library Journal*, suppl., 127(5): 15.

National Council of Teachers of English. 2003. NCTE members approve resolutions on composing with nonprint media and students' right to their own language. News release, December 1. http://www.ncte.org/about/press/rel/115075.htm.

New York City Board of Education. 1993. *Pan American educational resources & cultural materials.* Brooklyn: Office of Bilingual Education, New York City Board of Education.

Olsen, Laurie. 1998. The Unz/Tuchman "English for Children" initiative: A new attack on immigrant children and the schools. *Multicultural Education* 5 (Spring): 11–13.

Oran, Sally M. 2003. From the mountain to the mesa: Scaffolding preservice teachers' knowledge about the cultural contexts of literacy. In *Multicultural issues in literacy research and practice*, ed. Arlette Ingram Willis, Georgia Earnest Garcia, Rosalinda B. Barrera, and Violet J. Harris, 167–184. Mahwah, NJ: L. Erlbaum Associates.

Ovando, Carlos Julio, and Virginia P. Collier. 1985. *Bilingual and ESL classrooms: Teaching in multicultural contexts.* New York: McGraw Hill. (Quoted in Lessow-Hurley 2000, 8)

Peregoy, Suzanne F., and Owen F. Boyle. 1993. *Reading, writing, and learning in ESL: A resource book for K–8 teachers.* Tempe, AZ: Bilingual Press.

Perry, Theresa, and Lisa Delpit, eds. 1998. *The real Ebonics debate: Power, language, and the education of African-American children.* Boston: Beacon Press.

Rosberg, Merilee. 1995. *Exploring language through multicultural literature.* ERIC Report. Cedar Rapids, IA. ED 389 175.

Rosendo, Miriam. 2000. Book browse: A creative approach to meaningful language learning. *Multicultural Teaching* 19 (Autumn): 33–38.

Rudin, Ernst. 1996. *Tender accents of sound: Spanish in the Chicano novel in English.* Tempe, AZ: Bilingual Press/Editorial Bilingue.

Schon, I. 2005. *El gato garabato (The cat in the hat). Booklist* 101(13): 1208.

———. 2004a. Libros de ciencias en Español. A selection of recent science trade books in Spanish. *Science and Children* (March): 43–47.

———. 2004b. Board books, supernatural tales and more: Children's books in Spanish. *Language* (February): 39.

———. 2004c. Latinos, Hispanics, and Latin Americans. *Book Links* (January): 44–48.

———. 2004d. Bilingual books: Celebration vs. confusion. *Booklist* 101(1): 136–138.

———. 2004e. *Recommended books in Spanish for children and young adults: 2000–2004.* Lanham, MD: Scarecrow Press.

———. 2003a. From the U.S. and abroad: Books in Spanish for children and adolescents. *Multicultural Review* (December): 43–46.

———. 2003b. Huicholes to Monstruos: Books in Spanish from Spanish-speaking countries. *Language* (November): 37–39.

———. 2003c. Noteworthy books in Spanish for adolescents. *VOYA* (August): 190–192.

———. 2003d. From Newbery winners to Islam. Books in Spanish for adolescents. *CR* 37(2): 40–43.

———. 2000a. From Cinco lobitos to Los tres cerditos: Children's books in Spanish from around the world. *Childhood Education* 80(2): 93–95.

————. 2000b. *Recommended books in Spanish for children and young adults, 1996 through 1999.* Lanham, MD: Scarecrow Press.

————. 1993. *Books in Spanish for children and young adults: An annotated guide.* Metuchen, NJ: Scarecrow Press.

Singh, Majari, and Lu Mei-Yu. 2003. Exploring the function of heroes and heroines in children's literature from around the world. ERIC Digest. Bloomington, IN: ERIC Clearinghouse on Reading English and Communication, 1–3. ED47709.

Smallwood, Betty Ansin. 2002. Thematic literature and curriculum for English language learners in early childhood education. ERIC Digest. Washington, DC: ERIC Clearinghouse on Languages and Linguistics. ED470 980.

————. 1991. *The literature connection: A read-aloud guide for multicultural classrooms.* Reading, MA: Addison Wesley Publishing Company.

Smallwood, Betty Ansin, Wendy McDonell, Rob Clement, and Ruth Lambach. 1993. Ask the TJ. *TESOL Journal* 2(4): 45–47.

Smallwood, Betty Ansin, et al. 2002. *Integrating the ESL standards into classroom practice. Grades pre-K–2.* Washington, DC: Teachers of English to Speakers of Other Languages.

Tamayo, Lincoln, Rosalie Porter, and Christine Rossell. 2001. The text of the Massachusetts initiative. An initiative petition for law: An act related to the teaching of English in public schools. http://onenation.org/matext.html.

Torres-Zayas, Adalin. 2004. *Current issues: Books in Spanish for young readers.* Workshop. Barahona Center for the Study of Books in Spanish for Children and Adolescents, California State University, San Marcos.

Truscott, Diane M., and Susan Watts-Taffe. 2003. English as a second language, literacy development in mainstream classrooms: Application of a model for effective practice. In *Multicultural issues in literacy research and practice*, ed. Arlette Ingram Willis, Georgia Earnest Garcia, Rosalinda B. Barrera, and Violet J. Harris, 185–202. Mahwah, NJ: L. Erlbaum Associates.

Weinstein-Shr, Gail. 1992. *Stories to tell our children.* Boston: Heinle & Heinle.

5

Peace and Children's Literature

Since the 1970s, much has been written about peace and violence in children's literature. There are many resources for teachers who want to learn about this literature and how best to use it in the classroom.

In the 1970s, book editors and authors began to write about the criteria teachers should use to evaluate how violence is depicted in books for youth (Giblin 1995; Jordan 1973). In 1987, a volume of *Children's Literature* was devoted to the topic of violence in books for youth. The International Board on Books for Young People at http://www.ibby.org was founded to promote international understanding and goodwill through books for children and teenagers. In 1998, the theme for the *26th Congress of the International Board on Books for Young People* in New Delhi, India, was *Peace through Children's Books*. In 2000, *The Lion and the Unicorn* published a themed issue titled "Violence and Children's Literature" (Goodenough 2000b). In 2001, Kate Agnew and Geoff Fox's *Children at War: From the First World War to the Gulf* was published. This work is not limited to a review of novels written for young people but extends to "autobiographies, popular fiction, comics, story papers, and picture books" (1). Most recently, the 2005 theme for the sixth IBBY regional conference was *Children's Books: Messengers of Peace*. Since 1953 the Jane Addams Book Awards have been presented to books that "effectively promote the cause of peace, social justice, world community" (http://home.igc.org/~japa/jacba/index_jacba.html).

A body of literature for a youth audience after September 11, 2001, is devoted to the events of that day and their aftermath. The 1990s and 2000s have been marked by the publication of new realistic literature. Books about gang violence, homelessness, poverty, HIV (human immune deficiency virus), guns, and bullying have been written, in part, in the service of what some call bibliotherapy, or helping youth deal with the stress in their lives, and what others call identification of the reader with the story and events (Stamps 2003, 26).

All of these resources range in coverage from topics of war, urban society, increasing societal violence, and globalization to alienation, fairytales, and trauma. Each one in some way considers the question (Goodenough 2000a, v), "Will honest representations of the human capacity for evil overwhelm the young mind in despair?"

Age Appropriateness

Evaluating books about peace and violence for age appropriateness is important because many works include materials for younger and older audiences in the same volume (Goodenough 2000a, vi). For example, *The Big Book for Peace* (Durell and Sachs 1990) and *911: The Book of Help* (Cart 2002) include pieces for both youth and adult audiences.

This is also the case for books based on the lives of young people. Some of these include autobiographical essays or essays based on interviews with youth. At first glance, these works appear to be books written for young audiences about young people, but in some cases, these are documents of sociological research. Careful reading of the front matter of books can determine the appropriate audience for a book. The front matter, or introduction, includes a specific statement of the purpose of a work and the intended audience.

Bibliotherapy

Fairy tales and storytelling have provided an escape to "secret spaces" where readers and listeners can "frame, interpret and relieve atrocious anxieties" (Goodenough 2000a, v). Stories soothe people in trauma by leading them to use their imaginations to mediate, repair, and preside over the invention of new meanings in a new world (viii). Stories communicate the ideology of peace but also communicate how conflict is a part of life and how conflict resolution leads to growth (Kulkarni and Hulikavi 1998, 137). When using books to help traumatized children, some suggest considering how the story depicts relationships with others, relationship with self, and the human relationship with nature (137).

Sue Ellen Bridgers's novel *All We Know of Heaven* (1996) is a story based on her cousin's experience with domestic violence during the depression. Bridgers speculates that there may be "a strong role for young adult literature in examining the realities of abusive, confining relationships" (Bridgers 2000, 72). She suggests that perhaps a book about such a relationship could help a reader who may find himself or herself be in violent relationship come to a realization about his or her own situation (72).

Realism

During the 1960s, realistic fiction written for teens addressed many topics and did not guarantee happy endings. In 1967, S. E. Hinton "created a form of teen literature that takes on tough issues" when she wrote *The Outsiders*, a story about "greasers" and "socs." The "socs" (socials) are the "popular, wealthy kids." The "greasers" are the "less popular school outcasts."

The tension between the two peer groups leads to a rumble in which a "greaser kills a soc." *The Outsiders* has been criticized for romanticizing violence (Murphy 2004). Teacher Shelby Salley says that "at a deeper level, the book advocates nonviolence and encourages young people to break down the barriers between peer groups" (Noz 1999). Salley's students relate the peer conflicts described in *The Outsiders* to the social and class peer conflicts that have been described in school shooting tragedies, and other school violence, during the 1990s (Noz 1999). Hinton was seventeen when *The Outsiders* was published. The author was motivated to write the novel because she "was mad about the social situation" at her high school "where everyone got in their little group and wouldn't make friends outside it" (http://www.sehinton.com).

During the 1970s, realism in young adult fiction was criticized for promoting "faith in a pathogenic, miserable and hopeless condition of being, which is, allegedly, our realistic condition" (Jordan 1973, 140–145).

In 1974, Robert Cormier published *The Chocolate War*, a story about high school bullying and the pressure to conform. *The Chocolate War* continues to come under challenge. In 2003, it was challenged as unfit for younger readers because "the story does not have a positive message about how to deal with a gang, bullies or peer pressure" (Hill 2005). Objection was also raised because the "main character resists; he is brutally beaten, and also learns that the religious instructors who ran the school were as bad as the bullies who were students" (Hill 2005). But teachers report that students continue to "identify with the storyline" of *The Chocolate War* and comment on the truth of the book and that "stuff like this happens in school all the time" (Axiotis et al. 1999, 27).

Horror novels grew in popularity among teenage and younger readers in the 1980s as Stephen King titles and R.L. Stine's *Goosebumps* series were widely read. During the late 1990s, popular culture combining intense violence with humor was a trend that began with movies like *Scream*.

Reviewer Kathleen Isaacs writes that in the 2000s "the amount of violence in books published for teens seems to be multiplying, and the descriptions include ever more disturbing detail" in the best of literature (2003, 50). Isaac reports that many of her middle school students "prefer not to read these books" because they are students who are "more familiar with the possibilities [of violence] and less knowledgeable about actual pain and suffering" (51). Isaacs thinks the current book market that includes increasingly violent books for youth has been driven by the media's inaccurate and overly violent portrayal of society (51).

Young authors' stories are shaped by events that surround them. Like S. E. Hinton, Nick McDonnell published the bestselling novel *Twelve* (2002) when he was seventeen years old. In the front matter, an inscription reveals how, like Hinton, his writing was shaped by the experiences of his generation. It reads: "[C]an we please all stand and have a moment of silence for those students who died. And now can we have a moment of silence for those students who killed them" (McDonell 2002).

Science Fiction

Science fiction is fiction that has used "science for violence and war," and this gives science a "narrow and sensationalistic" bad image even though "science is an abstraction that is not good or bad" (Salwi 1998, 113). Popular, violent, juvenile science fiction depicts war as "exciting and fun" because it leads to "dramatic action." Peace is sometimes seen as monotonous and boring (Salwi 1998, 110). However, science fiction also includes "the horrors of wars in their stories to emphasize the importance of peace" (Salwi 1998, 111). In Arthur C. Clarke's *3010: The Final Odyssey,* man achieves "peace through technology." Salwi Dilpi and Ira Saxena write science-fiction stories about peace. Dilpi believes there is "a need to write about the various problems of peace itself from a scientific perspective . . . in the form of science fiction" (Salwi 1998, 113).

War Stories

Contemporary juvenile literature includes books that present realistic, nonromantic depictions of war. Realism has expanded war fiction to include works that "confront the moral dilemmas posed by more modern wars, with no simplistic accounts of good guys versus bad and no pat definitions of what constitutes heroism" (Myers 2000a, 327–336). In 1995, Masha Rudman described the scope of war literature. It concerns "how people behave with each other" and "how communities are built or destroyed." It depicts the development of "competition, bullying, and friendship" and demonstrates the skill of peacemaking" (Rudman 1995, 369). The IBBY Congress recommends using literature that can restore the confidence and security of those children who suffer from the trauma of wars and tragedies.

Nonviolence

IBBY also recommends using children's books that use realism to "inspire peace without paralyzing with fear" (International Board on Books for Young People 1998, 467; Myers 2000a, 327–336). There is a need to take advantage of the economic prosperity of peaceful times to publish books that instill a nonnuclear, nonviolent philosophy in children. A philosophy of love, truth, and nonviolence can "equip children to live peacefully with strangeness in society" (Saxena 1998, 106). Books can help readers "cope with life's situations" by including kindness and "reassurance in the goodness of humanity" (107). Such a philosophy can also inspire children to action (Saxena 1998, 104; Salwi 1998, 109).

For example, the nonfiction book *Sadako and the Thousand Paper Cranes* (Coerr 1977) recounts for grade-school audiences the story of Sadako Sasaki's folding of 1,000 paper cranes to survive leukemia induced by exposure to the Hiroshima nuclear bombing ten years earlier in 1945 (104). Sadako's statue holding a paper crane is located in Hiroshima Peace Park. In 1993, Coerr published *Sadako,* a picture-book version of the same story, for a younger audience.

Katherine Scholes's early reader picture nonfiction book *Peacetimes* (1989), reissued as *Peace Begins with You* (1990; 1994), captures the spirit of the nonviolence movement including advice for how to become a peacemaker (Saxena 1998, 105). Known for its beautiful illustrations, this book introduces the concept of peace and the meanings of needs, rights, wishes, compromise, and resolution in everyday personal life, telling how peace can feel "warm, bright, strong, or calm, cool, and gentle." It goes on to discuss the same topics on an international level and with respect to the earth (Saxena 1998, 105; *Peace begins with you* 1990).

Natural Disaster

Organizations also pursue relief through programs designed to connect books and readers. In 2005, in Aceh, Sumatra, IBBY set up a worldwide tsunami relief program voluntary collection among its National Sections to support children's literature projects in the Asian countries that were affected by the tsunami. Donations are used to purchase books and set up libraries. The premise is that "reading and children's books are very effective in alleviating children's sorrows after tragedy" and that providing books and readers can support this end (IBBY 2005).

Reality-based Literature

The 1990s and 2000s ushered in a new generation of realistic fiction and nonfiction related to war, gangs, school violence, and guns. These books from different genres address contemporary young people in the media generation.

Nonfiction

In nonfiction youth literature young people write about their experiences in life using a journalistic, sometimes therapeutic style. Young authors have created thematic, photoessay collections to give young readers stories in which they can identify with experiences, feelings, and personal appearance. Books discuss topics that many young people face but that may not be commonly discussed in classrooms. Young people write about their experiences with violence, HIV education, abuse, and life on the streets. They write about exposure to drugs, handguns, police brutality, and poverty. Common themes in their stories include their ability to tap their inner resources, finding hope and changing lives.

In *Voices from the Streets. Young Former Gang Members Tell Their Stories* (1996), S. Beth Atkins turned her interviews with young people into stories to help readers identify with why people join gangs, whether the reason is ethnic association, protection, yearning for "family" life, poverty, lack of education, or lack of job opportunity. Atkins carries a message of hope by including stories about how people can leave gangs. She asserts that "between 1980 and 1993 gang related murder of and by juveniles . . . increased fourfold." The stories highlight courage, time, dedication, hard work, and a strong commitment to the self-determination and desire to change that it takes to leave a gang (ix).

Collections of essays by and for young people inform and inspire young readers. Youth Communication was founded by Keith Hefner in 1980 in response to the overly censored high school presses (Kay, Estepa, and Desetta 1998, 278). In Youth Communication publications, youth journalists improve their own writing as they write stories they believe will "benefit their peers" (279). In *Things Get Hectic: Teens Write about the Violence that Surrounds Them/Youth Communication* (1998), adult editors guide teenage journalists in selecting and crafting stories (Kay, Estepa, and Desetta 1998). Stories describe violence in the home and on the street, gangsta' rap, women and rap, mosh pits, gay bashers, anti-Arab media, violent movies, guns, weapons, sexual assault, relationship violence, police and the criminal justice system, and stories of war and violence in immigrant's home countries.

In *Hear These Voices: Youth at the Edge of the Millennium*, author Anthony Allison invites readers to identify with the stories and to relate to the community and love depicted in them (1999, ii). Stories are about abandoned street children, child prostitutes, HIV-positive teens, drug addicts, and conflict resolution programs. Readers of these stories are encouraged to seek help from an adult if the adults in their lives are not taking responsibility for the well-being of the young person.

Common themes in "voices" nonfiction include a plea for adults to take responsibility, a commitment to remaining hopeful, and a dedication to finding new solutions for problems. Finally, a message in these books is that "young people do not seek violence, enjoy it or get used to it" and that they want help and someone to listen to them.

Gangs

There is a lack of books about street violence and gangs for young readers and reluctant young adult readers. Gang literature is often autobiographical and intended to inform readers about how to get out of a gang and what to expect if you join a gang.

In *It Doesn't Have to Be This Way. A Barrio Story* (1999), Luis J. Rodriguez presents a bilingual book in a picture-book format. The author explains his experience in a gang, his work now as a counselor, and his hope of showing young people their options. Rodriguez explains how young people join gangs "to belong, to be cared for, and to be embraced" (3). In this picture book is a scene of a friend who has been shot and is lying in the street. This disturbing image depicts the reality of violence.

Always Running: La Vida Loca, Gang Days in L.A. (1993) by Luis Rodriguez was written for older readers and has been challenged for depictions of graphic violence and sexual assault.

The founder of the Crips gang in Los Angeles, Stanley Tookie Williams, has coauthored a series of children's books warning young readers about the dangers of gang life. Williams, a convicted murderer, on death row, coauthored the series *Tookie Speaks Out against Gangs*. The series includes the book *Gangs and Violence* (1996). The proceeds from the sale of Williams's books go to the Institute for the Prevention of Youth Violence and other organizations for peace (Forecasts 1998). Williams has also been nominated for the Nobel Peace Prize for his antigang efforts. Still, many question the ability of Williams to speak with honesty and authenticity, considering his own history of violence and crime.

School Shootings and Gun Violence

During the 1990s, school shooting incidents included the Columbine High School killings in 1998 (Orr 2003, 13). Suicide rates among youth rose. Bullying in schools increased as "one-third of U.S. students . . . experienced bullying either as the target or the perpetrator" (25). A *Time* magazine poll in 2000 indicated that parents felt "better about the issue of school violence, while children were feeling worse and one third of children surveyed reported witnessing a violent incident, while less than 10 percent of parents suspected that their children had ever seen anything" (26).

In Todd Strasser's *Give a Boy a Gun* (2000), the author lobbies, persuades, and convinces the audience that in the United States "gun use and gun availability is horribly, insanely out of control" and dedicates his book to ending youth violence and charges readers with the goal of making change on the issues of banning semiautomatic assault-type weapons and gun control. Strasser lists many books and Web sites of many organizations devoted to stopping gun violence among youth (143–146).

One frequently referenced juvenile book about shootings by children is *Making Up Megaboy* (1998) by Virginia Walter. The story centers on other people's responses to teenage boy Robbie, who has retreated into an imaginary cartoon world and who has shot the owner of a liquor store using his father's handgun. The book is full of illustrations that are "integral to this story and add a surreal tone and mood" and reflect the perspective of Robbie (Zvirin 1998, 1009; Courtot n.d.). Zvirin writes that, "along with Walter Dean Myer's *Scorpions* (1988) and Sonia Levitin's *Adam's War* (1994), this is part of a growing number of novels for the age group that focus on the tragic outcome of guns in the hands of children" (1009). *Making Up Megaboy* is told from multiple perspectives. Robbie's perspective is communicated through the drawings included in the book. Although one reviewer wrote that the book "reads like a CNN news report," reviewers agree it is a good conversation starter that makes no judgments and presents no lessons (Courtot n.d.; Guira 1998; Zvirin 1998, 1009). It is accessible to the media generation because the graphics provide visual representations of characters (Courtot n.d.; Guira 1998).

Some recent titles include stories that describe "the conditions that might lead to" school violence (Isaacs 2003, 51). Ron Koertge's *The Brimstone Journals* (2001) and Alex Flinn's *Breaking Point* (2002) are "well-written and thoughtful titles useful for discussing some of the underlying problems" (51).

In *Just One Flick of a Finger* (1996), Marybeth Lorbiecki creates a picture book with illustrator David Diaz, winner of the Caldecott Medal for 1994's *Smoky Nights* about the Los Angeles riots. In *Just One Flick of a Finger*, Jack fears being bullied and takes his father's gun to school. His friend Sherm confronts him about it. Later, Jack accidentally shoots Sherm, and Sherm is hospitalized. Some reviews praise the language in hip-hop-style verse and the urban text and images that "capture the tension and fear of an urban schoolyard menaced by guns" (*Just One Flick of a Finger* 1996). Reviews have also called the book patronizing, "unrealistically and sentimentally hopeful," heavy-handed, with "contrived solutions," and simplistic and moralistic (Rochman 1996; Del Negro 1996; Ammon 1997). Perhaps a testament to the different readings the book offers or simply a difference in readers' views, reviewers propose age ranges for which the book is appropriate from "ages six and up" to "for older readers" beginning with grade 6 through grade 12.

The Unhappy Ending

Robert Cormier's books are known for breaking the convention of the happy ending. Parents have objected to the pessimism in *The Chocolate War* and *I Am the Cheese* (Iskander 1987, 7). Sylvia Patterson Iskander proposes that Cormier's stories bother people because they "leave no room for any thing but pessimism about the survival of Cormier's protagonists" (9). Because there is no happy ending, readers continue to think about the book and about moral responsibility suggested by the books (18). Cormier wrote that his message is that "evil only occurs when we allow it to occur; it does not blossom by itself" (18). This interpretation of unhappy endings suggests a role for those who present books to readers.

Framing Violent Content

In the late 1990s and 2000s, villainy in stories did appeal to children. The books in *A Series of Unfortunate Events* by Lemony Snicket, also known as Daniel Handler, became bestsellers. Each book in the series addresses readers, warning that what they are about to read is "extremely unpleasant" and that "there is nothing to be found in these pages but misery, despair, and discomfort, and you still have time to choose something else to read" (Snicket 1999, 2001). Handler thinks that young people relate to the idea that rewards are often unrelated to good behavior (Bowers 2002).

In children's literature "the appeal of the violence and its effect on the child are determined to a great extent by context, by the way in which the violence is framed" by teachers (Tatar 1998, 83). Teacher Darcy Lockman suggests "appalling activities" for teachers to use to teach the series (Lockman 2002, 50). The most intriguing of these suggestions is to ask students to think of other literary villains, such as Count Olaf, and to list what they have in common. She asks students to describe what they would say if they encountered Count Olaf, and how he might react to them. Lockman suggests students think of new settings for an adventure in the series and write to the author to suggest it. These empowering activities situate readers in control of their responses to stories (50).

Other strategies for framing the content of violent stories with students include having students read John Gardner's reworking of the Beowolf epic, *Grendel* (1971) or other books about "perennial conflicts." Students may then role-play as they hold peace talks and develop peace contracts, based on the conflicts in the story. Any stories that include conflicts are opportunities for teachers to ask students to argue either side of the conflict in a debate, then to switch sides (Coghlan 2000, 86–87).

Jennifer Armstrong argues that narrative in children's literature can help transmit "civilization" to young readers (2003, 191). Narrative texts provide readers with more options. Narrative is "a string of decisions, reactions, consequences," and reading stories is "one of the best ways to learn that there are many possible outcomes to every set of circumstances" (194).

Selection Criteria

The IBBY Congress recommended that in a world in which they are overexposed to violence, children need to be presented with nonviolent solutions to the conflicts shown in stories. Nonviolence is designated as "strength of conviction . . . and . . . values such as love, tolerance, friendship, justice and forgiveness" (IBBY 1998, 467). Author June Jordan recommended a "new realism" as one in which "usable" information supercedes the "reality of some particular bad news" (Jordan 1973, 45).

Some teachers worry that teaching peace using literature means they must stop teaching certain classics that include a measure of violent content (Coghlan 2000, 85). Many agree that violence has played a delightful and appealing role in books for youth who do not read to identify, or to find therapy, but who read because they love stories (Tatar 1998, 68). The success of the Lemony Snicket series is evidence that young readers appreciate good stories and accept that bad things happen to good people in them (Yolen et al. 2002, 32).

Many think that it is not possible to protect young readers from the knowledge of sad, dangerous, or evil situations. They think it is more important to write honestly for young readers. For example, many important stories of people's experiences during wars appear in Hebrew and Jewish literature. These stories are widely read because they focus on messages of love, humor, and hope. They depict courage and optimism of characters in tragic circumstances (Yolen et al. 2002, 34).

Many think that literature does not need to inform young people about bad news in the world, and they oppose bibliotherapy. They argue that realism in reading is not necessary therapy for those already encountering difficulties. They recommend that such readers may enjoy books of humor, fantasy, or historical fiction (Yolen et al. 2002, 33). Children who are victims of war would benefit more from books about "close family relationships, stories with humor, and with characters who exercise some control over their lives" than from picture books about war (33).

These values of infusing books with hope and human feeling are emphasized in criteria developed for teachers to evaluate books that include themes of violence (Giblin 1995). In addition to assessing the age appropriateness of a story, teachers should assess the emotional reality in a story and the level of honesty with which characters are portrayed (31). Describing the rationale of the evil characters for their behavior deepens the story. The depth of "themes, nuances, patterns, and connections" within stories, and the treatment of emotion and feeling, or the humanization of stories, can broaden the understanding of the reader (31). Finally, how thoughtfully the author has researched and presented the subject matter in its overall context helps readers consider the broader themes of the story within American or global society (31).

Other criteria about specific topics have been suggested. For example, Rudman (1995) suggests evaluation criteria for books about war. The cause of wars should not be portrayed simplistically, caused by one incident, and stories should not glorify battle (370). Fact should be distinguishable from opinion and well researched. Other criteria include not trivializing "the realities of war"; not depicting peace as suddenly won; not depicting the end of war as the end of problems (371). For books about bullies, the protagonist should not have to become the bully's best friend, convert the bully to nonviolence, or perform a heroic act to fit in (371). Books should be at the "appropriate developmental level" and not be too "grisly, violent, or sophisticated as to confuse, frighten or overwhelm young readers" (371).

Conclusion

Part of contemporary culture includes the unchecked content of the Internet. Computer security in schools cannot ensure against the delivery of spam to email inboxes. Violent events in the world are broadcast over the Internet. People have grown accustomed to, if also weary of, dealing with violent content in media. In this context, teachers, parents, and storytellers often think about how to present the "unspeakable and the unrepresentable" in an "ethically responsible way" (Myers 2000, 445).

Case: Always Running

Always Running: La Vida Loca, Gang Days in L.A. (1993) by Luis J. Rodriguez has won a Carl Sandburg Literary Award (1993), and a *Chicago Sun-Times* Book Award in 1994. Rodriguez, a former gang member, received an "Unsung Heroes of Compassion" award from the Dalai Lama for his writings (Herendeen 2003a).

Rodriguez wrote *Always Running* to warn his son away from gang life. He wrote it to tell "the raw truth to show youngsters that gang" life is not "glamorous" (*Modesto Bee* 2003c). He says he gets hundreds of letters from young people who quit gangs or did not join after reading his story. Rodriguez acknowledges that the book is "hard," "graphic," "not a book for everybody," and that it contains more violence than sex. Rodriguez agrees that parents should decide whether their children should read the book or not, instead of banning the book.

In fall 2003, a home-schooling parent complained because of the graphic sex and violence in the novel *Always Running*. She visited the high school principal, where the book was used and said other parents had complained to her but feared their children's grades would suffer if they complained about the book.

Always Running was part of the Modesto City Schools Passport to Literature program and was approved for use with the eleventh grade. School policy stated that English Department chairs would review a book that was proposed for reconsideration, then send their recommendations to the school board. Administrators in the school system had, in the past, been instructed to offer parents information about some of the books students were assigned, including annotations of each book, so that parents could ask for alternative assignments if readings were objectionable (Herendeen 2003b).

The administration pulled the book from use in the class where it was being taught before an official review could take place. The teacher was not blamed for using the book. The administrator who pulled the book claimed that it had "slipped through" the review process and had not been looked at "carefully enough." He questioned the writing quality and the literary value of the novel (Herendeen 2003b).

On November 9, 2003, the *Modesto Bee* ran an article clarifying the circumstances of pulling the book without formal review (*Modesto Bee* 2003c). The book had not been banned because it was still available in the school library. The home-schooling parent who complained was within her rights as a taxpayer to complain about the curriculum. School administrators had disrupted a teacher's teaching plans and had ignored school board policy on review of books (*Modesto Bee* 2003c).

The teacher who was using the book said she chose it from the state list of recommended books. She wanted a contemporary novel that was "relevant, educational, and interesting." She wanted something for students who often questioned the relevance of readings to their lives.

According to the *Modesto Bee*, in 2003 gangs represented "a serious problem in Modesto," and at least half of the homicides in Modesto in 2003 were gang related. The article pointed out that teens "know about this violence . . . talk about it . . . worry about it . . . know things their parents don't," and they navigate these problems (2003c).

The teacher said the book helped her to "get kids interested in reading." The reluctant readers in her class were asking "if they could read ahead" in this book. The teacher said that none of the students in her class or their parents had complained about using the book. She observed that no one had asked her about how teaching the book was going. She reported that halfway through the unit the book was pulled, disrupting her class planning from October to January. The teacher noted that this was difficult because students were not "ready to be done with it yet" (*Modesto Bee* 2003c).

Students who had been reading the book in class became involved by "fighting with their heads, not with their hands," said their teacher. Students wrote to school board members, arguing to keep the book in the curriculum (*Modesto Bee* 2003a). One sixteen-year-old student said the book is "cool," "emotional," and understandable. He said he encountered gangs everyday outside his house and that this book "reinforced his decision not to join a gang." Another student wrote that the novel discourages those not in gangs from joining and encourages those who are in gangs to find a way out (*Modesto Bee* 2003c).

Letters to the editor of the *Modesto Bee* addressed the issue. One educator argued that the district "buckled in to an individual who wants to make the choice for the rest of us" (Paull 2003). Literature "isn't about the world as it should be: its context is always the world as it is." *Always Running*, like other great literature, "allows us to witness its characters wrestling with real obstacles toward the achievement of a moral consciousness" (Paull 2003). In another letter, a citizen argued on behalf of the book that *Always Running* was written as a warning against gang involvement and not to titillate readers (Goodman 2003).

The executive director of the Modesto Teachers Association said the administrators violated policy and had to take the matter back to the board that approved the book. The book was reviewed by a committee of high school English Department chairs. They recommended reinstating the book.

In December 2003, the school board heard twelve speakers on the topic. People objected to the graphic sex and violence in the book and voiced concern that the parental notification process about book content might not be understood by parents with limited English-language skills (Johnson 2003). They worried that those who do not read the book may be ridiculed by their peers. Other arguments were that "students who have been sexually assaulted would be forced to relive the experience by reading the book's detailed rape scene." Such a reading might also conflict with the district's code of conduct that was committed to making students feeling safe and comfortable in school. Another argument was that the "anti-gang message could be accomplished without excessive descriptions of sex and violence." Art Rodriguez's book *East Side Dreams* (1999) was recommended as an alternative reading that points out "the downside of gang life . . . without gratuitous sexual and violent details" (Johnson 2003). According to the *Modesto Bee*, *Always Running*'s author Luis J. Rodriguez gave a statement to the board: "Yes, my book is graphic. Yes, it's shocking at times. But it's also literary, educational, and redemptive. Like so much good literature" (Johnson 2003).

The board agreed that the decision of whether a student reads the book is the parent's decision but stated that they would "prefer that teenagers read Rodriguez's work in a supervised setting" (Johnson 2003). Board members voted 4 to 3 in favor of allowing the book back into the classroom. They did not like the idea of censoring the book and argued that controversial topics are found in works by Shakespeare and that "the controversial parts make up a small portion of the book and vilify, not glorify, that behavior" (Johnson 2003).

In September 2004, Luis Rodriguez was the keynote speaker at the Central Valley Educational Summit for teachers and community members in Modesto; his address was titled "Closing the Achievement Gap for Poor and Minority Children in Modesto and Stanislaus County" (*Modesto Bee* 2004).

Discussion Questions

1. Why did the home-schooling parent object to the book?

2. What is the difference between using *Always Running* for instructional purposes and making it accessible in the library without instruction?

3. What was the result of ignoring the school policy for reconsidering a book?

4. How might the graphic violence in *Always Running* affect the book's literary quality? What arguments were made in favor of the book's literary quality?

5. How do you respond to the suggestion to use a different, less graphic book to deliver the same information? Is this possible? What is the purpose of literature?

6. What is the difference between violence that is glorified in literature and violence that is used to describe a real situation?

7. What is the literary purpose of graphic violence, sexuality, or rough language?

8. Do the students' responses about the relevance of the book add to the literary quality of the book?

9. What do you think about the teacher's choice for encouraging reluctant readers?

10. How would you decide what readings to use with different age groups?

11. What priorities were expressed by the school board?

12. Using role-playing, have a discussion about this case. Take a position as the teacher, an administrator, a student, the author of the book, a parent, and a school board member.

References

Agnew, Kate, and Geoff Fox. 2001. *Children at war. From the First World War to the Gulf.* New York: Continuum.

Allison, Anthony. 1999. *Hear these voices. Youth at the edge of the millennium.* New York: Dutton Children's Books.

Ammon, Bette. Just one flick of a finger. *Voice of Youth Advocates* 20(2). Children's Literature Comprehensive Database. http://clcd.odyssi.com (accessed August 25, 2005).

Armstrong, Jennifer. 2003. The writer's page: Narrative and violence. *Horn Book Magazine* 79(2): 191–194.

Atkins, S. Beth. 1996. *Voices from the streets. Young former gang members tell their stories.* Boston: Little, Brown.

Axiotis, Vivian M., James R. Harstad, Katharine J. Heintschel, and Bonnie Molnar. 1999. What young adult books have you used successfully to teach the classics? *English Journal* 88(3): 27–29.

Barton, Stan. 2002. Good and bad books. *Washington Post*, July 13.

Bowers, Keith. 2002. Creeping out the kids. Will the real Lemony Snicket please stand up? *Berkeley Express*, December 25.

Bridgers, Sue Ellen. 2000. Learning a language of nonviolence. *English Journal* 89(5): 71–73, 93.

———. 1996. *All we know of heaven.* Wilmington, NC: Banks Channel Books.

Canada, Geoffrey. 1998. Foreword. In *Things get hectic: Teens write about violence that surrounds them/Youth Communication*, ed. Philip Kay, Andrea Estepa, and Al Desetta. New York: Simon and Schuster.

Cart, Michael, ed. 2002. *911: The book of help.* Chicago: Cricket Books.

———. 1996. *From romance to realism: 50 years of growth and change in young adult literature.* New York: HarperCollins Children's Books.

Coerr, Eleanor. 1993. *Sadako.* New York: Putnam.

———. 1977. *Sadako and the thousand paper cranes.* New York: Putnam.

Coghlan, Rosemarie. 2000. The teaching of anti-violence strategies within the English curriculum. *English Journal* 89(5): 84–89.

Coles, Robert. 1987. The child's understanding of tragedy. In *Children's literature*, vol. 15, ed. Margaret Higgonet and Barbara Rosen, 1–6. New Haven, CT: Yale University Press.

Courtot, Marilyn. n.d. Making Up Megaboy (review). Children's Literature Reviews. *Children's Literature Comprehensive Database.* http://clcd.odyssi.com.

Del Negro, Janice M. 1996. Just one flick of a finger. *Bulletin of the Center for Children's Books* 50(1). Children's Literature Comprehensive Database. http://clcd.odyssi.com (accessed August 25, 2005).

Durell, Ann, and Marilyn Sachs. 1990. *The big book for peace.* New York: E. P. Dutton Children's Books.

Flinn, Alex. 2002. *Breaking point.* New York: HarperTempest.

Forecasts: Children's books. 1998. *Publisher's Weekly* 245(25): 43.

Future classics. Books. 1993–1994. *American Visions* 8(6): 35.

Giblin, James Cross. 1995. Violence, children, and children's books. *School Library Journal* 41(11): 30–31.

Goldberg, Beverly. 2000. Fallen angels resurrected. *American Libraries* 31(10): 17.

Goodenough, Elizabeth. 2000a. Introduction to violence and children's literature. Special issue, *Lion and the Unicorn* 24(3): v–ix.

———, ed. 2000b. Violence and children's literature. Special issue, *Lion and the Unicorn* 24(3).

Goodman, Michelle. 2003. A warning, not titillation. *Modesto Bee*, November 27.

Guira, Shirley. 1998. *Making up Megaboy. Alan Review* 25(3). Children's Literature Comprehensive Database. http://clcd.odyssi.com. (accessed August 25, 2005).

Herendeen, Susan. 2003a. Panel supports book list selection: Always running, pulled for review, is reinstated. *Modesto Bee*, November 19.

———. 2003b. District removes books after parents' objection. Author says raw tale of gangs not for everyone. *Modesto Bee*, November 1.

Higgonet, Margaret, and Barbara Rosen, eds. 1987. *Children's literature*. Vol. 15. New Haven, CT: Yale University Press.

Hill, Mary Jo. 2005. Cormier still stirs dissent; Chocolate war controversy roles. *Telegram & Gazette* (Worcester, MA), February 27.

Hinton, S. E. 1967. *The outsiders*. New York: Viking Press.

Honawar, Vaishali. 2002. Parents to debate "appropriate books in schools." *Washington Times*, April 21.

International Board on Books for Young People. 2005. Help the children hit by the tsunami disaster. http://www.ibby.org/index.php?id=257.

———. 1998. *26th Congress of the International Board on Books for Young People. Peace through Children's Books. Proceedings*. New Delhi, India: Indian BBY, Association of Writers and Illustrators for Children.

Isaacs, K. T. 2003. Reality check. A look at the disturbing growth of violence in books for teens. *School Library Journal* 49(10): 50–51.

Iskander, Sylvia Patterson. 1987. Readers, realism and Robert Cormier. In *Children's literature*, vol. 15, ed. Margaret R. Higgonet and Barbara Rosen, 7–18. New Haven, CT: Yale University Press.

Janeczko, P. 1977. Interview with Robert Cormier. *English Journal* 66: 10–11.

Johnson, Elizabeth. 2003. Trustees vote 4–3 for book. It shouldn't be on reading list, critics of "Always Running" claim. *Modesto Bee*, December 16.

Jordan, June. 1973. Young people: Victims of realism in books & life. *Wilson Library Bulletin* 48: 140–145.

Kay, Philip, Andrea Estepa, and Al Desetta. 1998. *Things get hectic. Teens write about violence that surrounds them./Youth Communication*. New York: Simon and Schuster.

Koertge, Ron. 2001. *The brimstone journals*. Cambridge, MA: Candlewick Press.

Kulkarni, Suneeta, and Prasanna Hulikavi. 1998. Books for traumatized children. Content analysis of peace and violence in children's books. In *26th Congress of the International Board on Books for Young*

People. Peace through Children's Books. Proceedings. New Delhi, India: Indian BBY, Association of Writers and Illustrators for Children.

Lockman, Darcy. 2002. Meet the author: Lemony Snicket. *Instructor* 112(3): 50–51.

Lorbiecki, Marybeth. 1996. *Just one flick of a finger.* New York: Dial Books.

May, Jill P. 1995. *Children's literature and critical theory: Reading and writing for understanding.* New York: Oxford University Press.

McDonell, Nick. 2002. *Twelve.* New York: Grove Press.

Modesto Bee. 2004. Achievement gap. September 15.

———. 2003a. Book ban, reinstatement offers valuable lessons. November 21.

———. 2003b. Book ban reinstatement offers valuable lessons. November 11.

———. 2003c. Curriculum censored. Important book wrongly pulled from classrooms on 1 complaint. November 9.

Murphy, Bernadette. 2004. A taste for blood taints Hinton's new venture (book review). *Los Angeles Times,* September 14.

Myers, Mitzi. 2000a. Storying war: A capsule overview. *Lion and the Unicorn* 24(3): 327–336.

———. 2000b. "No safe place to run to": An interview with Robert Cormier." *Lion and the Unicorn* 24(3): 445–464.

Myers, Walter Dean. 1988. *Scorpions.* New York: Harper & Row.

Noz, Kristen. 1999. 7th graders have message about violence. *Richmond Times,* May 18.

Orr, Tamara. 2003. *Violence in the schools. Halls of hope, halls of fear.* New York: Scholastic.

Paull, Laura. 2003. Letter to the editor. *Modesto Bee,* November 19, sec. B.

Peace begins with you. 1990. Children's Literature Reviews. *Children's Literature Comprehensive Database.* http://clcd.odyssi.com.

Recommendations. 1998. *26th Congress of the International Board on Books for Young People. Peace through Children's Books. Proceedings.* New Delhi, India: Indian BBY, Association of Writers and Illustrators for Children.

Rochman, Hazel. 1996. *Just one flick of a finger. Booklist* 92 (19–20): Childrens' literature comprehensive database. http://clcd.odyssi.com (accessed August 25, 2005).

Rodriguez, Luis J. 1999. *It doesn't have to be this way. A barrio story.* San Francisco: Children's Book Press.

———. 1993. *Always running: La vida loca, gang days in L.A.* Willimantic, CT: Curbstone Press.

Rudman, Masha Kabakow. 1995. *Children's literature.* 3rd ed. New York: Longman Publishers.

Salvadore, M. B. 1988. Review of *Fallen angels* by Walter Dean Myers. *School Library Journal* (June–July): 118.

Salwi, Dilip M. 1998. Peace through science fiction? In *26th Congress of the International Board on Books for Young People. Peace through Children's Books. Proceedings*. New Delhi, India: Indian BBY, Association of Writers and Illustrators for Children.

Sanchez, Lionel. 2004. Beheading images seen in classrooms: School district puts two on paid leave after complaints from students, parents. *San Diego Union Tribune*, May 15.

Saxena, Ira. 1998. A Ghandian way for children. In *26th Congress of the International Board on Books for Young People. Peace through Children's Books. Proceedings*. New Delhi, India: Indian BBY, Association of Writers and Illustrators for Children.

Scholes, Katherine. 1990. *Peace begins with you*. San Francisco: Sierra Club Books.

———. 1989. *Peacetimes*. Australia: Hill of Content Publishers.

Snicket, Lemony. 2001. *The ersatz elevator. A series of unfortunate events. Book six*. New York: Harper-Collins Publishers.

———. 1999. *The bad beginning. A series of unfortunate events. Book one*. New York: HarperCollins.

Stamps, Lisa. 2003. Bibliotherapy: How books can help students cope with concerns and conflicts. *Delta Kappa Gamma Bulletin* 70(1): 25–29.

Strasser, Todd. 2000. *Give a boy a gun*. New York: Simon and Schuster Books for Young Readers.

Tatar, Maria. 1998. "Violent delights" in children's literature. In *Why we watch: The attractions of violent entertainment*, ed. Jeffery Goldstein, 69–86. New York: Oxford University Press.

Walter, Virginia. 1998. *Making Up Megaboy*. New York: DK, Ink.

Williams, Stanley "Tookie." 1996. *Gangs and violence. Stanley "Tookie" Williams, with Barbara Collman Becnel*. New York: Rosen/Powerkids Press.

Yolen, Jane, et al. 2002. How books tell the world's bad news to children. *Lilith* 27(3): 32–39.

Zvirin, Stephanie. 1998. Making Up Megaboy. *Booklist* 94(12): 1009.

6

Children's Literature and People with Disabilities

Perhaps no group has been as overlooked and inaccurately presented in children's books as individuals with disabilities. Most often they were not included in stories and when they were, many negative stereotypes prevailed such as characters who were pitiful or pathetic, evil or superheroes, or a burden and incapable of fully participating in the events of everyday life. Often the difference or disability was the main personality trait emphasized to the reader; not a balance of strengths and weaknesses.

(Blaska 1996, 11)

Changes since 1975

Since the 1970s, changes in publishing books for children that include characters with disabilities have given teachers much to consider when selecting books. One reason for this is the effect of IDEA, the Individuals with Disabilities Act. Before implementation in 1975, "approximately 1 million children with disabilities were shut out of schools and hundreds of thousands more were denied appropriate services" (Office of Special Education and Rehabilitative Services 2003). By 1978, the government required public schools be opened to "students whose physical or mental disabilities had previously excluded them from the 'mainstream' educational settings or opportunities" (Robertson 1992, 1).

The influence of practical changes as a result of IDEA on children's literature is clear. Between 1940 and 1976, approximately 311 juvenile books featuring characters with disabilities were published in the United States (Harris and Baskin 1988, 56). These characters were stereotypical, treated in a childlike manner, had their conditions romanticized, and had their limitations described in unrealistic ways. Characters' physical problems commonly were caused by polio (Harris and Baskin 1987, 188). Other inaccurate depictions included overrepresentation of blind characters, considering their numbers in the general population. Often characters were drawn who avoided the world, and sometimes humorous or figurative expressions about disabilities were included (Robertson 1992, 1).

The shift in school attendance meant that students before 1975 had fewer personal experiences they could refer to in order to "balance negative or stilted portrayals" of the characters with disabilities they found in fiction (Robertson 1992, ix, 2). The influence of IDEA in practice was that children with disabilities attended neighborhood schools and were in contact with more teachers, students, librarians, readers, and authors.

After 1976, there was an increase in publication. Between 1976 and 1982 alone, 350 juvenile books that included characters with disabilities were published in the United States (Harris and Baskin 1988, 57). As awareness changed, so did juvenile literature about people with disabilities. The 1960s and 1970s realism of young adult literature gave readers more stories about social conflict. This trend also offered readers more realistic depictions of the problems associated with particular disabilities. Family life was depicted more realistically. Even so, stories included unrealistic, easy solutions (Baskin and Harris 1977, 42).

Between 1977 and 1987, characters with disabilities began to be more carefully developed and conditions more carefully described. In addition, "less severely disabled characters" and mild and moderate forms of disorders were more frequently included (Harris and Baskin 1984, 188).

Criticism, Disability Bias, and Disability Consciousness

Literature and disability awareness changed rapidly, but libraries still offered books that represented authority and could not go unchallenged (Saunders 2000, 3). For this reason, Baskin and Harris took on the job of evaluating the depiction of disability in books in use. Since their initial publication in 1977, analysis of the depiction of disability in juvenile literature appears in bibliographies, research, and criticism and has become standard in review sources. This gauge of disability bias in juvenile literature over the decades does not reflect social values as much as it reflects the expertise, focus, and philosophy of the critic. Among the bibliographers, researchers, and critics on the topic are people with different abilities, teachers, literary critics, social workers, medical researchers, family members, and advocates.

Bibliographies

Many bibliographies recommend teaching approaches, activities, and supplemental resources in addition to information about specific books. Some bibliographies are nonevaluative booklists, but most do evaluate books. Some bibliographies are the result of content analysis research projects that try to answer questions about the representation of a specific condition. Careful reading of the method and presentation used by the bibliographer is important.

Notes and *More Notes from a Different Drummer*

The first major bibliographic source on juvenile literature and disability was published in 1977. Baskin and Harris's *Notes from a Different Drummer* "identified, described and critiqued works written between 1940 and 1975 that contained disabled characters" and "demonstrated each title's usefulness in building a fair or balanced perception of exceptional people" (Roberston 1992, 2). This resource "encouraged readers to consider the flaws and strengths of each title before selecting it" (3). Each entry includes an analysis of how "impairments are treated" (Baskin and Harris 1977, xii). At the time, authors felt they should not organize books by condition because this seemed like labeling characters by condition. Instead, they included a subject index of conditions.

Notes from a Different Drummer raised awareness of reviewers and the publishing industry about sensitivity to people with different abilities (2). In 1984, *More Notes from a Different Drummer* continued this work, "evaluating books published through 1981" (Robertson 1992, x). The *Different Drummer* books evaluated fiction that was in print and out of print, intended for infants to adolescents. The books included those written in foreign countries and distributed in the United States and excluded religious press books but not books with religious characters (xi).

Updating *Notes* for the 1980s and 1990s

In 1985, a bibliography of nonfiction titled *Accept Me as I Am: Best Books of Juvenile Nonfiction on Impairments and Disabilities* (Friedberg, Mullins, and Sukiennik 1985) expanded readers' resources. For the 1992 edition, this title was changed to *Portraying Persons with Disabilities: An Annotated Bibliography of Nonfiction for Children and Teenagers*.

In 1992, Debra Robertson's *Portraying Persons with Disabilities: An Annotated Bibliography of Fiction for Children and Teenagers* continued the *Notes* series. Evaluating books published between 1982 and 1991, Robertson identifies specific impairments and the plot themes that include the "featured characters who are disabled." She omits full annotations for "seriously flawed titles" (xi). She recommends a group of books from the *Notes* bibliographies so that readers will have a complete reference to titles published since 1940.

Robertson's works represent subtle and important enhancements to evaluation. She set standards of evaluation that "not every impairment portrayed has to be critical to the action," that a disability in a story does not have to be a "metaphor for the protagonist's development," and that what characters say and do is important, not what they cannot do (xii). Books are arranged according to disabling condition in the "spirit of service and not to demean" (xi, 2). A review of the growth of fiction publishing for children in the 1980s and 1990s is included.

Specific Conditions and Impairments Bibliographies

In 1994, Lisa Kupper published *A Guide to Children's Literature and Disability: 1989–1994*. This bibliography describes books about specific conditions and impairments. It was intended to help parents and professionals identify books with stories about children with like conditions and impairments. Books feature the personalities, friendships, challenges, accomplishments, and daily lives of people with disabilities (3). Topics include ADHD (attention deficit hyperactivity disorder), blindness, cerebral palsy, deafness, learning disabilities, serious or life-threatening conditions, and physical disabilities. Each entry describes what disability or main theme is in the story, and entries are divided into Juvenile Picture Books, Juvenile Easy Reader, Juvenile Fiction, and Young Adult books (3). This source lists references to finding aids for materials before 1989 and publishers' contact information for all of the books listed.

Characters in Company with Others

In *Kids, Disabilities and Regular Classrooms: An Annotated Bibliography of Selected Children's Literature on Disability* (1996), Gary Owen Bunch lists "fictional stories involving characters with disabilities in company with others without disabilities." Bunch includes books that attract readers and help readers "realize that disability is one aspect of a person and that every one is more alike than different" (1). This bibliography also includes informational books to describe specific conditions such as autism and AIDS (acquired immunodeficiency syndrome) and discuss causes, treatments, and appearance. The purpose of including informational books is that "being informed supports understanding and acceptance" (1). Books are listed that depict characters as people first and disability as one aspect of their lives (1). Books are grouped by disability or condition of challenge and ordered by reading or instructional age, and books suitable for being read aloud are noted. The Bunch bibliography includes the following themes: "challenges overcome; love found or lost; mysteries and detectives; bullies and heroes; adventure and humor . . . in which regular students and students being included can see all people having a rightful place in the world as one among a diversity of others" (2).

Importance of Careful Reading

To save time and selection of inappropriate materials, teachers should carefully read the purpose of any bibliography they use to select books. While this may seem obvious, bibliographies are created for many reasons and many audiences and do not always list recommended materials. For example, *Children's Literature and Disability: Resources You Can Use* (2001) from the National Information Center for Children and Youth with Disabilities lists ninety-five sources for finding information about AD(H)D, autism, Down syndrome, hearing impairment, learning disabilities, mental retardation, physical disabilities, serious medical or life-threatening conditions, sibling issues, visual impairment, and other disabilities. There is a disclaimer that the list is "not an endorsement of any of the books" and encourages users to carefully evaluate all materials.

Raising Awareness and Psychological Support

Psychological Effects

Gary Bunch argues that "students with disabilities benefit from being surrounded by peers who possess more than a passing understanding that a person with any type of disability is a person first . . . and is not defined by the disability" (1996, 3). In this spirit, Blaska (1996) recommends that books from disability literature "should be incorporated into every program and not limited to classes with children with disabilities in order to educate all children about varieties of ability and disability" (13).

Since the 1970s, one goal of using juvenile fiction that included characters with disabilities was to ease the tension of mainstreaming practices. Stories were used to reduce "rejecting behaviors," model "appropriate interaction," and "allow people to explore social exchanges" (Baskin and Harris 1977, 48). Stories could help normalize experiences and clarify feelings (48). Books could promote self-acceptance, provide information about disabilities, increase the comfort level with people who have disabilities, foster empathy, and facilitate accepting behavior (Landrum 2001, 252; Bunch 1996, 3).

Bunch writes that what "differentiates disabled children from youngsters in other minority groups is the nearly complete absence of close adult models either to consult with or to emulate . . . [and] the psychological benefits of group identification and cohesion are largely absent" (Bunch 1996, 13). Reading a social act can shape a classroom community, promote caring, and form positive attitudes (3).

In the 1980s, studies suggested that more was needed than information and interaction to reduce rejecting behaviors. Change in "perceptions occurs when reading includes . . . follow-up discussion or activities and stories that present characters with disabilities accurately, realistically, and positively" (Landrum 2001, 252). Other studies suggested that being read to, bibliotherapy, and guided reading might help change attitudes about disability (Blaska 2003, 6).

By the 1990s, the consensus was that books, along with teacher guidance, could "help children understand and accept persons with disabilities." Books help when teachers use activities that highlight the "critical information to be learned" and when they explain the accuracy or inaccuracy of depiction of abilities and characteristics (Blaska 1996, 12). Bunch recommends selecting books for the classroom and library that could be easily included in read-aloud sessions. Bunch recommends not including books about disability solely because someone in the class has that disability (Bunch 1996, 5). Also, Bunch recommends stories that are appropriate for discussions that help readers see the other's point of view, using "what if" as a discussion prompt.

Kathy Saunders (2000) suggests teaching methods and language that include all individuals in the human family. Saunders proposes getting young people to imagine possibilities for designing abilities for doing things. Saunders suggests using stories that are not steeped in pity and do not include a tragic ending. She recommends stories in which characters with disabilities are just living a life like the other characters. Bunch believes that "children belong together and that . . . teachers who are serious about including children will have a plan for the use of such literature with the overall program so that everyone feels included" (1996, 1). The power of literature is that it can "make difference familiar and not strange and frightening." Bunch recommends recognizing students with special needs in the "materials of the classroom, the curriculum adaptations, or literature" to promote a welcoming and secure classroom (1996, 2).

Individual teachers "must decide that these are a necessary part of the curriculum" and believe that "deliberate selection" of "affirming literature" is important for "promoting equity respecting disability" (Bunch 1996, 3, 5). Teachers can also counter the influence of negative bias, subtle bias, and bias by omission in books (Blaska 1996, 14). Teachers can incorporate inclusive activities and present realistic and positive role models through literature (14).

Medical Interpretations and Sociopolitical Contexts

Authors and illustrators may not have had ready access to the information they needed to craft unbiased depictions of characters with disabilities in the past. Today, there are easily accessible and sufficient research materials to help authors develop accurate characters. In 1987, Carol Gill described medical and sociopolitical models that she applied to occupational therapy. According to Gill, "disability activists charge that the medicalization of rehabilitation" allowed society to avoid responsibility for accommodating people with disabilities (1987, 53).

Stories that "medicalize" characters with disabilities function in the same way. Using the medical model, the critic might ask, To what extent does a story present a disability as abnormal or focus on diagnostic categories to describe a character? Gill's sociopolitical model recommends that occupational therapists acknowledge the complexity, goals, interests, and needs of people. They should acknowledge human needs like relationships, sexuality, artistic expression, and recreation and recognize societal barriers that impede meeting these needs (50, 53). They should support self-esteem and challenge stereotypes like "childlike," "weak," "lacking in judgment," and "incapable of enjoying life." Gill believes occupational therapists should "address the reality of what life is like for disabled persons" and fit services to the "patient's needs, values, and interests" (54).

Applying this to authorship, contemporary authors might be expected to depict the reality of life for characters with disabilities and to reflect characters' needs, values, and interests as complete and complex human beings. Contemporary authors could be expected to accurately acknowledge the social lives of characters for the time period of the story. In others words, for the time and location of a story, an accurate depiction of character experiences might include information about "job discrimination, unequal access to education and community resources, isolation, interpersonal rejection and prejudice" (53). The social context is one that acknowledges that physical perfection, youthfulness, achievement, and extreme independence are not the only desirable values and that people with disabilities are whole, deserving of basic rights and full and equal rights without gratitude or perceiving these as charity (52). The sociopolitical model helps people to reflect on "social aspects of disability" and on "society's response to disability" and to read stories with raised awareness of the author's depiction of disability in the story (54).

Literary Devices Interpreted in Classical Works

Classic texts, the "cultural artifacts that reflect society's perceptions," are often regarded as respectable and prestigious (Harris and Baskin 1987, 188). Many critics agree that books "transmit values," offer interpretations, model behavior, "inform, redirect, and shape understandings and responses" (Harris and Baskin 1987, 188; Margolis and Shapiro 1987, 18).

Mythic tales and classics in children's literature contain many negative stereotypes and inhumane perceptions about people with disabilities (Baskin and Harris 1977, 38, 42). Mythic stories punished unapproved behavior with disabling conditions (18). In fairy tales, body's form and ability represented the "quality of the inner person" (20).

Notes from a Different Drummer provides analysis of mythic, prescientific literature in fairy tales and in nineteenth-century literature. It describes the use and interpretation of disability as literary symbolism (Baskin and Harris 1977, 22). Blindness has often been used as a metaphor for individual, social, or global unwillingness to deal with an issue (24). In the nineteenth century, characters with disabilities had "restricted, particularized roles," were "models of forbearance and humility," or were "punished malefactors." Disability reflected the attitude of the time as "object lesson," "paragon of virtue," and "unfortunate victims" (Baskin and Harris 1977, 39–40). Finally, the extent to which folklore involves a disability is so great that "a comprehensive report and analyses of myths and legends involving disability" could fill an extensive volume (Robertson 1992, xi).

Inhumane depictions and interpretations of people who have disabilities in literature confront teachers with decisions. Margolis and Shapiro (1987) argue that classics are "powerful tools by which civilization perpetuates . . . values" and that "English teachers have a unique opportunity and responsibility to counter . . . injustice suffered . . . [and] caused by such stereotypical portrayals" (18). They suggest teaching methods for addressing cultural allegorical symbols of the "evil prosthesis of Captain Hook," the "fear-inducing . . . wooden leg of Captain Ahab," and the "pitiable crutch of Tiny Tim" (18). They suggest that students explore the origins of stereotypes with research to explain the use of blindness as punishment in myths, the deformity of *Rumpelstiltskin*, the witch's crutch in *Hansel and Gretel*, and the witch in *Snow White* who must turn ugly and hunchbacked to do evil (18). Margolis and Shapiro suggest the impact of negative images of disability in classical literature can be used to heighten awareness to help readers and teachers understand this power. They do not recommend censoring stories but recommend discussing and explaining symbolism so that "damaging messages are negated" (21).

Margolis and Shapiro argue that "when literature is taught without an explanation of the moralistic meaning assigned to disabilities, those with impairments may find it difficult to overcome deeply entrenched prejudices which interfere with their rights as citizens to live and work where they choose, obtain an education, and, in some instances, even survive" (21). They recommend a formal method of literary analysis in which teachers ask students to consider how characters are portrayed as whole people, or as literary devices. In so doing, teachers begin a dialogue about how disability has been used as a literary device to symbolize inner evil, to foretell events, and to set a tone of terror. They can discuss how "literary treatment of disability often used artificial scenarios in which a disabled person overcame a significant ailment in no time at all through the agency of faith or pious suffering or death that subsequently enlightened all who had known them" (Robertson 1992, 3).

Students can question whether characters with a disability are depicted as recipients of pity, as burdens, as uncomplaining heroes. They can question if characters are drawn as competent people with abilities who can provide for themselves and interact with others in "mutually rewarding ways" (Margolis and Shapiro 1987, 20). Margolis and Shapiro recommend students interview people with disabilities about how they are treated in life and about their feelings about how they are portrayed in literature (19).

Kathy Saunders (2000) questions this approach, arguing that these efforts take more time than expected and that often not enough classroom time is set aside for a sufficient discussion of the historical context of the book and the negative stereotype. Saunders does not propose removing all texts with negative implications from circulation and admits that books with negative stereotypes and portrayals may be useful for informed debate. Still, she points out that there may be books in the classroom library that include negative stereotypes and that are read independently with no intermediary to challenge disablist ideas (3).

Saunders recommends adapting stories as she has in *Happy Ever Afters. A Storybook Guide to Teaching Children about Disability*. She offers "story lines and illustrations which can be used and adapted so that positive concepts and coping strategies can be introduced to even the youngest children" (xi).

Literature also demonstrates what an author understands about disability. This understanding might be based on the information available at the time a book was written and based on the author's assumptions or research (Keith 2001).

The realism of the 1970s did not guarantee "accuracy, balance, or extensive data" (Baskin and Harris 1977, 34). In 1977, Baskin and Harris reported on incorrect descriptions of symptoms, treatments, and prognoses in books written about characters with disabilities. They reported "misrepresentation of societal conditions," improbable behavior by those with disabilities and those responding to them, labels like "stupid," idiot-savant stereotypes, and miraculous cures (50, 51, 53). Inaccurate illustrations minimized or obscured disabilities (54).

Trends in Evaluation, Criteria, and Guidelines

While evaluation standards have not necessarily changed that much since the 1970s, more people are writing about the topic. They voice diverse opinions that add to the breadth of evaluation standards to consider. By far, the most widely discussed and influential criterion is character development (Baskin and Harris 1977, 34). That so many lengthy lists and specific evaluation concepts and processes exist are testament to the extent to which negative stereotypes pervade juvenile fiction. Teachers who are aware of "what constitutes constructive and unprejudiced portrayals" may be better able to counter bias found in literature (188). The first very influential evaluation guidelines were written in *Notes from a Different Drummer*.

Evaluation criteria help professionals analyze books and inform authors interested in raising their awareness about character depictions. Many ideas have evolved and been incorporated into general selection guidelines. These include accurate depictions of culture, inclusion, and social experiences. They include ideas about the importance of specificity. Selection guidelines for intermediate books have been recommended. Detailed evaluation systems like the DICSEY Code (discussed later in the chapter) have been developed.

Baskin and Harris Evaluation Standards

In 1977, Barbara Baskin and Karen Harris broke ground by proposing attention to the following issues when considering books that include disability. Are characters used as devices to send social messages, depict racial issues, romanticize stories, minimize or deny a disability, or provide a search for self? Do they serve as the suffering payment in exchange for grace and enlightenment, an agent for the deliverance of others, an example of a faith cure, or a catalyst for others' growth?" (Baskin and Harris 1977, 32).

In 1988, Harris and Baskin offered guidelines for "constructive and unprejudiced portrayals of people" with disabilities (56). In addition to literary quality, high standards of accuracy, including "etiology, prognosis, and remediation therapy," are essential. Personal, family, and societal realities should be included, as well as honest approaches to impairment in all genres, including fantasy, historical fiction, and science fiction. Omission and distortion of characters for political purpose or propagandizing should be avoided (56). Books whose characters affirm that people with disabilities share the same essential human needs, desires, and aspirations as their readers are recommended. Books are recommended that show how the bonds that unite people are more important than the differences (59).

Depiction of Culture, Inclusion, and Accuracy of Social Experiences

In her article "Literature for Minority Handicapped Students" (1986), Marguerite C. Radencich describes books with stories about disability in different cultural communities. These include American Indian, Americans of European descent, Jewish Americans, black Americans, and Latin Americans. Radencich's report of varied depiction of disability across cultural groups includes a caveat to carefully review the books when using them.

A shift in evaluation and publishing reflected a growing awareness about the importance of describing the diversity of ability accurately. Critics called for characters who represented "the population with varying abilities" because "diversity is not limited to heritage" (Blaska and Lynch 1998, 11).

Importance of Specificity about People to Selection

In 1989, Constance Mellon recommended books focus on the child, not the disability. She recommends using books with factually accurate depictions of specific disabilities (47). The aspects of the disability should be revealed "not as the main focus of the book, but through the unfolding of a story" (47). The book does not have to include "every aspect of the disability" (47). Mellon argued that teaching one book that includes one disability "does not help teachers and children understand" that other disabilities like blindness, spina bifida, or epilepsy have their own features (46). Mellon recommends avoiding books that focus on the differences caused by the disability, that is, books that feature a wheelchair on the cover or that name the disability in the title or that refer to people as "poor little thing" or "brave little soul." She recommends avoiding stories in which "healed children are happy normal children while disabled children overcome trials" (47).

Selecting Intermediate Literature

Ruth Landrum (2001) proposed selection criteria for intermediate literature (252). In plots, characters with disabilities should face similar conflicts to those of their peer group. The climax may include the disability but should not focus on it. Seeking a cure for a disability is not a means of giving a character a normal life, and attitude does not cause disability, prevent it, or create cures. Information about any disability in a story should be accurate. Emotional range should be found in characters, including anger, sadness, joy, love, pride, and shame. Strength, independence, competency, self-determination, and sexuality in adolescence should be characteristics available to characters. Family, friends, and society are available to characters with disabilities. Characters are not restricted to roles of heroes or victims but are able to be multidimensional characters (254). The theme of disability is not a cause or a lesson. Characters with disabilities initiate and actively participate in plots. Words such as *handicapped*, *lame*, *crippled*, and *special* should be avoided in referring to characters (254). Tragic or hopeless stories are due to the "human condition and not the character's disability" (255).

Use of the Personal Response in Evaluation

One approach to book evaluation includes gauging one's own emotional reactions to a book (Smith-D'Arezzo 2003, 75). Reviewers might ask if they like the book, if they would recommend it, if they feel connections in it, then can write up their initial reactions to a book. Books should appeal to children, and teachers should feel positive about discussing books with children. Special education topics require accurate and realistic portrayals for readers. Historical context and school settings that are portrayed accurately provide a realistic view of special education to readers (90). Characters can be people who readers want to befriend and shown as characters with realistic flaws (76, 77). The plot should be believable and not give characters abilities they did not have at the beginning of the book (88).

The DICSEY Code for Evaluating Literature

A fear of becoming disabled, or the feeling that this is a remote possibility, is common (Saunders 2000, 4). When a realistic understanding of the lives of people who have disabilities is developed, children gain a realistic view of minor conditions. They may also accept assistance if they become disabled, more readily develop relationships with friends who become disabled, accept a minor caring role, and pursue their complete potential (5).

Kathy Saunders (2000) developed the DICSEY Code framework for evaluating literature to help teachers develop questions according to ability aspects. DICSEY stands for Disability, Image, Control, Society, Enabled, and Young carers (32). Book entries include title, author, the plot, characters, and discussion questions based on DICSEY categories. D (Disability) questions ask how disability affects everyone and asks readers to consider new ways of doing things. I (Image) questions ask what images from stories only give part of the truth. C (Control) questions encourage discussion of the human desire to manage our own lives. S (Society) questions are about the rules of society and laws and how we change these to make it easier for everyone to participate. E (Enabled) questions ask about the need for an environment that allows people with disabilities to do things for themselves. Y (Young carers) questions are those that help people discuss how care giving can affect schoolwork, friendships, and self-care. Saunders provides pages of items to think about under each DICSEY topic. These concepts are meant to guide teachers in thinking of questions to use to discuss books with children.

Content Analysis

Scholars use content analysis research to explain literature. While Joan Blaska has done the most extensive and up-to-date work in this area, Mary Anne Prater (2000, 2003) developed a multiple categories approach for analyzing books. In addition, content analyses continue to be done on groups of books that include or are about general topics such as learning disabilities and about specific topics such as ADHD.

Content Analysis by Joan Blaska

Joan Blaska's *Using Children's Literature to Learn about Disabilities and Illness* (1996, 2003) is a result of research the author did to examine children's literature that includes a character with a disability or illness. Blaska believes that instead of beginning to include literature about disability when a child with a disability becomes part of the class, all children "should have the opportunity to lean about diversity of ability much like they learn about cultural diversity" (7).

Blaska's resource includes informational chapters and an annotated bibliography. Blaska's 1996 edition resource reviews over 175 books published for those from birth to eight years of age between 1985 and the early 1990s. Books are classified as outstanding, very good, fair, or not recommended. An annotated bibliography and a cross-referencing index are included. The source includes fiction and nonfiction and represents ten disability areas and six chronic illnesses. The annotations describe the stories. The cross-reference indexes are given for disability, for chronic illness, and for how disability is treated within a story.

In informational chapters she discusses thematic approaches used by early childhood educators, and she offers lesson plans for forty-eight different themes. She includes activities for teaching about disabilities, publishers of children's books, books by title, and a list of disability organizations. She discusses inclusionary programs, whole language, literacy approaches, and reading aloud. She offers suggestions about how to teach about disabilities and chronic illnesses with preschoolers and young children. What distinguishes Blaska's resource are her suggestions and resources for teaching about differences in addition to the resources she provides about teaching about disability.

Blaska gives an overview of sixteen disabilities and six chronic illnesses, including suggestions for responding to questions from young children. She outlines a book selection process and describes the review approach, rating system, and subject categorization approach she used. Blaska recommends books that reflect "respect and responsibility, discuss issues of inclusion, and that include the use of first person language" (1996, 51). Blaska evaluates characterization, setting, plot, theme, narrative, and illustrations. She includes a copy of the Images & Encounters profile, a checklist to help reviewers evaluate books according to inclusion and depiction of persons with disabilities. The profile includes guidelines for evaluating story, tone, attitudes, information presented, language used, integration, art, style. Books are assigned a yes or no on each criterion, based on whether it is addressed positively or negatively, or an NP (not present) if the criterion was not present in the story line, illustrations, or language (51).

Mary Anne Prater's Approach to Multiple Categories

Characters who are accurately depicted and who are emphasized as people with disabilities as an aspect of their lives are the current evaluation standard for literary excellence. Mary Anne Prater's "Using Juvenile Literature with Portrayals of Disabilities in Your Classroom" (2000) describes forty-six books published before 1985. Criteria for inclusion on the list included literary quality. For each book, the list describes the disability portrayed, curriculum connection, grade level, affective content, name of the character who has the disability and if the character plays a major, supporting, or minor role. The type of information that might be taught and discussed about specific disabilities is listed. Prater recommends that the "characteristics of individuals with mental retardation, including stereotypic ideas about these individuals," might be discussed. Prater's style of bibliography allows for the child character to be first and not defined by his or her disability.

Content Analysis Related to AD(H)D

Content analysis for empirical research accuracy is also an approach for assessing books. Diana Mayer Demetrulias (2000) studied twenty-one fiction and nonfiction books published about attention deficit (hyperactivity) disorder since 1980. She found that the depictions of the disorder reflect current empirical research findings about AD(H)D and that the books are sensitive to families. Her study did not evaluate literary quality. A descriptive annotated list of the books is provided. For young children, two books use elephant and turtle characters, and another book is a sibling story. Informational books for young children explain the body as a racecar and offer strategies for behavior (Demetrulias 2000, 39). Books for older children are mostly informational and involve young people more. These books answer frequently asked questions, suggest ways young people can help themselves, and offer the perspectives of young adults themselves, describing their diagnosis experience and how they responded, and perspectives from adults who were diagnosed as teens. Two fiction stories include a sibling story (40).

Content Analysis Related to Learning Disabilities

Janet I. Gold describes in nonevaluative detail nine books that address learning disability in stories and in children's own voices and proposes approaches for the classroom such as recording texts so slower readers can listen and follow the text at the same time (Gold 1983, 614). Gold recommends discussions of characters' strengths and weaknesses, how to cope with name calling, how to release frustration, and considering what things the character in the story with a learning disability (LD) thought he would never learn about but did and how he did it (616).

Mary Anne Prater also studied books that included characters with learning disabilities (2003). She found that LD played a major role in the story line and that the characters with LD were dynamic and main characters. In other words, the individual with a learning problem is finally diagnosed, treated, and made better with the character's self-esteem. Parents were commonly depicted as denying the LD and resisting evaluation. She found that fewer picture books depict LD since it is a "hidden disability" and that many juvenile books are out of date (59). She found that most of the books she read were about the LD.

Conclusion

In addition to literary stories, many juvenile books are published for use by the medical, rehabilitative, and social work communities to provide information and explanation to young people, their families, and other professionals about specific "conditions" for informational purposes. Juvenile literature does not yet include much about the experiences of young people who have multiple disabilities.

It seems that no one writing on the topic advocates eliminating books that include unfavorable portrayals, and others write that this would endanger the "right to free access to information and interpretation" (Baskin and Harris 1977, 49). While these ideas are open to the interpretation of individual readers, they are examples of the sophistication with which professionals are currently examining literature that includes characters with disabilities.

Case: *Summer of the Swans*

In 1970, Betsy Byars published *The Summer of the Swans*, and the book was awarded the John Newbery Medal in 1971. Byars was inspired by her experience tutoring two children with learning difficulties through a volunteer program sponsored, in 1968, by West Virginia University. For Byars this "stunning experience" allowed her to be around "kids who were having real problems in learning" and to learn "how much they suffered . . . because they had learning difficulties" and "because of the way other kids treated them" (Byars 2000, 32). While the character of Charlie was not based on the children she tutored, Byars "did a lot of research on the character of Charlie in the Medical Library of W.V.U." She found "three case histories of kids who had had brain damage because of high-fevered illnesses when they were babies." Byars writes that all the details of Charlie's life "were from those case histories," and nothing was made up. Published in April 1970, the book did not sell well and was not widely well reviewed but did win the 1971 Newbery Medal (Byars 2000, 32).

In 1976, *Summer of the Swans* was criticized because the character with disabilities functions to provide a crisis from which "comes the insight and energy for the central character's passage to adulthood" (Baskin and Harris 1977, 31). In 2001, Landrum noted that Charlie does not actively participate in the plot, that Charlie "seems to exist outside the story," and that the dialogue emphasizes what Charlie cannot do more so than what he can (253). The critique goes on to say "the text implies that initially Charlie was rejected by some family members due to his disability" and that he "remains a one-dimensional being whose only developed trait is his disability" (253). Landrum suggests that Charlie is portrayed as a disability rather than as a child with a disability.

Byars presented the character of Charlie as a character among other characters with problems. The author allows for the point of view of the child with the disability to be read and understood by the readers. She also allows for the point of view of others affected by the disability to emerge in a way that makes *Summer of the Swans* a human story, not defined by Charlie's disability. Instead, it is about the emotions and identification of the characters with the reader. The literary quality of the story is acknowledged by merit of the Newbery Medal. Themes in the novel include overcoming not fitting in, and developing friendships.

Discussion Questions

1. Read *Summer of the Swans* and evaluate and discuss the book.

2. What are the major themes of the book?

3. How is Charlie portrayed?

4. Are there any stereotypes at play in the book?

5. What relationships does Charlie have?

6. What needs are expressed by Charlie?

7. Is Charlie portrayed as a disability in the book or as a whole person? Why did you answer this way?

References

Baskin, Barbara H., and Karen H. Harris. 1988. *More notes from a different drummer: A guide to juvenile fiction portraying the disabled.* New York: R. R. Bowker.

———. 1977. *Notes from a different drummer: A guide to juvenile fiction portraying the handicapped.* New York: R. R. Bowker.

Bauer, Carolyn J. 1985. Books can break attitudinal barriers toward the handicapped. *School Counselor* 32: 302–306.

Blaska, Joan Kay. 2003. *Using children's literature to learn about disabilities and illness.* 2nd ed. Troy, NY: Educator's International Press.

———. 1996. *Using children's literature to learn about disabilities and illness.* Moorehead, MN: Practical Press.

———. 1994. Inclusion and depiction of individuals in award-winning and highly recommended children's books. Unpublished manuscript. (Quoted in Blaska 2003)

Blaska, J. K., and E. C. Lynch. 1998. Is everyone included? Using children's literature to facilitate the understanding of disabilities. *Young Children* 53(2): 36–37.

Bunch, Gary Owen. 1996. *Kids, disabilities and regular classrooms: An annotated bibliography of selected children's literature on disability.* Toronto: Inclusion Press.

Byars, Betsy. 2000. Byars, Betsy, 1928– , Autobiography feature. In *Something about the author,* vol. 108, ed. Alan Hedblad, 23–29. Detroit, MI: Gale Group.

———. 1970. *Summer of the Swans.* New York: Viking Press.

Demetrulias, Diana Mayer. 2000. The depiction in juvenile literature of children with attention deficit disorder. *Journal of Youth Services in Libraries* 13(2): 36–42.

Friedberg, Joan Brest, June B. Mullins, and Adelaide Weir Sukiennik. 1985. *Accept me as I am: Best books of juvenile nonfiction on impairments and disabilities.* New York: Bowker.

Gill, Carol. 1987. A new social perspective on disability and its implications for rehabilitation. *Occupational Therapy and Health Care* 7(1): 49–55.

Gold, Janet T. 1983. "THAT'S ME!" The LD child in literature. *Academic Therapy* 18: 609–617.

Harris, Karen H., and Barbara H. Baskin. 1988. Treatment of disabilities in young adult fiction. *Education Digest* 53(7): 56–59.

———. 1987. Evolution of disability characterization in young adult fiction. *Educational Horizons* 65 (Summer): 188–191.

Keith, Lois. 2001. *Take up thy bed and walk: Death, disability and cure in classic fiction for girls.* New York: Routledge.

Kronick, Doreen. 1986. Children's books and games. Books about handicaps. *Academic Therapy* 21 (January): 373–376.

Kupper, Lisa, ed. 1994. *A guide to children's literature and disability: 1989–1994.* Washington, DC: National Information Center for Children and Youth with Disabilities. ED389 114.

Landrum, Judith. 2001. Selecting intermediate novels that feature characters with disabilities. *Reading Teacher* 55(3): 252–258.

Margolis, Howard, and Arther Shapiro. 1987. Countering negative images of disability in classical literature. *English Journal* 76(3): 18–22.

Marlowe, Mike, and George Maycock. 2001. Using literary texts in teacher education to promote positive attitudes toward children with disabilities. *Teacher Education and Special Education* 24(2): 75–83.

Mellon, Constance A. 1989. Exceptionality in children's books: Combining apples and oranges. *School Library Journal* 35(14): 46–47.

Morrison, William F., and Harvey A. Rude. 2002. Beyond textbooks: A rationale for a more inclusive user of literature in preservice special education teacher programs. *Teacher Education and Special Education* 25(2): 114–123.

National Information Center for Children and Youth with Disabilities. 2001. *Children's literature and disability. Resources you can use.* 2nd ed. Washington, DC: National Information Center for Children and Youth with Disabilities. ED389 114.

Office of Special Education and Rehabilitative Services. 2003. Archived information. An overview of the bill to provide a broad understanding of some of the changes in IDEA '97. http://www.ed.gov/offices/OSERS/Policy/IDEA/overview.html.

Prater, Mary Anne. 2003. Learning disabilities in children's and adolescent literature: How are characters portrayed? *Learning Disability Quarterly* 26(1): 47–62.

———. 2000. Using juvenile literature with portrayals of disabilities in your classroom. *Intervention in School and Clinic* 35(3): 167–176.

Quicke, John. 1985. *Disability in modern children's fiction.* Cambridge, MA: Brookline Books.

Radencich, Marguerite C. 1986. Literature for minority handicapped students. *Reading Research Instruction* 25 (Summer): 288–294.

Rasinski, Timothy V., and Cindy Gillespie. 1992. *Sensitive issues: An annotated guide to children's literature K–6.* Phoenix, AZ: Oryx Press.

Robertson, Debra. 1992. *Portraying persons with disabilities: An annotated bibliography of fiction for children and teenagers.* 3rd ed. New Providence, NJ: Reed Publishing (USA).

Saunders, Kathy. 2000. *Happy ever afters. A storybook guide to teaching children about disability.* Staffordshire, England: Trentham Books Limited.

Smith-D'Arezzo, Wendy M. 2003. Diversity in children's literature: Not just black and white issue. *Children's Literature in Education* 34(1): 75–94.

Stelle, Lucinda C. H. 1999. Review of children's literature: Children with disabilities as main characters. *Intervention in School and Clinic* 35(2): 123–128.

7

Gender

Many educators think that the gender of a child is constructed at an early age. The books children read inform their understanding of gender. That children use information to "form gender perceptions" is supported by Kohlberg's theory of cognitive and moral development, social learning theory, and gender schema processing theory (Greever, Austin, and Welhousen 2000, 325). Exposure to sexist images is "likely to have detrimental effects on the development of children's self-esteem, particularly on that of girls and on the perceptions children have of their own and of others' abilities and possibilities" (Paterson and Lach 1990, 186).

Authors, teachers, and publishers influence what children learn about gender from books (Louie 2001, 143). In the 1970s, feminists raised awareness about gender bias and stereotypes in children's books. Experimental forms of fiction emerged to parody, reverse, and raise awareness about gender bias and stereotypes. These forms allowed readers to see the many ways that books portrayed gender. By the 1990s, critics' focus had turned from analyzing books for gender bias and stereotypes. Instead, they began to analyze books for the construction of gender identity. There are many resources teachers can use to identify and evaluate books for gender representation and to find examples of interesting titles related to the construction of gender through children's literature.

History

In spite of the attention to gender in children's literature, the history of gendered children's literature is recent. Books for boys emerged by the mid-1800s, "complemented by domestic stories for girls (Segel, 168)" (Marshall 2004, 261). Even though boys and girls both read adventure stories, these were known as a genre for boys (281).

During the 1970s, the feminist movement raised awareness among teachers and librarians about the representation of gender in books. Feminist studies suggested that female characters were underrepresented in children's books and that "stereotypical portrayals of girls and women in books that received Caldecott Awards or Honors reinforced gender bias" (Marshall 2004, 259; Rudman 1995, 177; Louie 2001, 142). Studies of children's books in the 1980s and 1990s "found more female characters depicted but concluded that the portrayal of women and girls remained narrow" (Marshall 2004, 259). Representation of more males than females in children's literature continued into the 1990s (Louie 2001, 142). Contemporary children's literature reflects "growing awareness of the change in gender role definitions and behaviors" and the concerns of an "increasingly independent and enlightened public" (Rudman 1995, 177). Awareness has also grown among authors, illustrators, and publishers (Louie 2001, 142).

Responsibility

Fox (1993) writes that teachers, authors, and publishers "should acknowledge society's . . . attitudes about women" (85). Fox argues that to remain "aloof" and "unaware" is to "commit . . . crimes" of sexism (86). Teachers can "avoid blithely passing on damaging, static traditions that inhibit growth" by analyzing books for sexism (Coats 2001, 408). On the other hand, teachers are warned that overanalyzing books for sexism might lead to collections that are "harmlessly clean: simple, cheerful, relentlessly realistic" and that lack the magic of children's classics that lead all readers on an unconscious "search for self" (Wullshlager 1991).

Teachers may or may not feel responsible for gender-fair teaching using children's books. Some teachers take seriously a responsibility to "become more aware of gender-related issues, examine their own biases, and engage children in situations where perceptions can be discussed openly" (Greever, Austin, and Welhousen 2000, 329). Greever and colleagues write that a teacher's view of gender is based on what he or she learned as a child, and perceptions of gender have changed since he or she grew up. This awareness helps teachers explore and "come to terms with their own biases" (329).

A teacher preparation program at Texas A&M University develops teacher self-awareness about gender bias in children's literature by asking teachers to discuss their own questions about gender bias together, to examine books for gender bias, and to debate that there is "no longer a need to be concerned about gender bias in children's literature" (Walker and Foote 1999–2000, 89–90). Self-testing for self-awareness is sometimes used with students who answer questions about admirable gender traits and compare these. They also list what they believe are occupations for men and women. These techniques rely on the idea that every one is at a different place with respect to "attitudes toward masculine and feminine characteristics and roles" (Rudman 1995, 179).

Authors are also responsible for gender stereotypes and breaking them. Gender stereotypes persist in children's literature because it is "unrealistic to expect authors to write their stories with gender restrictions placed on them" (Louie 2001, 143). Authors may or may not feel responsible for writing gender-fair books. Pinsent (1997) refers to a study showing "a strong tendency for male authors not to choose female protagonists though female writers are willing to write about males" (76). Virginia Hamilton (2001) says that she combines "fact, memory, and imagination combine to make plot and characters" and that she "writes fictions and not sociology" (21, 23). Author Mem Fox (2001) tries to balance the scales in children's literature by writing "anti-sexist" children's books and has made a commitment to "make the main character a girl, to show people that girls . . . are active and interesting, courageous, feisty people" (67). Fox gives male and female characters "permission" to escape gender-based social expectations (Fox 1993, 85).

Publishers also influence content and many now have "guidelines to authors and artists to assist them in using nonsexist, nonracist language and images" (Rudman 1995, 181).

Political Agenda of Stories

Children's literature is political when used to promote a "more just social order" in the classroom (Rice 2002, 40). It has been argued that because books contain an author's views about gender, "there is no such thing as a politically innocent book for kids" because books contain an author's views about gender (Short 2001, 186). For example, author Mem Fox (1993) admits that unless she pays attention to sexism, the lessons she has learned about gender stereotypes slip into her writing (86).

As a genre, feminist children's books since the 1960s reject "stereotypical gender roles," and some have "overt ideological agendas" (Trites 1997, 4). Some recommended reading lists suggest books about the developmental needs of young people with respect to gender (Short 2001, 191). Other recommended books are those that address boys' and girls' developmental needs. Many recommended books "give the reader a chance to think about or internalize the wider issues of being a girl" (Collins 1998, 35–36).

Gender-fair teaching means teachers acknowledge the bias and stereotypes in books, expand the choices of gender messages offered, and give students more options "in how they think about themselves and others" (Short 2001, 191). Many teachers are not comfortable taking on "a political agenda and voice" because it feels as though they are imposing their views on students (189). Educators struggle with raising "children's awareness of gender positioning/issues without creating controversy" and recognize the "discourse of the school needs to change . . . for educators to be willing to implement critical literacy activities that focus on gender" (Rice 2002, 39–40).

Student comfort is also an issue. Student "talk itself is gendered," and unless moderated, literature discussions may break down into "gendered talk" where girls talk about emotions and relationships and boys talk about action and plot (Short 2001, 191). Boys' voices may dominate literature discussions unless students are grouped into girl majority or all-girl groups or unless ways are found to encourage all students to take part (Short 2001, 191; Fredrickson 2000, 304). Encouraging talk means helping students vent anger about "not being heard, disagreeing with readings and opinions, debating gender, power dynamics, and prejudice" (Fredrickson 2000, 306). It means encouraging "students to look at both sides of a given issue" and not to "blend in, but to stand out and speak up" (306–307).

In *Beauty, Brains, and Brawn: The Construction of Gender in Children's Literature* Susan Lehr explores how classroom life reinforces "culturally gendered roles for girls and boys" (Lehr 2001, 2). Lehr argues that the attention boys and girls get in the classroom is a function of what they demand. Teachers have reported that when they gave as much attention to girls as to boys that boys reacted with "anger, hostility, and resentment" (2).

Sexism in Literature

Sexism in society and schools damages girls and boys (Walker and Foote 1999–2000, 89). Language arts programs that address developmental needs with respect to gender are those that encourage boys and girls to read books "with strong girls as central characters" (Collins 1998, 34). Everyone benefits from stories with balanced, realistic, and unbiased gender portrayals.

In "Ten Quick Ways to Analyze Children's Books for Sexism and Racism" (Council on Interracial Books for Children 1980), many starting points for analysis are suggested. Evaluators can analyze books for stereotypes, tokenism, active and passive roles, standards for success, and roles for women. They can consider the relationships and heroes in a story. The effect of a book on a child's self-image might be considered, in addition to the perspective and background of authors and illustrators, the use of sexist language, and the copyright date of a book.

Feminism and Children's Literature

Feminism does not refer only to female emancipation. In *Waking Sleeping Beauty: Feminist Voices in Children's Novels*, contemporary feminist Rebecca Seelinger Trites defines feminism as the "belief in the worth of all individuals" and "the premise that all people should be treated equally" (1997, 2). "Feminism" has many interpretations with respect to children's literature. A balanced treatment of this is found in *Girls, Boys, Books, and Toys: Gender in Children's Literature and Culture* (Clark and Higonnet 1999). Essays relate the history of mainstream feminism to children's literature. Some feminist modes of thinking are analyzed as outdated. The "recuperative task of feminist criticism . . . adding/restoring authors to the canon" is explored (Kidd 2000, 675).

Feminism has added to and changed children's literature. Story revisions, reversals of gender stereotypes, rejection of traditional roles, metaphorical stories, and relationships between female characters that strengthen the female protagonist's voice are examples of how literature has been enhanced (Trites 1997, x).

Feminist Books

A feminist children's novel is one that empowers characters, allowing them autonomy, self-expression, self-determination, and self-awareness. It affirms and celebrates a character's agency, individuality, choice, and nonconformity (Trites 1997, xi, 6–8). Characters acknowledge compassion, interconnectedness, and communication (5). Gender does not permanently impede the character's development, and characters overcome gender-related conflicts and destroy traditions of oppression (4, 6). Characters are aware of when and how they are controlled, transcend oppression, and females succeed at traditionally male tasks (5). Authors of feminist novels include Virginia Hamilton, Patricia MacLachlan and Cynthia Voigt, Francesca Lia Block, Ursula K. LeGuin, Margaret Mahy, Mildred Taylor, and Barbara Wersba, Rosa Guy, Angela Johnson, and Minfong Ho (9).

Antisexist and Nonsexist Books

Antisexist books are about the subject of gender and "challenge sexist assumptions" that it is better to be a boy. These books are sometimes absurd or humorous (Pinsent 1997, 81).

Nonsexist fiction helps readers imagine the potential of females by presenting a world in which gender discrimination does not exist and in which males and females are "shown in equal numbers, performing similar tasks and behaving similarly" (Sue Adler, quoted in Claire et al. 1993, 111).

Emancipatory Fiction

Feminist interpretations of gender representations in books began to give way, in the 1990s, to studies that focused less on bias and more on the construction of gender identity. Feminism's role with respect to analysis of children's literature has expanded and pays more attention to "class, race, and age" and the depiction of feminist values rather than focusing on "egalitarian depictions of gender" (Clark, Kulkin, and Clancy 1999, 72; Coats 2002, 208). In addition to feminist books, *emancipatory fiction* is also recommended. This term refers to books that are emancipatory to males and females from all ethnic and cultural backgrounds. Books that "provide an insight into female values and the strength provided by women's comradeship," that "consider the whole person in the whole community," and that "involve strong female characters, but not at the expense of undervaluing males because of their sex" are also recommended by Pinsent (1997, 85). Pinsent recommends "emancipatory fiction for males" including *Flour Babies* (Fine 1992) and *Henry's Baby* (Hoffman 1993) (88).

Girls and Sexism

One concern is that omission of female characters or portrayal of them in subservient roles not only takes power from female readers but confirms "unconscious prejudices of male readers" (Pinsent 1997, 77). Portraying characters equally helps female readers imagine their potential and male readers imagine "women on equal terms" (77).

Stereotypes are being undone. Ruth O. Saxton (1998) describes the construction of a "new girl" in contemporary fiction by women. The "new girl" is "not an object of the marriage market," marriage is not a qualification for her adulthood, and motherhood does not limit her artistic or self fulfillment" (xx). She is "who she will become," and her maturity and survival relate to her level of resistance of "the generic mold" as she comes to terms with the "values and mores of U.S. womanhood" for which "the body is a battleground over which conflicting cultural values are fought" (xx).

Influence of Liberal Feminism on Girls

Feminist scholars in the 1970s studied how books for young people portrayed women and girls. Dominance of liberal bias in feminist social science research has been credited with influencing the children's book market to incorporate liberal feminist content (Clark, Kulkin, and Clancy 1999, 71). Studies raised the awareness of publishers, authors, awards committees, parents, and teachers about the visibility and voice of female characters in children's books (71, 80). This awareness helped girls "battle messages that tell them they are second best, or victims, or human beings measured by the beauty of their bodies and the pliability of their minds (Bauermeister & Smith, 1997, viii)" (Heine and Inkster 1999, 427).

Literature exerts a powerful influence on "girls' need to become emotionally whole, confident adults" (Collins 1998, 34). Balanced, realistic, and unbiased gender portrayals counter the "negative effect that gender stereotypes have on the self-esteem and self-worth of girls" (Heine and Inkster 1999, 427; also see Rudman 1995, 177).

Feminist pedagogy can also counter negative effects of gender stereotypes in literature. Using feminist pedagogy to teach literature means teaching that feminism is a positive force. It reveals stereotypes, compares masculinist with feminist ideology, and validates that "youth culture has the ability to change" the masculinist worldview (Coats 2002, 208). Feminist teachers validate female voices in the classroom equally with male voices and discuss "gender-linked and non-gender specific strengths" of characters in books (Trites 1997, 142).

The Amelia Bloomer Project highlights quality books for youth that exhibit feminist viewpoints and ideals. The books on the Project's lists identify picture books and, intermediate and young adult books that include "significant feminist content, excellence in writing, appealing format, and age appropriateness for young readers" (http://www.libr.org/FTF/bloomer.html). The list is sponsored by the Feminist Task Force of the Social Responsibilities Round Table of the American Library Association.

The Women's Studies Librarian's Web site at the University of Wisconsin lists resources of books for girls (http://www.library.wisc.edu/libraries/WomensStudies). These include the Women's National Book Association's list of "Eighty Books for the 21st Century Girls" (http://www.wnba-books.org/anniversaries/80women.html). This list is made up of favorite titles that "provide smart, capable and talented female role models for further generations of girls."

Expanding Gender Identity

Some critics argue that gender identity is constructed by diversity in culture, by history, by commercial media, and other factors (Marshall 2004, 258). Using books and activities that "encourage children to explore both non-stereotypical reading choices and behavior" is part of "gender-fair" instruction that challenges children to consider "gender issues even as they learn gender" (Chick 2002, 19, 23).

Gender-fair instruction refers to using books of excellent literary quality that "avoid stereotyping characters into gender-roles" and that show "characters as individuals, with their own strengths and weaknesses" so that readers may see that a person is more than his or her gender identity (Marshall 2004, 259; Pinsent 1997, 89; Chick 2002, 19).

Gender-fair instruction does not attempt to establish a "gender-egalitarian model" but to "find a range of portrayals" and to raise awareness in readers that gender prejudice exists and can work against people (Diekman and Murnen 2004, 382). It means creating "gender-diverse" collections in schools and teaching about gender without imposing personal opinions (Short 2001, 186).

Such instruction is not meant to omit books that depict stereotypical roles but to add books that allow "boys and girls to expand their definitions of masculinity and femininity" (Short 2001, 187; also see Rice 2002, 33). Analyzing how the design of stories is influenced by culture helps readers resist gender expectations and consider alternative solutions for characters and for themselves (Roberts, Cecil, and Alexander 1993, x; Marshall 2004, 260; Chick 2002). It allows them to "confirm, broaden or modify their own gender identity" (Roberts, Cecil, and Alexander 1993 x; also see Marshall 2004, 260; Chick 2002).

Gender fairness shifts the focus from sex roles to examine "how gender is produced within particular cultural practices" (Marhall 2004, 261). Analysis is focused on gender as a "socially produced identity" as opposed to a "universal category with one single meaning" (268). Being a girl or boy may have multiple meanings influenced by many social and cultural factors (269).

For example, in searching for a positive female role model in books, researchers found characteristics that added to a positive model but not a single definition of a positive female role model (Heine and Inkster 1999, 428). Researchers considered many factors including "personal characteristics, issues, problem-solving methods, relationships, stereotypes, and underrepresented or misrepresented groups among young female lead characters in recent children's literature" that contributed to a positive character (428).

Gender Positive!: A Teachers' and Librarians' Guide to Nonstereotyped Children's Literature, K–8 (Roberts, Cecil, and Alexander 1993) describes books and activities useful for expanding notions of gender identity. Books include nonstereotypic gender portrayals. Recommendations for supplementing and replacing books that "misinform children about gender roles" are offered. Books that demonstrate "life choices" for girls and boys not limited by gender are suggested (xiii). Activities are suggested that help readers "cope with stereotypic messages" and "prepare them for the real and changing world they will face as adults" (xiii; also see Chick 2002, 19).

Boys and Sexism

In the 1990s, the men's movement raised awareness about male stereotypes in American culture. Books published about boys' lives included *Real Boys: Rescuing Our Sons from the Myths of Boyhood* (Pollack 1999), *Raising Cain: Protecting the Emotional Life of Boys* (Kindlon and Thompson 1999), and *The Wonder of Boys* (Gurian 1996). Many teachers read these books "to explore and reflect on their own belief systems" (Greever, Austin, and Welhousen 2000, 329).

Expectations for male behavior "are so deeply ingrained that most people are unaware of them" (329). Boys who "violate or try to ignore" these expectations are "taunted or ostracized by significant adults or peers" (329). Expectations about male behavior are reinforced by stories that depict, for example, the male duties of fighting dragons, rescuing fair maidens, and marrying (Wolf 2004, 170). In particular, war books sometimes exaggerate the male stereotype as "anonymous aggressors with weapons, fighting machines who follow orders mindlessly" (Desai 2001, 88). Soldiers are shown as "part of the background of a violent world, perhaps off-stage but ever threatening and impersonal, like a looming hurricane" (88). Desai writes about the need for more "emphasis on expanding behavior choices for boys in the classroom" and "examining the implications of those limited male choices on attempts to teach conflict resolution" (91).

Content analyses suggest that male characters are often restricted to male gender roles, while female characters have masculine and feminine gender behaviors available to them. There is a lack of books that depict boys as nurturing, caring, cooking meals, using household artifacts, and taking care of children (Diekman and Murnen 2004, 381–382; Poarch and Monk-Turner 2001, 70). This fails to show boys and girls the people boys can become (Diekman and Murnen 2004, 381–382). In one reader response study, readers demonstrated "unacceptance of nontraditional male characteristics" (Rice 2000, 229). Boys' responses reflected a rigid expectation about males' "stereotypical position"; however, girls responded in ways suggesting that they have broader "cultural definitions of gender" (230). The role of fathers in children's books is ill-defined (Valpy 1996, 302). Books that include fathers often depict them as "stern, remote, judgmental figures, frowning critically at their children's mistakes" (302).

One technique that has been recommended for transcending restricted gender roles is reading against the grain. Readers read themselves into the roles of characters not of their own gender and consider the qualities depicted for this character in the story. This allows readers to imagine the position of the character based on gender identity and to consider broader solutions for the character (Rice 2000, 230). Males who read female characters may find the "feminine side of their nature is liberating, allows for tender feeling and need for emotional expression" (Pinsent 1997, 77). Students can explore the subtleties of gender stereotypes in literature from a personal level and using a critical approach (Temple 1993, 92).

The Assumption of Boys' Books and Girls' Books

Findings from gender-based research on reading patterns that have been reported in practitioner journals have influenced how teachers select books to encourage reading. These decisions are sometimes based on generalized assumptions about gendered reading that are not definitive.

In *"Reading Don't Fix No Chevys": Literacy in the Lives of Young Men* (2002), Michael W. Smith and Jeffrey D. Wilhelm describe a study they did to "take a close look at a wide variety of adolescent boys . . . to understand them personally, to understand their literate behaviors and to come to understand how to teach them in improved ways" (xx). In the chapter "What's Going Down: A Review of the Current Concerns around Boys and Literacy," the authors present a "Summary of Research on Gender and Literacy." Here they offer a "quick statement of findings" they believe are compelling about the differences between boys and girls on literacy tasks. Although Smith and Wilhelm do not present the summary as a generalized list—and in fact, warn against generalization—concepts from the summary have made their way into practitioner literature as a basis for recommending practice (10; also see Jones and Fiorelli 2003, 9).

These general statements have been challenged by other scholars. For example, the general idea that boys are more inclined to read nonfiction than girls has been questioned because this finding may be related to factors such as lack of attention to encouraging girls to read informational books (Doiron 2003, 16). Ray Doiron (2003) cites research to suggest that "both boys and girls enjoy reading stories including novels and easy fiction books" but that "boys choose both fiction and non-fiction while girls choose more fiction" (15).

Although many think that girls will read boys' books, but boys will not read girls' books, there is little evidence to suggest that boys reject books with female protagonists. Boy and girl readers enjoy stories in which female protagonists are "powerful, resourceful, and active" when males are not shown negatively and when stories are well constructed and inventive (Pinsent 1997, 76; Louie 2001, 144; Rudman 1995, 181; Short 2001, 187).

Requests for more "boy-centered hero books" that would attract boy readers leave some wondering, "How much is the cause of girls' empowerment being forfeited for the sake of stimulating reluctant boys to read?" (Temple 1993, 90).

Fairy Tales and Folktales

Much has been written and discussed about gender stereotypes and the relationship of the female to folk- and fairy tales (Bottigheimer 1986; Wariner 1995; Zipes 1986). Masha Kabakow Rudman provides a comprehensive treatment of the topic (1995, 181). Stereotypes in fairy tales demonstrate "models of female development based on patriarchal assumptions" (Keyser 1989, 158). Although the oral tradition of fairy tales and folktales was a means women used to communicate about ideas and experiences, this role was overshadowed in Western literature based on "19th century European values and ideas" as tales were "transcribed from oral tradition by Grimm and Andrew Lang" (Rudman 1995, 183). In these transcriptions, "males became rescuers, controllers, intellectual extroverts, active, take physical risks, initiators" (183). Female protagonists became limited as weak, demure, passive, obedient characters who need rescuing, and who are rewarded by wedding the rescuer and serving him (183; also see Pinsent 1997, 79). Only the female servants, witches, fairy godmothers, and wicked stepsisters could be shown as "powerful and intelligent, ugly, strong, and obedient," and "active female heroines" were either "evil or nonhuman" (Rudman 1995, 183). This depiction warned female readers against rebellion and nonconformity (Keyser 1989, 158).

During the 1970s, feminism played a role in correcting stereotypes in the genre of fairy tales and folktales, resurrecting lost versions and forgotten tales, and revising stories for gender fairness. *Womenfolk and Fairytales* (Minard 1975), *Tatterhood and Other Tales: Stories of Magic and Adventure* (Phelps 1978), *The Maid of the North: Feminist Folktales from around the World* (Phelps 1981) are books that give new life to old tales (Pinsent 1997, 80).

Although some object to tampering with historically accurate cultural values, fairy tales and folktales have also been written and revised using feminist principles (Louie 2001, 148). *Dr. Gardner's Fairy Tales for Today's Children* (Gardner 1980) presents stories that do not mythologize or enhance romantic love with magical powers and do not include happily ever after stories. Another approach has been role reversal of the victim in stories to an active role, for example, in *The True Story of the 3 Little Pigs* (Scieszka 1989). Stories are also popular that switch genders and gender roles of characters. These include *Prince Cinders* (Cole 1987) and *The Paper Bag Princess* (Pinsent 1997, 80). When parodies of fairy tales are used with children or young adults, it is recommended that the original versions of the stories be reviewed with students. In addition, younger children may not be able to conceptualize the meanings of parody in stories (80).

Coming of Age in Fantasy and Science Fantasy

Fantasy stories help females theorize options for coming-of-age rituals that are frequently limited for women to "pregnancy, childbirth, and marriage" (Attebery 1996, 290). Coming-of-age stories "enhance the experiences girls need to become emotionally whole, confident adults," and science fantasy has more power than traditional fantasy because it believably presents "changes in economic systems, family structures, political relationships, even language" (Collins 1998, 34; also see Attebery 1996, 298). The "route to maturity" can be more than marriage (Attebery 1996, 299). Because a fantasy convention is that "a task undertaken be completed within the narrative," this means that "maturity is hard-won, but worth the winning, and the female heroes represent an unprecedented range of models for development," including "power and self-knowledge" (299). Fantasy fiction that includes girls coming of age without a male character required include "Diana Wynne Jones's *The Spell-Coates* (1979), Virginia Hamilton's *Justice and Her Brothers* (1978), Michaela Roessner's *Walkabout Woman* (1988), and Suzette Haden Elgin's *Ozark Trilogy* (1981)" (Attebury 1996, 298). The importance of coming-of-age stories is recognized by the GRRLStories Web site at http://www.grrlstories.org by Corinne Platt. This site provides information about coming-of-age rites and ceremonies for girls across America. It invites girls to tell their own stories and have a "choice in the story they create for themselves."

Girls' Series Books

In *Nancy Drew® and Company: Culture, Gender, and Girls' Series* (Innes 1997) the female protagonists in girls' series are described as "not always a teenager, who, with or without friends, has exciting adventure after exciting adventure in a series of books that focus on her experiences" (3). These include Trixie Belden, Cherry Ames, and Nancy Drew, among others. Other series have been organized around activities—for example, "Automobile Girls, Adventure Girls, Camp Fire Girls, College Girls, Moving Picture Girls, Radio Girls, Red Cross Girls, and Motor Maids" (3). Gender identity is constructed in these popular books based on the current state of the "culture's values, mores, and biases" (10).

Pairing Historical Fiction and Contemporary Classics

Although many themes in earlier fiction persist in contemporary fiction, pairing contemporary with historical texts is a technique to help readers compare the treatment of males and females in literature during different eras (Rudman 1995, 186). Carol Jago (2000) recommends pairing *The Scarlet Letter* by Hawthorne (1850) with *Jasmine* by Mukherjee (1989); *A Doll's House* by Ibsen (1889) with *Top Girls* by Churchill (1982); *Jane Eyre* by Bronte (1847) with *Annie John* by Kincaid (1985); *The Awakening* by Chopin (1899) and *Mama Day* by Naylor (1988); and *Daisy Miller* by Miller (1877) with *Breakfast at Tiffany's* by Capote (1958, 127).

Themes of "romantic fulfillment, rejection of romance, individuation from mother, maternal loss or presence, physicality, experience of her body in the culture, sex or denial of sex" persist, and Ruth O. Saxton suggests many discussion questions to explore these themes in ways that provide historical comparison (Saxton 1998, xi, xviii). Saxton recommends questions that will help students compare stories set historically with contemporary stories (xviii).

Interaction with Texts

Interaction with texts helps "children who have traditional definitions of masculinity and femininity . . . move beyond their initial response to the nontraditional gender role" (Rice 2002, 39). It allows students to discuss nonstereotypical gender behavior while maintaining distance from their perceptions of their own gendered behavior (Greever, Austin, and Welhousen 2000, 329).

Examples of interaction with text include readers switching the genders of characters who initiate action (Rudman 1995, 185). It includes revising stories to fit contemporary life or writing traditional tales that reverse expected gender roles (Attebery 1996, 294). It includes rewriting stories to include themselves as the main character and choosing a course of action (Rice 2002, 35). Students can use this interaction to learn what male and female traits are valued in a story and to discuss whether they value these traits.

Criteria and Selection

Balancing gender in literature choices, while at the same time increasing reading choices, helps students come to expect "diversity of gender roles among cultural groups" (Short 2001, 195). Reviewing for gender fairness means considering how books value male or female occupations, traits, and contributions. It means considering how what characters are able to do in a story is related to their gender. It means considering the portrayal of competition, parental roles, the depiction of clothing, and the use of language (Rudman 1995, 182; Diekman and Murnen 2004, 381; Roberts, Cecil, and Alexander 1993, xi).

In "Six Characteristics to Consider When Examining Children's Books for Positive Gender Role Models," Heine and Inkster (1999) evaluate whether or not girls are portrayed with "a range of admirable emotions and traits, including perseverance, courage, independence, and resourcefulness" (429). They consider how characters mature or come of age. They ask readers to determine the character's perspective on many things including gender images, gender-appropriate behavior, roles, body image, and physical beauty (429).

Stories that support girls' developmental needs depict girls' struggle "to be their integrated selves" and depict "conflict and change in the lives of real girls" (Collins 1998, 35).

Booklists and Bibliographies

Booklists include those in bibliographic essays. For example, Belinda Louie (2001) recommends many books "in which girls have space to express their feelings" with the gender issue noted (145). These include: "*Baseball Ballerina* (gender roles); *Heather Has Two Mom-*

mies (gender roles); *I Live with Daddy* (gender roles); *Granny the Pag* (aging); *What Jaime Saw* (coping with abuse); *White Wash* (coping with racism); *Speak* (rape survival); *I Was a Teenage Fairy* (beauty/self-image); *The Skin I'm In* (skin color); and *Finding My Own Voice* (assertiveness)"(145).

Greever, Austin, and Welhouse (2000) list books that portray nonstereotypical male roles and expectations, including *Oliver Button Is a Sissy* (de Paola 1979) and *Marvin Redpost: Is He a Girl?* (Sachar 1993) (329). Lists also group books to emphasize a particular gender identity theme. For example, Carol Jago (2000) developed lists with creative titles like "10 Classics for Girls Certain They Will Never Meet Prince Charming" and "10 Classics for Boys (and Girls) Who Love Action and Hate Long Descriptions of Drawing Rooms and Landscapes" (153). Heine et al. (1999) list books with positive girl characters including historical, contemporary, and fantasy character descriptions. Rice (2002) lists books for early readers that include nontraditional gender roles (40).

Gender Positive! (Roberts, Cecil, and Alexander 1993) includes a bibliography of over 200 books for "children in the formative elementary school years (K–8)," with annotations about gender portrayal (xi). Kathleen Odean's bibliographies for boys' and girls' books are *Great Books for Boys: More Than 600 Books for Boys from 2 to 14* (1998) and *Great Books for Girls: More Than 600 Recommended Books for Girls, Ages 3 to 14* (2002). Heine et al. (1999) recommend "*Let's Hear It for the Girls: 375 Great Books for Readers 2–14* (Bauermeister and Smith 1997), *100 Books for Girls to Grow On* (Dodson 1998) and *Once Upon a Heroine: 450 Books for Girls* (Cooper-Mullin and Cove 1998)" (423).

Bibliographies also appear regularly in reading, educational, and library journals. For example, Cheryl Karp Ward published an annotated bibliography, "It's a Girl Thing" in *Voices from the Middle* (2001, 64). Patrick Jones and Dawn Fiorelli published bibliographies of books for boys in *Teacher Librarian* (2003, 12, 13).

Jon Scieszka's Web site "Guys Read" (http://www.guyread.com) was inspired by the author's desire to motivate guys to read using a Web site where men and boys can post book suggestions and opinions. Scieszka is not trying to define what makes a "guy book." Instead, he hopes to let guys know what other guys are reading (Scieszka 2003, 18).

Case: Web Site Reviews

Jon Scieszka, author of *The Stinky Cheese Man and Other Stupid Fairly Tales* (1992) and *The True Story of the 3 Little Pigs* (1989) by A. Wolf, was a teacher for ten years. His experiences, and reading Smith and Wilhelm's study (2002), inspired him to start the "Guys Read" Web site (http://www.guyread.com). Scieszka lists reasons that boys might struggle with reading: because they "develop slower than girls," they have a competitive learning style that works against them, they are asked to read books that are not appealing, or they are not motivated to read. In addition, boys need "positive male role models for literacy" because "the majority of adults involved in kids' reading are women," and boys may not see it as a masculine activity (http://www.guysread.com/about_guys_why.html). The mission of the site is to "motivate boys to read by connecting them with materials they will want to read" (http://www.guysread. com/about_guys_mission.html). The site exists to "call attention to boys' literacy," to "expand our definition of reading," to include many formats that "count as reading," and to give boys a forum for choosing what they enjoy and finding out what they want.

The Women's Studies Librarian's Web site at the University of Wisconsin lists resources on girls' development that include resources for finding books for girls (http://www.library.wisc.edu/libraries/WomensStudies/girlsdev.htm). These include the Women's National Book Association's list of "Eighty Books for the 21st Century Girls" (http://www.wnba-books.org/anniversaries/80women.html). This list is made up of favorite titles that "provide smart, capable and talented female role models for further generations of girls."

Discussion Questions

1. Review the Web sites mentioned. Discuss the qualities of these sites and how you might use them in your work as a teacher.

2. What would you add to or change about these sites?

3. What specific gender-based needs are met by these Web sites?

4. What characteristics of individual readers are described at these sites based on gender?

5. How could you encourage boys and girls to read genres they might not select on their own?

Study: Reading against the Grain

Mem Fox writes that in South Australia teachers teach overtly about gender. In reading against the grain activities, teachers reread stories with young children, asking them to notice what the males and females are doing in the story. Teachers ask students if what the males and females in the story are doing are what males and females really do.

Still, Fox believes you can ruin a good book by too much analysis of sexism because a book may have a great many other wonderful attributes that are swept under the carpet simply because of one aberrant piece of sexism. You have got to look at the whole book and say, "Well, for this reason and for this reason, this is a great book and it's a pity they slipped up here" (Fox 2001, 68).

Discussion Questions

1. What is the purpose of the reading against the grain exercise described by Mem Fox?

2. Select a children's picture book and read against the grain.

3. Switch the gender of the characters in the story.

4. What did this exercise reveal, if anything? How did it change the story or your view of the story?

5. Act out or rewrite the story, from the point of view of a character in the story that is not your gender. Make any changes you like.

6. Discuss the changes you made to the story from the perspective of role-playing a different gender than your own. Why did you make the changes? How did they change the story for the reader?

7. Discuss the gender expectations you find in the story. How do these compare to contemporary gender expectations?

References

Asselin, M. 2003. Bridging the gap between learning to be male and learning to read. *Teacher Librarian* 30(3): 53–54.

Attebery, Brian. 1996. Women's coming of age in fantasy. In *Only connect: Readings on children's literature*, 3rd ed., ed. Sheila Egoff, Gordon Stubbs, Ralph Ashley, and Wendy Sutton, 288–300. New York: Oxford University Press.

Bottigheimer, Ruth B., ed. 1986. *Fairy tales and society: Illusion, allusion, and paradigm.* Philadelphia: University of Pennsylvania Press.

Brancato, R. F. 2001. "In defense of: *Are you there God? It's me! Margaret*, Deannie, and Blubber—Three novels by Judy Blume." In *Censored books: Critical viewpoints*, ed. N. J. Karolides, L. Burress, and J. M. Kean, 87–97. Lanham, MD: Scarecrow Press.

Braxton, B. 2003. Bait the boys and hook them into reading. *Teacher Librarian* 30(3): 43–44.

Bryan, L., D. Owens, and Linda Walker. 2004. Y-RAP (Young Readers Art Project). A pragmatic solution for reluctant readers. *Reading Improvement* 41(4): 235–240.

Cart, Michael. 1996. *From romance to realism: 50 years of growth and change in young adult literature.* New York: HarperCollins Children's Books.

Chick, Kay A. 2002. Challenging gender stereotypes through literature: Picture books with strong female characters. *Journal of Children's Literature* 28(2): 19–24.

Christian-Smith, Linda K. 2000. More than crime on her mind: Nancy Drew as woman hero. In *A necessary fantasy?: The heroic figure in children's popular culture*, ed. Dudley Jones and Tony Watkins, 87–110. New York: Garland.

Claire, H., et al., eds. 1993. *Equality matters.* Clevedon: Language Matters. (Quoted in Pinsent 1997, 81, 84)

Clark, Beverly Lyon. 1996. *Regendering the school story: Sassy sissies and tattling tomboys.* New York: Routledge.

Clark, Beverly Lyon, and M. R. Higonnet, eds. 1999. *Girls, boys, books, toys: Gender in children's literature and culture.* Baltimore, MD: Johns Hopkins University Press.

Clark, Roger, Heidi Kulkin, and Liam Clancy. 1999. The liberal bias in feminist social science research on children's books. In *Girls, boys, books, toys: Gender in children's literature and culture*, ed. Beverly Lyon Clark and M. R. Higonnet, 71–82. Baltimore, MD: Johns Hopkins University Press.

Clothier, M. 1999. TechReport: Site encourages kids to read. *Atlanta Journal and Constitution*, May 16.

Coats, Karen. 2002. Dangerous intersections: Feminists at work. *Childrens' Literature* 30: 205–210.

———. 2001. Fish stories: Teaching children's literature in a postmodern world. *Pedagogy: Critical Approaches to Teaching Literature, Language, Composition and Culture* 1(2): 401–409.

Cole, Babette. 1987. *Prince Cinders*. New York: Putnam.

Collins, Carol Jones. 1998. The way we do the things we do: Required reading lists and girls. *Knowledge Quest* 26(4): 34–37.

Council on Interracial Books for Children. 1980. Ten quick ways to analyze children's books for sexism and racism. In *Guidelines for selecting bias-free textbooks and story books*, 24–26. New York: Council on Interracial Books for Children.

Crabb, P. B., and D. Bielawski. 1994. The social representation of material culture and gender in children's books. *Sex Roles* 30: 69–79.

de Paola, Tomie. 1979. *Oliver Button is a sissy*. New York: Harcourt Brace Jovanovich.

Desai, Christina M. 2001. Picture book soldiers: Men and messages. *Reading Horizons* 42(2): 77–98.

Diekman, Amanda B., and Sara K. Murnen. 2004. Learning to be little women and little men: The inequitable gender equality of nonsexist children's literature. *Sex Roles* 50(5–6): 373–385.

Dodson, Shireen. 1998. *100 books for girls to grow on: Lively descriptions of the most inspiring books for girls, terrific discussion questions to spark conversation, great ideas for book-inspired activities, crafts, and field trips*. New York: HarperCollins.

Doiron, Ray. 2003. Boys books, girls books. Should we re-organize our school library collections? *Teacher Librarian* 30(3): 14–16.

Ernst, S. B. 1995. Gender issues in books for children and young adults. In *Battling dragons: Issues and controversy in children's literature*, ed. Susan Lehr, 66–78. Portsmouth, NH: Heinemann.

Fine, Anne. 1992. *Flour babies*. New York: Little, Brown.

Fox, Mem. 2001. Author profile. In *Beauty, brains, and brawn: The construction of gender in children's literature*, ed. Susan Lehr, 67–69. Portsmouth, NH: Heinemann.

———. 1993. Men who weep, boys who dance: The gender agenda between the lines in children's literature. *Language Arts* 70(2): 84–88.

Fredrickson, Elaine. 2000. Muted colors; Gender and classroom silence. *Language Arts* 77(4): 301–308.

Gamallo, Isabel C. Anievas. 1998. Subversive storytelling. The construction of lesbian girlhood through fantasy and fairy tale in Jeanette Winterson's *Oranges are not the only fruit*. In *The girl: Constructions of the girl in contemporary fiction by women*, ed. Ruth O. Saxton, 119–134. New York: St. Martin's Press.

Gardner, Richard A. 1980. *Dr. Gardner's fairy tales for today's children*. Cresskill, NJ: Creative Therapeutics.

Greever, Ellen A., Patricia Austin, and Karyn Welhousen. 2000. William's doll revisited. *Language Arts* 7(4): 324–329.

Gurian, Michael. 1996. *The wonder of boys: What parents, mentors, and educators can do to shape boys into exceptional men*. New York: Putnam.

Hamilton, Virginia. 2001. Author Profile. In *Beauty, brains and brawn: The construction of gender in children's literature*, ed. Susan Lehr, 21–23. Portsmouth, NH: Heinemann.

Heine, Pat, and Christine Inkster. 1999. Strong female characters in recent children's literature. *Language Arts* 76(5): 427–434.

Hoffman, Mary. 1993. *Henry's baby*. New York: Dorling Kindersley.

Horning, K. T. 2001. *From cover to cover. Evaluating and reviewing children's books*. New York: Harper-Collins.

Inness, Sherrie A., ed. 1997. Introduction. In *Nancy Drew® and company: Culture, gender, and girls' series*, 1–13. Bowling Green, OH: Bowling Green University Popular Press.

Jago, Carol. 2000. *With rigor for all: Teaching the classics to contemporary students*. Portland, ME: Calendar Island Publishers.

Jones, Dudley, and Tony Watkins. 2000. *A necessary fantasy? The heroic figure in children's popular culture*. New York: Garland.

Jones, Patrick, and Dawn Cartwright Fiorelli. 2003. Overcoming the obstacle course: Teenage boys and reading. *Teacher Librarian* 30(3): 9–13.

Keyser, Elizabeth. 1989. Feminist revisions: Frauds on the fairies? In *Children's Literature*, vol. 17, ed. Francelia Butler, Margaret Higonnet, and Barbara Rosen, 156–170. New Haven, CT: Yale University Press.

Kidd, Kenneth. 2000. Material girls and boys. *Michigan Quarterly Review* 39(3): 674–678.

Kindlon, Daniel J., and Michael Thompson. 1999. *Raising cain. Protecting the emotional life of boys*. New York: Ballantine Books.

Lehr, Susan. 2001. The hidden curriculum: Are we teaching young girls to wait for the prince? In *Beauty, brains, and brawn: The construction of gender in children's literature*, ed. Susan Lehr, 1–18. Portsmouth, NH: Heinemann.

Louie, Belinda Y. 2001. Why gender stereotypes still persist in contemporary children's literature. In *Beauty, brains, and brawn: The construction of gender in children's literature*, ed. Susan Lehr, 142–151. Portsmouth, NH: Heinemann.

Marshall, Elizabeth. 2004. Stripping for the wolf: Rethinking representations of gender in children's literature. *Reading Research Quarterly* 39(3): 256–270.

Mead, Alice. Author profile. In *Beauty, brains, and brawn: The construction of gender in children's literature*, ed. Susan Lehr, 152–155. Portsmouth, NH: Heinemann.

Mora, Pat. 2001. Author profile. In *Beauty, brains, and brawn: The construction of gender in children's literature*, ed. Susan Lehr, 157–161. Portsmouth, NH: Heinemann.

Odean, Kathleen. 2002. *Great books for girls: More than 600 recommended books for girls, ages 3–14*. New York: Ballantine Books.

———. 1998. *Great books for boys: More than 600 books for boys from 2 to 14*. New York: Ballantine Books.

O'Keefe, Deborah. 2000. *Good girl messages: How young women were misled by their favorite books*. New York: Continuum International Publishing Group.

Parille, Ken. 2001. "Wake up and be a man": *Little women*, Laurie and the ethic of submission. In *Children's literature*, vol. 29, ed. Elizabeth Lennox Keyser and Julie Pfeiffer, 34–51. New Haven, CT: Yale University Press.

Paterson, Sheryl Bender, and Mary Alyce Lach. 1990. Gender stereotypes in children's books: Their prevalence and influence on cognitive and affective development. *Gender and Education* 2(2): 185–197.

Phelps, Ethel Johnston. 1981. *The maid of the North: Feminist folktales from around the world*. New York: Holt, Rinehart and Winston.

———. 1978. *Tatterhood and other tales: Stories of magic and adventure*. Old Westbury, NY: Feminist Press.

Pinsent, Pat. 1997. *Children's literature and the politics of equality*. New York: Teachers College Press.

Poarch, Renae, and Elizabeth Monk-Turner. 2001. Gender roles in children's literature: A review of non-award-winning "Easy-to-Read" books. *Journal of Research in Childhood Education* 16(1): 70–76.

Pollack, William. 1999. *Real boys. Rescuing our sons from the myths of boyhood*. New York: Henry Holt and Company.

Rice, Peggy S. 2002. Creating spaces for boys and girls to expand their definitions of masculinity and femininity through children's literature. *Journal of Children's Literature* 28(2): 33–42.

———. 2000. Gendered readings of a traditional "feminist" folktale by sixth-grade boys and girls. Special Issue: Reader Response. *Journal of Literacy Research* 32(2): 211–236.

Roberts, Patricia L., Nancy L. Cecil, and Sharon Alexander. 1993. *Gender positive!: A teachers' and librarians' guide to nonstereotyped children's literature, K–8*. Jefferson, NC: McFarland.

Rudman, Masha Kabakow. 1995. *Children's literature*. 3rd ed. New York: Longman Publishers.

Sachar, Louis. 1993. *Marvin Redpost: Is he a girl?* New York: Random House.

Saxton, Ruth O., ed. 1998. *The girl: Constructions of the girl in contemporary fiction by women*. New York: St. Martin's Press.

Scieszka, Jon. 2003. Guys and reading. *Teacher Librarian* 30(3): 17–18.

———. 1989. *The true story of the 3 little pigs*. New York: Viking.

Short, Kathy G. 2001. Why do educators need a political agenda on gender? In *Beauty, brains, and brawn: The construction of gender in children's literature*, ed. Susan Lehr, 186–192. Portsmouth, NH: Heinemann.

Smith, M. W., and J. D. Wilhelm. 2002. *"Reading don't fix no chevys": Literacy in the lives of young men*. Portsmouth, NH: Heinemann.

Temple, Charles. 1993. "What if beauty had been ugly?" Reading against the grain of gender bias in children's books. *Language Arts* 70(2): 89–93.

Town, Caren J. 2004. *The new southern girl*. Jefferson, NC: McFarland.

Trites, Roberta Seelinger. 1997. *Waking Sleeping Beauty: Feminist voices in children's novels*. Iowa City: University of Iowa Press.

Valpy, Michael. 1996. Fathers fare poorly in children's books. In *Only connect: Readings on children's literature*, 3rd ed., ed. Sheila Egoff, Gordon Stubbs, Ralph Ashley, and Wendy Sutton, 300–302. New York: Oxford University Press.

Vandergrift, Kay E. 1995. Female protagonists and beyond: Picture books for future feminists. *Feminist Teacher* 9(2): 61–70.

Von Drasek, Lisa. 2002. Boy, oh, boy—books! *Teaching PreK–8* 33(2): 72–73.

Walker, Carole, and Martha M. Foote. 1999–2000. Emergent inquiry: Using children's literature to ask hard questions about gender bias. *Childhood Education* 76(2): 89–91.

Ward, Cheryl Karp. 2001. It's a girl thing. *Voices from the Middle* 9(2): 64–66.

Wariner, Marina. 1996. The absent mother: Women against women in old wives' tales. In *Only connect: Readings on children's literature*, 3rd ed. Sheila Egoff, Gordon Stubbs, Ralph Ashley, and Wendy Sutton, 278–287. New York: Oxford University Press.

———. 1995. *From the beast to the blonde: On fairy tales and their tellers*. New York: Farrar, Straus, Giroux.

What is the best thing a teacher-librarian can do to encourage boys to read? 2003. *Teacher Librarian* 30(3): 32–33.

Wolf, Shelby Anne. 2004. *Interpreting literature with children*. Mahwah, NJ: Lawrence Erlbaum Associates.

Wullshlager, J. 1991. Twilight of the enchanters. *London Financial Times*, March 30.

Zipes, Jack, ed. 1986. *Don't bet on the prince: Contemporary feminist fairy tales in North America and England*. New York: Methuen.

8

Literature with GLBTQ Characters, Themes, and Content

Contemporary bibliography uses *GLBTQ* to refer to "gay, lesbian, bisexual, transgendered, questioning." Collections are more relevant to classroom communities that include GLBTQ students and family members when they include more than just heterosexually focused fiction. Including books that include GLBTQ characters, themes, and culture in classroom libraries expands reading choices for all students and improves school climate by acknowledging and respecting sexuality differences in people. Teachers select books for their literary quality and to improve self-esteem, to offer role models, to create safe spaces in schools, and to broaden views of sexuality and community for all students (Greenbaum 1994, 71; Caywood 1993, 50). Early GLBTQ fiction in the 1960s and 1970s included books that emphasized stereotypes or homophobia or homosexuality as a character's problem. Fiction in the late 1990s and 2000s is characterized by authentic stories and characters that include the GLBTQ experiences and themes as a usual part of life and culture.

Demand for Books

Lack of information about available good books has left many excellent titles out of collections. In the past, the assumption that there are no gay or lesbian students in schools has been used as a reason to think there is no demand for GLBTQ content books (Anderson 1992, 62; Greenbaum 1994, 71). Because "gay, lesbian, and bisexual teens and preteens make up a substantial percentage" of library users, and because their family members are an even larger group, collections that include GLBTQ content are often well used (Anderson 1992, 62). The assumption that there was no demand may be attributable to lack of awareness on the part of professionals and societal prejudice. These factors may have contributed to hesitancy on the part of young people to ask for books (62).

1960s

John Donovan's novel *I'll Get There, It Better Be Worth the Trip* (1969) is often referred to as the first book that discusses a teenager and homosexuality. It has been criticized for including a theme of punishment for homosexuality (Jenkins 1998a, 299; Norton and Vare 2004, 65). The story is about Davy, who is thirteen-years-old and adjusting to his parents' divorce and who meets a male friend; the two kiss and share a sexual experience. After the boys' experience, Davy's dog is hit by a car and killed. The characters' responses to homosexuality in the book are to view it as a choice and something that might be forgotten with heterosexual experience (Cart 1996, 224).

Mixed book reviews of Donovan's novel demonstrate the divergent criteria critics used to evaluate gay-themed literature for youth at the time (Fuoss 1994, 162; Senick 1978, 52). The book has been described as being about homosexuality, among many other things; as being suitable only for adult counselors; and as a guilt-ridden response to homosexuality that would reinforce fears of GLBTQ youth (Senick 1978, 52).

1970s

Before the sexual revolution, "children's books avoided homosexuality or any kind of sexuality" (Cooper 2000, 10). The popularity of the problem novel created space in the marketplace for authors to write about taboo topics (Cart 1996, 189). Young adult problem novels told stories of adolescent development, including sexuality, from the point of view of the young adult (Jenkins 1998a, 298; Cart 1996, 299). The young adult problem novel form was suited to lesbian and gay coming-out themes because this form often included stories of intense "sexual attraction, social rebellion and personal growth" (Kidd 1998, 114).

Often the "problem" in gay-themed problem novels was homophobia and not homosexuality (Kidd 1998, 114; Cooper 2000, 10). Bad things happened to gay characters and those close to them in books in the 1970s. They suffered death, violence, rape, or institutionalization, and many critics interpreted this as a punishment trend. Included in this group of novels are *Sticks and Stones* (Hall 1977), *The Man without a Face* (Holland 1972), and *Trying Hard to Hear You* (Scoppettone 1974) (Garden 2001, 22; Cart 1996, 197; 2004; Norton and Vare 2004, 65). Homosexuality was sometimes depicted as a "temporary stage" for protagonists (Cart 1996, 225; Jenkins 2003, 49).

Roger Sutton, editor of *Horn Book Magazine*, noted that at least some books in the 1970s included homosexuality that was positive and that depictions improved (Cooper 2000, 10). *Ruby* (Guy 1976) featured a black, lesbian character. M. E. Kerr's novel *I'll Love You When You're More Like Me* (1977) included an upbeat, "well-adjusted" gay character and had a humorous tone (Cart 2004).

1980s

Literature in the 1980s introduced books about gay parents, AIDS, and falling in love. The 1980s brought the first literary novel, literature from other countries, and bibliographic resources for finding books. Norma Klein wrote about a gay parent in *Breaking Up* (1980), and A. M. Homes wrote about gay parents in *Jack* (1989). M. E. Kerr's *Night Kites* (1986) acknowledged the homosexuality of a male character with AIDS (Cart 1996, 214).

In 1982, British author Aidan Chambers's book *Dance on My Grave* was issued in the United States. In the 1980s and 1990s, U.S. publications of British, Australian, New Zealander, and Canadian authors demonstrated the universal experiences of gay and lesbian teenagers (Cart 2004). These authors included Paula Brock, David Rees, William Taylor, Jean Ure, Kate Walker, and Diana Wieler.

Annie on My Mind and Nancy Garden

Published in 1982, Nancy Garden's now-classic work *Annie on My Mind* was the first lesbian young adult novel. It depicts a couple that remains together at the end of the book and an emotional teen love story (Jenkins 2003, 48). The book has been banned, burned, and at the center of a "1994 federal courts case, in which a U.S. District judge in Kansas ordered the book returned to school library shelves" (Jenkins 2003, 49). It was one of the 100 most frequently challenged books between 1990 and 2000, according to the American Library Association (http://www.ala.org/ala/oif/bannedbooksweek/bbwlinks/100mostfrequently.htm).

In an interview with Christine Jenkins in 2003, Garden describes her experiences with the book over time and reflects on how the market has changed. In the book, high school senior Liza Winthrop falls in love with Annie Kenyon. The cover art of the 1982 edition is a stereotypical depiction of lesbians and shows two people not looking at each other, "not relating to each other" (Jenkins 2003, 50). In 1984, the first paperback cover shows Annie looking much older than Liza. The cover art for the 1992 edition shows two individuals who love each other (50).

Nancy Garden believes that the taboo against GLBTQ-themed literature for children is gone (Garden 2001, 22). When her books were removed from the shelves in Olathe, Kansas, but then ordered back by the courts, Garden says she realized that it was "extremely important in this kind of situation to try to understand the other side's position and to listen to the other side" (Jenkins 2003, 49). Garden responds to those who think her books harm young people by saying that it "is a natural impulse for most adults" to want to protect young people from harm but that it is "also important to prepare teens for the world they'll meet as adults and to help them understand it and form their own reactions to it" (49). Garden asserts that it is better for teens to "encounter difficult subjects when they still have loving adults—like their parents and teachers and librarians—to talk to them" (49).

Annie on My Mind has been celebrated as a classic and is on the American Library Association's "Best of the Best Books for Young Adults" list. *School Library Journal* selected it as one of the most influential books of the twentieth century (Jenkins 2003, 48). In 2003, Nancy Garden was awarded the Margaret A. Edwards Award for lifetime achievement in writing.

Picture Books

Publication of picture books has met with similar resistance. Kenneth Kidd (1998) argues that the "reticence about sexuality in general in children's books" and the "lingering belief that homosexuality . . . is incompatible with, or even antithetical to, childhood and its culture" have limited the growth of GLBTQ-themed books for young children (114). Alyson Publications published two groundbreaking titles: *Heather Has Two Mommies* (Newman 1989) and *Daddy's Roommate* (Willhoite 1990).

Heather Has Two Mommies

Picture book publication depicting children with same-sex parents began in 1989 with Leslea Newman's self-publication of *Heather Has Two Mommies*. Newman wrote the book to meet the needs of families who had no books to read to their children that showed their type of family and to help "children with lesbian mothers feel good about themselves and their families" (Newman 1997, 150). Newman had no political agenda but wanted children "to see their own image reflected back to themselves within the culture at large" and wanted to enhance self-esteem by providing positive images (149–150). She wanted to send the message that the "most important thing about a family is that all the people in it love each other" (150).

Having sent the book to over fifty publishers, Newman decided to publish the book herself in 1989 and to market it using a letter-writing fund-raising/sales campaign. The successful sales proved there was an audience for a book portraying "a child and two lesbian mothers in a positive way" (150).

Alyson Wonderland

Alyson Publications, one of the "first gay and lesbian presses, founded in 1980 by Sasha Alyson," started the Alyson Wonderland imprint in 1990. The goal was to "create and set apart books especially for children . . . that explored and acknowledged the contemporary need for recognizing all types of families, not just the typical mother-father archetype" (Yampbell 1999, 31). Alyson published Newman's book. Since that time, the imprint has tried to publish a new picture book every two years (32). *Heather Has Two Mommies* and John Willhoite's *Daddy's Roommate* remain the two Alyson Wonderland titles that have made money.

Objections and Challenges to Heather

Objections to Newman's book include showing different kinds of families, negative reactions to the anatomical details depicted in the book, and the use of the words *sperm*, *egg*, *breasts*, and *belly* to describe pregnancy (Ford 1998, 129). Critics have noted that images of a lesbian getting pregnant through artificial insemination may not be understood by small children (129). Newman has been called "one of the most dangerous writers living in America" (Newman 1997, 149). Both Newman and Willhoite have been accused of promoting sodomy, militancy, prostitution, bestiality, and incest. The books were removed from New York's Rainbow Curriculum designed in 1992 to teach respect for all racial and ethnic groups. School district officials objected to the inclusion in the curriculum guide of paragraphs on gay and lesbian characters and themes (152). Although school chancellor Joseph Fernandez supported content of the Rainbow Curriculum, the paragraphs were removed from the guide, and Newman's and Willhoite's books were removed from the bibliography of suggested books.

Newman describes a campaign by groups opposed to gay-themed books to remove *Heather Has Two Mommies, Daddy's Roommate,* and the book *Gloria Goes to Gay Pride* (Newman 1991) from library shelves in 1992. Across the country, books went missing from library shelves. Alyson Publications agreed to replace missing copies free of charge for the first 500 libraries who requested replacement copies for stolen books (Newman 1997, 152). Groups opposing Newman's book have even run ads in papers urging citizens to vote against library bond issues because the libraries refused to withdraw her book (151).

Leslea Newman's View

Newman argues that her book does not teach sex but that it is about family, and depicting only heterosexual families in books is dishonest (Newman 1997, 152). She urges teachers, parents, and librarians to remember students who have "lesbian or gay parents, siblings, aunts, uncles, grandparents, neighbors and friends" and not discount their experiences by pretending "there is only one type of family" (153). The tenth-anniversary edition issued by Alyson Publications in 2000 changed the anatomical descriptions related to artificial insemination. In this way, according to publisher Greg Constante, the original book that was "really more for adults" would better appeal to younger readers for whom it was purchased (Yampbell 1999, 33). Since the publication of *Heather*, Newman has written six picture books, five with gay or lesbian characters.

1990s

During the 1990s new books included more nonfiction to meet readers' informational needs, and fiction included a wider variety of characters and a broader range of topics. Between 1980 and 1999, 100 novels and story collections were published. Forty additional novels were published between 1999 and 2003 (Garden 2001, 22; Jenkins 2003, 49).

Informational Books

Roger Sutton's *Hearing Us Out: Voices from the Gay and Lesbian Community* (1994), Ann Herron's *Two Teenagers in Twenty* (1994), and Larry Dane Brimner's *Being Different: Lambda Youths Speak Out* (1995) are examples of collections of nonfiction narratives published during the 1990s Jacqueline Woodson's book *The Dear One* (1991) featured a black character, and R. J. Hamilton's *Who Framed Lorenzo Garcia?* (1995) featured a Latino character (Cart 2004).

Other forms of fiction besides realistic novels broadened choices for readers in the 1990s. *Am I Blue: Coming Out from the Silence* (1994), edited by Marion Bauer, is a collection of short stories by prominent authors about questions of sexuality and gender and includes comments from each of the authors. *Kissing the Witch* (Donoghue 1997) is a collection of fairy tales told from a lesbian perspective. Novels addressed issues like gay stereotypes in *Deliver Us from Evie* (Kerr 1994) and a parent's lesbianism in *From the Notebooks of Melanin Sun* (Woodson 1995). In *Earthshine* (1994) by Theresa Nelson, Slim McGranahan is the main character who chooses to live with her father who is living with AIDS and his partner. The story describes their daily lives, the friends they meet through a People with AIDS (PWA) support group, and how their community together celebrates life and learns about and experiences birth, dying, and death.

Books in the 1990s show a trend of moving away from homosexuality as a central topic, a trend away from presenting gay and lesbian protagonists, and a trend toward presenting gays and lesbians as secondary characters, according to content analysis studies conducted by Christine Jenkins (Jenkins 1998a, 302). These trends may indicate a shift to the "increased casual inclusion of gay and lesbian minor characters in straight YA novels" (Garden 2001, 22). Whatever the trends meant, by the late 1990s, authors' and critics' attention had shifted away from the importance of locating gay themes and characters in novels to the importance of evaluating books for literary quality.

Books about HIV Infection and AIDS

Based on his analysis of books for young people about HIV and AIDS, Robert McRuer (1998) argues that in the 1990s the "shift to understanding AIDS as everyone's disease" affected children's books as it "made it easy to exclude gay males" and homosexuality from books (134). Liberal arguments against reinforcing the stereotype that only gay men have AIDS supported this exclusion (134). Excluding gay males from books also erased "the critical understanding of social stigma and of community-based protective measures that gay men and lesbians . . . advanced for more than a decade" (139). This was "potentially lethal" because it removed from literature "the life-saving lessons learned in gay and lesbian communities during the AIDS epidemic" (135).

2000s

During the late 1990s, fiction with GLBTQ characters and themes was honored with mainstream book awards. Ellen Wittlinger's book *Hard Love* (1999) was named a Michael A. Printz Honor Book. In 2003, the Michael A. Printz Award for Excellence in Young Adult Literature went to *Postcards from No Man's Land* (1999) by Aidan Chambers. Garret Freymann-Weyr's book *My Heartbeat* (2002) was a Printz Award Honor Book in 2003 (http://www.ala.org/yalsa/printz). In 2003, Nancy Garden was awarded the Margaret A. Edwards award for lifetime achievement in writing books. Garden was recognized for "helping readers find the courage to be true to themselves" (http://www.ala.org/ala/yalsa/booklistsawards/margaretaedwards/maeprevious/2003nancygarden.htm). In 2004, Francesca Lia Block received this award for her work that enabled "teens to understand the world in which they live and their relationships with others and society" (http://www.ala.org/ala/yalsa/booklistsawards/margaretedwards/margaretedwards.htm). She is considered a groundbreaking author who uses a postmodern approach "to human sexuality that is so individual as to defy categorization" (Cooper 2000, 10).

Nancy Garden praises Block's books *Weetzie Bat* (1989), *Witch Baby* (1991), and *Cherokee Bat and the Goat Guys* (1992) for showing "sexual diversity in a matter of fact way" (Garden 1992, 7). Block's work has been praised for use of the "omniscient point of view" and for her intimate knowledge of her characters and her love and respect for them (Cart 1996, 237).

Future of GLBT Literature for Youth

In the 2000s, GLBTQ literature includes works recognized for literary merit and that tell human stories of all kinds. David Levithan's *Boy Meets Boy* (2003) has been praised for literary merit and for offering lovable characters whose homosexuality is casually accepted and for being the "first upbeat gay novel for teens" (Rochman 2003, 235). *Boy Meets Boy* appeared on Hazel Rochman's "Top Ten Romances for Teens" list for *Booklist* in 2003.

The "next generation of gay and lesbian books" is set in the context of "gay and lesbian culture" that now has "a very usual position in society, that of another part of human reproduction and human grouping" (Brass 2002, 44). Recommended authors in this next generation include Tea Bendun; Garret Freymann-Weyr; Brent Hartinger; Sue Hines; David Levithan; Lauren Myracle; Julie Ann Peters; Sara Ryan; and Alex Sanchez (Cart 2004; Norton and Vare 2004; Gallo 2004, 127).

School Environment

School environments include homophobia that affects all students. Homophobia contributes to "violence, taunting, and jokes" for gay and lesbian youth and may result in decreased self-respect, lowered self-confidence, "emotional isolation, physical and verbal abuse, parental rejection, depression, homelessness, dropout rate and suicide" (Day 2000, xii, xviii). Francis Ann Day cites the *Journal of Pediatrics* (1998) report that "gay students are four times more likely than straight ones to be threatened by weapons in school" (xi).

Homophobia and Heterosexism

Homophobia occurs when "some people believe that gays and lesbians, or people perceived as being gay or lesbian, are subhuman and/or evil, expendable, and worthy only of contempt" (Day 2000, xii). Scholars have quoted statistics and reports from the U.S. Department of Health and Human Services and published in the *American Journal of Public Health* that show that young gays and lesbians are more likely to attempt and commit suicide than other students. The reports state that this is, in part, a result of a "hostile and condemning environment, verbal and physical abuse, and rejection and isolation from family and peers" (Sedgewick 1998, 231; also see Cart 1999, 1810).

Homophobia is the "irrational fear or intolerance of lesbian and gay people" (Day 2000, xxiv). Heterosexism is "the assumption that all people are heterosexual or that heterosexuality is the superior sexual identity" (xxiv). Homophobia and heterosexism affect all young people. Homophobia makes boys "reluctant to communicate freely about their feelings or even to ask for help when they really need it." This occurs to the extent of "imposing a significant cost to the boys' health, safety and authentic sense of being" (Flood and Shaffer 2000, 4). Homophobia represses boys' freedom to "express emotional feeling," to exhibit feminine behavior, to express empathy, and to connect with the "qualities that support and sustain the intimacy and connection essential to healthy relationships" (4). Homophobia has discouraged authors and publishers from producing books that depict homosexual experience and life (Cart 1999, 1811). Homophobia causes gay children to grow up "feeling like outsiders" (Herren 2001b, 26).

Teachers and Academic Freedom

In the 1970s, antigay ballot initiatives passed across the country. In 1978, the *School Employees—Homosexuality Initiative Statute* was on the ballot in California and, sponsored by John Briggs, was known as the "Briggs Initiative." If passed, it would have provided for firing "schoolteachers, teachers' aides, school administrators or counselors for advocating, soliciting, imposing, encouraging or promoting private or public sexual acts . . . between persons of the same sex . . . or publicly and indiscreetly engaging in said acts" (Briggs 1977; also see Cruikshank 2003, 15). The initiative did not pass, but its presence on the ballot articulated the intolerance of people opposed to sharing information about homosexuality and helping gay teenagers. It discouraged teachers from helping gay students and raising awareness.

Creating Safe Spaces

Teachers help change school climate by offering life-affirming books that promote inclusion, depict relationships honestly, and honestly describe school settings (Norton and Vare 2004, 66, 69). Classrooms can be "safe spaces" for discussing gender and sexuality (Clark, Rand, and Vogt 2003a, 2). Classroom communities that value dialogue can support discussions of "sensitive social issues such as homosexuality" (Schall and Kauffmann 2003, 43).

In such discussion, "ideas and beliefs can be discussed rationally," and teens can "express their opinions frankly and freely" (Garden, quoted in Jenkins 2003, 50). Agreement is not required, just "true dialogue" that leads to growth (50). Schools may have a statement or policy against "hate violence that includes sexual orientation" (Allan 1999, 99).

English teachers can "acknowledge and support gay students in their classrooms and help straight students become more understanding and accepting" (Butt, quoted in Gallo 2004, 126). Teachers who are not judgmental may help students feel safe to be themselves (126). Books can be selected that destroy stereotypes that reinforce harassment (127). Many teachers consult the GLSEN (Gay, Lesbian and Straight Education Network) at http://www.glsen.org for support and ideas for creating safe spaces.

Teaching Experiences

High school English teacher Vicky Greenbaum (1994) assumes that "being open about your sexuality is a right." She points out the presence of gay and lesbian voices in literature to students and explains to them how homosexuality has been hidden in literature (71).

English teacher Anthony Consiglio does not focus on sexual orientation and homophobia when teaching about GLBTQ perspectives. He teaches students "self-exploration." Sexuality is an integral part of that. Consiglio teaches *Stone Butch Blues* (Feinberg 1993). The book includes a history of homophobia of the past several decades in the United States (Consiglio 1999, 72). Students ask complex questions and find that many of their questions are profound and valid—yet unanswerable (75).

Greg Hamilton taught *Jack* (1990) by A. M. Homes (Hamilton 2004, 107). Hamilton encourages students to set aside their own judgmental reactions and to make a "social critique" of the author's approach to the story (108). Students were allowed to make "negative and discriminatory remarks" to test their opinions in a public space, as long as they introduced their remarks saying, "This is what I believe" (108). Hamilton asks parents for help. He recommends teachers educate and prepare themselves and feel ready before teaching this way.

When Nan Phifer taught *Jack*, she asked students to write responses comparing the gay and heterosexual fathers in the book. One student responded negatively to the reading. Another student wrote that the book showed another "point of view towards gay people than just calling them fags" (Phifer 1994, 10).

Teacher Jessica Parker came out to her classroom and tried to "develop strategies to ensure" that the curriculum did not set homosexuals apart as the "other" (2001, 75). Parker integrates gay and lesbian fiction, nonfiction, and history into her "curriculum by placing it side-by-side with canonical literature" (77).

Christina Allan requires gay-themed titles as required reading selections so that students who are uncomfortable selecting an "overtly gay-themed book" for themselves can discuss non-heterosexual works (1999, 99).

William J. Broz (2001) keeps a "Safe Space" sticker "provided by the campus Bi-Sexual, Gay, Lesbian and Friends Association" on his office door. He encourages preservice teachers to learn about GLBTQ literature and to make books available to his own students (53).

Evaluation Criteria, Awards, and Resources

Books have been evaluated based on guidelines recommended by organizations and formalist, historical, cultural, and political literary analysis.

American Library Association—GLBTRT

In the late 1970s, the American Library Association, Social Responsibilities Round Table, Gay Task Force adopted as a set of guidelines *Evaluating the Treatment of Gay Themes in Books for Children and Young Adults* to assist librarians with book selection. While the organization has since become a separate roundtable, renamed the Gay, Lesbian, Bisexual, Transgendered Round Table (GLBTRT), the 1977 guidelines remain on the Web site. The guidelines are somewhat out of date with respect to language used to describe gay identity as a "valid life choice" and the recommendation that self-identified gay reviewers review GLBTQ books, but the guidelines are still useful.

The GLBTRT also sponsored a program about the "future of gay books for children" at the annual ALA conference in 2000. It produced *Bibliography for Gay Teens* at http://www.niulib.niu.edu/lgbt/bibteens.htm. Updated with fiction and nonfiction materials through 2004, the list is remarkable for its broad subject coverage.

Literary Quality

Roger Sutton, the first openly gay editor of the *Horn Book*, wants to see "well-rounded portraits of gays and lesbians" and realistic portrayals of life and is not interested in books written only to prove that homosexuality is all right (Cooper 2000, 9). Sutton thinks there are "certain standards of good literature" and that the goal of literature is not to provide role models but to show people as they are (9). He believes the story is more important than the need to give a positive picture (10).

Literary Analysis

Scholar Christine Jenkins borrows from historical analysis, black studies analysis, and cultural studies to analyze GLBTQ books (1998a, 306). To determine the level of respect for homosexuals in books, Jenkins analyzes books to see if homosexuality has been erased or if it is only included because a character is remarkable or persecuted. She analyzes whether homosexuality is shown as inhuman or transitional, if it is ignored, or if it is considered the same as "us" (309). Gay characters should not be defined by their sexuality, and stories should not all be about coming out and homophobia (308). Gays and lesbians fight for their rights, live "out" in a world in which their rights are not always respected, and are just characters living. Isolation from community, invisibility in the story, and victim status are not required (314).

Francis Ann Day and Evaluation Guidelines

In 2000, Francis Ann Day wrote *Lesbian and Gay Voices: An Annotated Bibliography and Guide to Literature for Children and Young Adults.* She assesses books for literary quality, authenticity, blatant homophobia, and heterosexism. Day's evaluation guidelines include assessing respectful language in books. She lists offensive terms like *lifestyle*, *preference*, *choice*, and *mannish* (xxiv). Characters should be identified with a variety of social groups, and relationships should be treated seriously, not limited to sex, and homosexuality should not be portrayed as a stage to outgrow (xxiv). She admonishes evaluators to beware of negative stereotypes of gay and lesbian characters, such as portrayals as pedophiles, inappropriate, exploitive, harmful, preoccupied with sex, and unable to maintain relationships (xxv).

Political Analysis

One perspective is that GLBTQ literature cannot be understood in an honest way without considering both its aesthetic qualities and its political meaning (Fuoss 1994, 160). Leslea Newman has been accused of writing *Heather Has Two Mommies* (1989) with a political agenda in mind. She asserts that she just wanted to tell a story after meeting a lesbian couple in town one day who complained that they had no books to read to their daughter about their type of family (Newman 1997, 149). Nancy Garden (2001) agrees that art and politics combine to change the world but that books written for "purely political reasons are likely to be tracts, not engaging stories" (22). Garden puts literary quality first in evaluation (22).

Bibliographies

A forthcoming title is, Michael Carts' and Christine Jenkins' *The Heart Has Its Reasons: Homosexuality in Young Adult Literature*. In 2000, Francis Ann Day wrote *Lesbian and Gay Voices: An Annotated Bibliography and Guide to Literature for Children and Young Adults*, with a foreword by Nancy Garden. It includes 275 annotated bibliographic entries for picture books, fiction, short stories, nonfiction, biography and autobiography, books for librarians, educators, parents and other adults, profiles of sixteen authors, and an appendix of additional resources. It was intended to be the first "authoritative source, critically annotated," for leading "teachers . . . to honest, accurate, gay-themed and gay friendly works for young people" (2000, xi).

Bibliographies are also included in journals in articles or as lists. For example, in 2001, *Booklist* published *Top 10 Gay and Lesbian Books for Youth* (Zvirin 2001, 1863). Other types of bibliographies are self-published, posted on Web sites, or delivered as parts of conferences. In 1982 Christine Jenkins and Julie Morris compiled and self-published *A Look at Gayness. An Annotated Bibliography of Gay Materials for Young People*. The Gay and Lesbian Educators of British Columbia (GALE-BC) at http://www.galebc.org offers the annotated bibliographies titled *Challenging Homophobia: A Teachers Resource Book* and *Book Resources: Fiction and Non-Fiction Resources for K–12*.

Awards and Organizations

ALA's GLBTRT presents the annual Stonewall Book Awards for fiction and nonfiction to "the best books with gay, lesbian, bisexual, and transgendered themes" (http://www.ala.org/ala/glbtrt/stonewall/stonewallbook.htm).

The Lambda Literary Foundation publishes the *Lambda Book Report*, a "monthly magazine devoted to reviewing books, interviewing authors, and following the trends in lesbian, gay, bisexual, and transgender publishing" including young adult and children's literature publishing (http://www.lambdalit.org/lbr_intro.html). This source includes criticism and discussion of the latest books and is carried by many public and university libraries. The Lambda Literary Awards annually recognize the best in GLBTQ literature and include a Children/Young Adult category.

The organization called the Publishing Triangle, Association of Lesbians and Gay Men in Publishing includes some books that are suitable for young adults on the list *100 Best Lesbian and Gay Novels* (http://www.publishingtriangle.org/100best.asp). This organization hosts a Queer Book Expo and provides a list of links to Web sites of writing competitions, publishers, writing organizations, writers' resources, lesbian writers' organizations, and zines at http://www.publishingtriangle.org/links.asp.

Case: *Rainbow* Books

Rainbow Boys (2001), *Rainbow High* (2003) and *Rainbow Road* (2005b) are books in a series by author Alex Sanchez that address themes of love and friendship. In *Rainbow Boys*, seventeen-year-old Jason attends a Rainbow Youth meeting for homosexual teens where he sees two other friends he already knows. *Rainbow Boys* is told from the alternating viewpoints of the three friends Jason, Kyle, and Nelson. The young men describe their experiences of coming out, express their feelings about love, romance, and sex, and struggle with their relationships with their parents in different ways.

A *Book Links* review of *Rainbow Boys* recommends the title for grades 9 through 12 and describes it as having "blunt terminology and graphic scenes" appropriate for "mature readers" (*Rainbow Boys* 2005, 34). A *Publisher's Weekly* review recommends the book for ages twelve and up and comments on the "hint of an educational agenda" in the book that includes "names of support groups and contact information in the book" (*Rainbow Boys* 2001, 62). Bob Witeck's review in *Lambda Book Report* (2001) gives no age recommendation and describes Sanchez's characters as likeable, sensitive, and balanced and the storytelling as "fluent, direct, and authentic" (21). Witeck writes that *Rainbow Boys*, published by Simon and Schuster, represents a "true crossover event in publishing" (21). Betty Evans's (2001) review in *School Library Journal* recommends the book for grade 9 and up and points out how the "gutsy, in-your-face debut novel speaks the language of real life for gay teens, that of the ecstasy, heartache, and humor of first love (and sex), that of daily harassment and fear, that of having what it takes to stand up and be proud of who you are" (169). Evans asks librarians to "make it available" in spite of likely challenges (169).

In 2004, in Owen, Wisconsin, a request was made to remove *Rainbow Boys* from the high school library because of the book's sexual content. The challenge was made by a former high school teacher and supported by parents who objected to the book's homosexual theme. A school district administrator decided to continue to make the book available to students in the tenth grade and older at Owen Withee Senior High ("Censorship Roundup" 2005, 20).

During the district review process, the administrator gave a reading of the book. According to the administrator, "most people who objected to *Rainbow Boys* had not read the book, but had only read excerpts that had appeared on the Internet" (20). *Rainbow Boys* has been selected as an ALA Best Book for Young Adults.

Author Alex Sanchez thinks that people who challenge books because of gay content hurt young people more than help them. He thinks young people are helped "by having full access to honest information and guided adult discussions about gay-straight themes" (Sanchez 2005a, 47). Sanchez thanks teachers who have stood up for gay-straight-themed books. He says that those who are challenged "by the prejudice of a parent or administrator and put into a position to defend such books . . . gain a deeper understanding of what it's like to be a young person struggling with gay-straight issues in America today" (48). Sanchez says that teachers may be "confronted with their own coming-out process, as individuals who understand the need to address gay-straight issues" (48).

Sanchez told Holly Atkins in an interview that the idea for *Rainbow Boys* came from his own coming-out issues (Atkins 2004). A section of his Web site at http://www.alexsanchez.com helps teens in their process of deciding "if, how, with whom, and when to come out" (Atkins

2004). He writes, in part, to provide youth with "access to information that allows them to analyze, interpret and come to their own conclusions about issues" (Atkins 2004). Trained as a youth and family counselor, Sanchez reports that, according to Human Rights Watch, more than 2 million lesbian and gay Americans are school age. Sanchez gets letters from readers who thank him for helping them come out to family and friends and letters to thank Sanchez for sharing the pain of name-calling and homophobia in his books (Sanchez 2005a, 46).

Sanchez asked a group of students what the one thing would be that he should tell teachers. The response was to let teachers know how much name-calling hurts and to ask them to intervene to stop the name-calling and not to look away (47). Sanchez thinks books that address homophobia can help young people "understand their emotional and sexual feelings" (47).

Discussion Questions

1. Read the book *Rainbow Boys.*

2. Compare the excerpts from the reviews of *Rainbow Boys.*

3. In recommending the book to readers, what age groups or grade levels do you think are appropriate?

4. How would you review the book?

5. What is the effect of the alternating viewpoints used to narrate *Rainbow Boys*?

6. What are parents' reactions to the book *Rainbow Boys* used in the curriculum? How can you determine these reactions?

7. How do you feel about teaching and holding literature discussions using gay-themed literature?

8. What does Sanchez mean when he says that teachers may be confronted with their own "coming-out process, as individuals who understand the need to address gay-straight issues"?

9. What is the role of the teacher, according to Sanchez?

References

Allan, Christina. 1999. Poets of comrades: Addressing sexual orientation in the English classroom. *English Journal* 88(6): 97–101.

Alvine, Lynne. 1994. Understanding adolescent homophobia: An interview with Bette Greene. *Alan Review* 20(2): 5. http://scholar.lib.vt.edu/ejournals/ALAN/winter94/Alvine.html.

Anderson, Douglas Eric. 1992. Gay information: Out of the closet. *School Library Journal* 38(6): 62.

Atkins, Holly. 2004. An interview with Alex Sanchez. *The Floridian*, December 13.

Barber, Karen. 1995. Letter from Boston. *Lambda Book Report* 4(9): 9. http://www.lambdalit.org/lbr_intro.html.

Bauer, Marion Dane. 1994. *Am I Blue?: Coming out from the Silence*. New York: HarperCollins.

Block, Francesca Lia. 1992. *Cherokee bat and the goat guys*. New York: HarperCollins.

———. 1991. *Witch baby*. New York: HarperCollins.

———. 1989. *Weetzie bat*. New York: HarperCollins.

Brass, Perry. 2002. Family: The new gay and lesbian culture meets the new family. *Lambda Book Report* 11(3): 44.

Briggs, John V. 1977. *School employees homosexuality initiative statute*. State of California. Los Angeles County Law Library. California Ballot Initiatives. http://www.lalaw.lib.ca.us/ballot.html.

Brimner, Larry Dane. 1995. *Being different. Lambda youths speak out*. New York: F. Watts.

Broz, William J. 2001. Hope and irony: *Annie on my mind*. *English Journal* 90(6): 47–53.

Campbell, Patty. 1993. The sand in the oyster. *Horn Book Magazine* 69(5): 568–573.

Cart, Michael. 2004. What a wonderful world: Notes on the evolution of GLBTQ literature for young adults. *The Alan Review* 31(2): 46–52.

———. 1999. Saying no to stereotypes. *The Booklist* 95(19–20): 1810–1811.

———. 1996. *From romance to realism: 50 years of growth and change in young adult literature*. New York: HarperCollins Children's Books.

Cart, Michael, and Christine Jenkins. Forthcoming. *The heart has its reasons. Homosexuality in young adult literature*.

Caywood, Carolyn. 1993. Reaching out to gay teens. *School Library Journal* 39(4): 50.

Censorship roundup. 2005. *School Library Journal* 51(2): 20.

Chambers, Aidan. 1999. *Postcards from no man's land*. London: Bodley Head.

———. 1982. *Dance on my grave*. New York: Harper & Row.

Clark, J. Elizabeth, Erica Rand, and Leonard Vogt. 2003a. Climate control. Teaching about gender and sexuality in 2003—Part 2. *Radical Teacher* 67: 2–3.

———. 2003b. Climate control. Teaching about gender and sexuality in 2003. *Radical Teacher* 66: 2–5.

Cockett, Lynn. 1995. Entering the mainstream: Fiction about gay and lesbian teens *School Library Journal* 41(2): 32–33.

Consiglio, Anthony. 1999. Gender identity and narrative truth: An autobiographical approach to bias. *English Journal* 88(3): 71–77.

Cooper, Michael. 2000. Influential and gay. Editor Roger Sutton shapes opinions on kid lit. *Lambda Book Report* 8(8): 9–10.

Cruikshank, Margaret. 2003. Reflection. *Radical Teacher* 67: 15.

Day, Francis Ann. 2000. *Lesbian and gay voices: An annotated bibliography and guide to literature for children and young adults*. Westport, CT: Greenwood Press.

Donoghue, Emma. 1997. *Kissing the witch. Old tales in new skins*. New York: HarperCollins.

Donovan, John. 1969. *I'll get there, it better be worth the trip; a novel*. New York: Harper & Row.

English, Hugh. 2003. Learning and unlearning historical sexual identities. *Radical Teacher* 66: 5–9.

Evaluating the treatment of gay themes in books for children and younger adults. What to do until utopia arrives. http://www.niulib.niu.edu/lgbt/bibthemeslit.htm.

Evans, Betty. 2001. *Rainbow boys. School Library Journal* 47(10): 169.

Fader, Ellen. 1994. Booklist: Nonfiction. *Horn Book Magazine* 70(4): 472.

———. 1991. *Understanding sexual identity: A book for gay teens and their friends* (book). *Horn Book Magazine* 67(2): 220.

Feinberg, Leslie. 1993. *Stone butch blues. A novel*. Ithaca, NY: Firebrand Books.

Flood, Craig P., and Susan Shaffer. 2000. Safe boys, safe schools. *WEEA Digest* (Newton, MA) (November): 3–11.

Ford, Elizabeth A. 1998. H/Z: Why Leslea Newman makes Heather into Zoe. *Children's Literature Association Quarterly* 23(3): 128–133.

Frangedis, Helen. 1988. Dealing with the controversial elements in *The catcher in the rye. English Journal* 77(7): 72–75.

Freymann-Weyr, Garret. 2002. *My heartbeat*. Boston: Houghton Mifflin.

Fuoss, Kirk. 1994. A portrait of the adolescent as a young gay: The politics of male homosexuality in young adult fiction. In *Queer words, queer images: Communication and the construction of homosexuality*, ed. Jeffrey R. Ringer, 159–174. New York: New York University Press.

Gallo, Don. 2004. The boldest books. *English Journal* 94(1): 126–130.

Garden, Nancy. 2001. Gay books for teens & kids: Coming into their own? *Lambda Book Report* 9(7): 22.

———. 1997. Gay fiction for kids: Is anyone out there publishing it? *Lambda Book Report* 6(4): 25.

———. 1994. Banned: Lesbian and gay books under fire. *Lambda Book Report* 4(7): 11–16.

———. 1992. Dick and Jane grow up gay: The importance of (gay) young adult fiction. *Lambda Book Report* 3(6): 7.

———. 1982. *Annie on my mind*. New York: Farrar, Straus and Giroux.

Gates, Gary J., and Jason Ost. 2004. *The gay and lesbian atlas*. Washington, DC: Urban Institute Press.

Gay and Lesbian Educators of British Columbia (GALE-BC). Challenging homophobia: A teacher's resource book, http://www.galebc.org/main.htm (accessed August 25, 2005).

———. 2001. Challenging homophobia in schools. *Teacher Librarian* 28(3): 27–30. Book resources: Fiction and non-fiction titles for K–12, http://www.galebc.org/main.htm (accessed August 25, 2005).

GLBTRT Newsletter (A publication of the Gay, Lesbian, Bisexual, Transgendered Round Table of the American Library Association). 2003. 15(2): 1–7.

Greenbaum, Vicky. 1994. Literature out of the closet: Bringing gay and lesbian texts and subtexts out in high school English. *English Journal* 83(5): 71–74.

Grizzle, Darrell. 2002. Fear & trembling at an ex-gay confab. *Gay & Lesbian Review* 9(1): 27–29.

Hamilton, Greg. 2004. Teaching the difficult. *English Journal* 94(2): 106–109.

Hamilton, R. J. 1995. *Who framed Lorenzo Garcia?* Los Angeles: Alyson Books.

Hanckel, Frances, and John Cunningham. 1979. *A way of love, a way of life: A young person's introduction to what it means to be gay.* New York: Lothrop, Lee & Shepard Books.

Happermann, Christine. 1998. Book reviews. *Horn Book Magazine* 74(3): 358–360.

Hearing us out: Voices from the gay and lesbian community. 1996. *English Journal* 85(1): 90.

Herald, Diana. 2000. Bibliography for gay teens. Gay Teens in the 21st Century: Access to the Future Preconference to the 2000 Annual Conference of the American Library Association. July 7. Gay, Lesbian, Bisexual & Transgendered Round Table of the American Library Association. http://www.niulib.niu.edu/lgbt/bibteens.htm.

Herren, Greg. 2001a. ACLU battles school district over gay books. *Lambda Book Report* 9(7): 6.

———. 2001b. Hearts and minds. *Lambda Book Report* 9(9): 26.

Herron, Ann. 1994. *Two teenagers in twenty: Writings by gay and lesbian youth.* Boston: Alyson Publications.

Homes, A. M. 1989. *Jack.* New York: Vintage Books.

Human Rights Watch. 2001. Hatred in the hallways III. Young and queer in America. May. http://www.hrw.org/reports/2001/uslgbt/Final-04.htm#P497_595577. (Quoted in Sanchez 2005a, 46)

Jenkins, Christine A. 2003. Annie on her mind. *School Library Journal* 49(6): 48–50.

———. 1998a. From queer to gay and back again. Young adult novels with gay/lesbian/queer content, 1969–1997. *Library Quarterly* 68(3): 298–334.

———. 1998b. Heartthrobs and heartbreaks: A guide to young adult books with gay themes. *Outlook* 1(3): 82–92.

———. 1993. Young adult novels with gay/lesbian characters and themes 1969–92: A historical reading of content, gender and narrative distance. *Journal of Youth Services in Libraries* 7: 43–55.

Jenkins, Christine A., and Julie Morris. 1982. *A look at gayness. An annotated bibliography of gay materials for young people.* 2nd ed. Ann Arbor, MI: Kindred Spirit Press.

Kerr, M. E. 1994. *Deliver us from Evie.* New York: HarperCollins.

———. 1986. *Night kites.* New York: Harper & Row.

———. 1977. *I'll love you when you're more like me.* New York: Harper & Row.

Kidd, Kenneth. 1998. Introduction: Lesbian/gay literature for children and young adults. Special Issue: Lesbian/Gay Literature for Children and Young Adults. *Children's Literature Association Quarterly* 23(3): 114–119.

Leslie, Roger. 2001. Lesbian and gay voices. Annotated bibliography and guide to literature for children and young adults (book review). *Booklist* 97(14): 1406.

Levithan, David. 2003. *Boy meets boy*. New York: Knopf.

McRuer, Robert. 1998. Reading and writing "immunity": Children and the anti-body. *Children's Literature Association Quarterly* 23(3): 134–142.

Mercier, Cathryn M. 2001. Professional reading 2000–2001. *Horn Book Magazine* 77(3): 289–299.

M.V.K. booklist: Nonfiction. 1995. *Horn Book Magazine* 71(1): 71.

Nelson, Theresa. 1994. *Earthshine. A novel*. New York: Orchard Books.

Newman, Leslea. 2000. *Heather has two mommies*. 2nd ed., 10th anniversary ed. Los Angeles: Alyson Wonderland.

———. 1997. *Heather* and her critics. *Horn Book Magazine* 73(2): 149–153.

———. 1991. *Gloria goes to gay pride*. Boston: Alyson Wonderland.

———. 1989. *Heather has two mommies*. Boston: Alyson Wonderland.

Norton, Terry L., and Jonatha W. Vare. 2004. Literature for today's gay and lesbian teens: Subverting the culture of silence. *English Journal* 94(2): 65–69.

Palmer, Jean. 1995. Am I blue? *KLIATT Review* 29(4): Children's literature comprehensive database, http://clcd.odyssi.com (accessed August 25, 2005).

Parker, Jessica. 2001. Language: A pernicious and powerful tool. *English Journal* 91(2): 74–78.

Phifer, Nan. 1994. Homophobia: The theme of the novel, *Jack. Alan Review* 20(2): 10. http://scholar.lib.vt.edu/ejournals/ALAN/winter94.

Queer resource list. 2003. *Radical Teacher* 67: 30–31.

Quinn, Mary Ellen. 2000. Lesbian and gay voices: An annotated bibliography and guide to literature. *Booklist* 97(6): 668–669.

Rainbow boys. 2005. *Book Links* 14(3): 34.

Rainbow boys (book review). 2001. *Publisher's Weekly*, November 26.

Rochman, Hazel. 2003. Top 10 youth romances. *Booklist* 100(2): 235.

Sanchez, Alex. 2005a. Open eyes and change lives. Narrative resources addressing gay-straight themes. *English Journal* 94(3): 46–48.

———. 2005b. *Rainbow road*. New York: Simon and Schuster.

———. 2003. *Rainbow high*. New York: Simon and Schuster.

———. 2001. *Rainbow boys*. New York: Simon and Schuster.

Schall, Janine, and Gloria Kauffmann. 2003. Exploring literature with gay and lesbian characters in the elementary school. *Journal of Children's Literature* 29(1): 36–45.

Sedgewick, Eve Kosofsky. 1998. How to bring your kids up gay. In *The children's culture reader*, ed. Henry Jenkins, 231–240. New York: New York University Press.

Senick, Gerard J., ed. 1978. Donovan, John 1928–   . In *Children's Literature Review*, vol. 3, 52. Detroit: Gale. 51–56.

St. Clair, Nancy. 1995. Outside looking in: Representations of gay and lesbian experiences in the young adult novel. *Alan Review* 23(1). http://scholar.lib.vt.edu/ejournals/ALAN.

Summer, Bob. 1995. Lambda rising expands on AOL. *Publishers Weekly* 242(36): 24.

Sutton, Roger. 1994. *Hearing us out. Voices from the gay and lesbian community.* Boston: Little, Brown.

Swartz, Patti Capel. 2003. Bridging multicultural education: Bringing sexual orientation into the children's and young adult literature classrooms. *Radical Teacher* 66: 11.

Webb. C. Anne. 1995. Taboo curriculum. *English Journal* 84(1): 120.

What to do until utopia arrives. 1976. *Wilson Library Bulletin* 50(7): 532–533.

Willhoite, Michael. 1990. *Daddy's roommate.* Boston: Alyson Wonderland.

Witeck, Bob. 2001. Their only mysteries themselves. *Lambda Book Report* 10(2): 21.

Wittlinger, Ellen. 1999. *Hard love.* New York: Simon and Schuster Books for Young Readers.

Woodson, Jacqueline. 1995. *From the notebooks of Melanin Sun.* New York: Blue Sky Press.

———. 1991. *The dear one.* New York: Delacorte Press.

Yampell, Cat. 1999. Alyson Wonderland Publishing. *Bookbird* 37(3): 31–33.

Zvirin, Stephanie. 2001. Top 10 gay and lesbian books for youth. *Booklist* 97(19–20): 1863.

Appendix
Book Review Resources

The following is a list of online resources for finding book reviews.

Alan Review. Electronic Archive of Past Issues. Ed. P.S. Carroll. Urbana, IL: Alan, The Assembly on Literature for Adolescents of NCTE, the National Council of Teachers of English. http://scholar.lib.vt.edu/ejournals/ALAN. Signed reviews of new young adult fiction and nonfiction books. Reviews include curricular thematic tie-ins. The *Alan Review* also includes author interviews and articles on young adult literature research and instruction.

Booklist. Ed. B. Ott. Chicago, IL: American Library Association. http://www.ala.org/ala/booklist. See *Youth: Special Lists and Features* section-/speciallists/speciallistsandfeatures1/youthspecial.htm. See *Reviews of the Month* section-/reviewsofmonth/reviewsmonth.htm.

Book Reviews at the Children's Literature Program. Ed. Alida Allison. Department of English and Comparative Literature at San Diego State University. http://www.rohan.sdsu.edu/~childlit/reviews. html. Signed reviews of children's books and young adult books. Books are reviewed by faculty and students associated with the Children's Literature Program at San Diego State University.

Bulletin of the Center for Children's Books. Ed. D. Stevenson. Urbana-Champaign: University of Illinois at Urbana-Champaign Graduate School of Library and Information Science. http://www.lis.uiuc. edu/puboff/bccb. Reviews by librarians and professors. Suggested reading levels and curricular uses. *Review Archives* are at http://www.lis.uiuc.edu/puboff/bccb/archive.html. Annual *Blue Ribbon* books are at http://www.lis.uiuc.edu/puboff/bccb/blueindex.html.

Children's Choices. Newark, DE: International Reading Association and the Children's Book Council. http://www.reading.org/resources/tools/choices_childrens.html. Voted on by children with the help of teachers, librarians, and children's literature specialists.

Children's Literature (themed reviews). http://www.childrenslit.com/th.htm. This organization, responsible for the production of the *Children's Literature Comprehensive Database*, offers free access to themed reviews. Includes Children's Literature Choices Award listings. http://www.childrenslit. com/clc.htm.

New York Times Book Review. New York: New York Times Co. http://www.nytimes.com/pages/books/ index.html. Signed critical reviews of books with one section dedicated to children's books.

Publisher's Weekly. New York: R.R. Bowker Co. http://publishersweekly.com. Signed critical reviews of books including children's and young adult books.

Recommended Books in Spanish. Ed. L. G. Schon, N. Algazi, M. Padilla Diamond, and M. Ruvinski. San Marcos: Barahona Center for the Study of Books in Spanish for Children and Adolescents, California State University. http://www.csusm.edu/csb/I.

School Library Journal. Ed. E. St. Lifer. New York: R. R. Bowker Co. http://www.schoollibraryjournal. com. Signed critical reviews of new general trade and paperback books. Reviews by youth services librarians and children's literature educators.

Spaghetti Book Club–Book Reviews by Kids for Kids! http://www.spaghettibookclub.org. Reviews written by children in the Spaghetti Book Club curriculum project schools. Curriculum leads students to meet language arts standards through the process of reading books and writing book reviews.

Teacher's Choices. Newark, DE: International Reading Association and the Children's Book Council. http://www.reading.org/resources/tools/choices_teachers.html. Includes annotated bibliographies of trade books for children and young adults that teachers have reviewed and "find to be exceptional in curriculum use."

VOYA (Voice of Youth Advocates). Ed. C. D. MacRae. Lanham, MD: Scarecrow Press. http://www.voya. com. Signed critical reviews for young adults reviewed by grade level, interest, popularity, and strength of writing. Source also reviews graphic novels.

Young Adults' Choices. Newark, DE: International Reading Association. http://www.reading.org/ resources/tools/choices_young_adults.html.

The following is a list of print journals and periodicals to consult for book reviews.

Bookbird. Ed. E. B. Freeman, B. A. Lehman, L. Ratcheva-Stratieva, and P. L. Scharer. Madrid, Spain: Instituto Nacional del Libro Español, The International Board on Books for Young People. Reviews of children's books published all over the world.

Book Links: Connecting Books, Libraries, and Classrooms. Ed. L. Tillotson. Chicago, IL: ALA, Booklist Publications. Unsigned, annotated, thematic bibliographies of children's books focused on particular core curricular areas. Author and illustrator interviews and essays and suggested activities are also provided.

Childhood Education. Ed. A. W. Bauer. Washington, DC: Association for Childhood Education International.

Children's Book Review Index (CBRI). Ed. D. Ferguson. Detroit, MI: Gale. Beginning in 1965, Index reviews of thousands of children's books, periodicals devoted to children's literature, and some media based on books.

Horn Book Guide. Ed. K. Flynn. The Horn Book Inc. Signed, critical reviews of hardcover trade children's books published in the United States not appearing in the *Horn Book Magazine.* Gives a rating from one to five and a suggested reading level. Includes a subject index.

Horn Book Magazine. Ed. R. Sutton. The Horn Book Inc. Signed reviews of the best children's and young adult books. Reviews appearing in the magazine are for those books submitted and judged to be the best by Horn Book reviewers.

Journal of Adolescent & Adult Literacy. Ed. T. Goodson. Newark, DE: International Reading Association. Critical reviews of new young adult books.

Kirkus Reviews. Ed. K. Breen (Children's). New York: Kirkus Service, Inc. Critical, unsigned reviews in the section dedicated to children's books.

Bibliography

Abrams, M. H. 1971. *Natural supernaturalism. Tradition and revolution in romantic literature.* New York: W.W. Norton, Inc.

Adams, Karen I. 1989. The "born-again" phenomenon and children's books. *Children's Literature Association Quarterly* 14(1): 5–9.

Agnew, Kate, and Geoff Fox. 2001. *Children at war. From the first World War to the Gulf.* New York: Continuum.

Alfaro, Cristina. 2004. Cross linguistic transfer: What must highly qualified teachers know? Lecture presented at San Diego State University, San Diego, Spring.

Allan, Christina. 1999. Poets of comrades: Addressing sexual orientation in the English classroom. *English Journal* 88(6): 97–101.

Allison, Anthony. 1999. *Hear these voices. Youth at the edge of the millennium.* New York: Dutton Children's Books.

Alvine, Lynne. 1994. Understanding adolescent homophobia: An interview with Bette Greene. *Alan Review* 20(2): 5. http://scholar.lib.vt.edu/ejournals/ALAN/winter94/Alvine.html.

Ammon, Bette. Just one flick of a finger. *Voice of Youth Advocates* 20(2). Children's Literature Comprehensive Database. http://clcd.odyssi.com (accessed August 25, 2005).

Anderson, Douglas Eric. 1992. Gay information: Out of the closet. *School Library Journal* 38(6): 62.

Armstrong, Jennifer. 2003. The writer's page: Narrative and violence. *Horn Book Magazine* 79(2): 191–194.

Asheim, Lester. 1983. Selection and censorship: A reappraisal. *Wilson Library Bulletin* 58: 180–184.

———. 1953. Not censorship but selection. *Wilson Library Bulletin* 28: 67.

Asimov, Nanette. 1998a. S.F. high schools to get diverse authors list. *San Francisco Chronicle*, March 21.

———. 1998b. School board strikes deal on books. Resolution stresses diversity, not quotas. *San Francisco Chronicle*, March 20.

———. 1998c. State's teachers agree—Book list too white. *San Francisco Chronicle*, March 14.

———. 1998d. New foe of race-based book lists. San Francisco proposal wrong, school chief says. *San Francisco Chronicle*, March 12.

———. 1998e. San Francisco weighs race-based reading list. 40% by nonwhites proposed in schools. *San Francisco Chronicle,* March 11.

Asselin, M. 2003. Bridging the gap between learning to be male and learning to read. *Teacher Librarian* 30(3): 53–54.

Associated Press State & Local Wire. 2004. Superintendent proposes dropping reference to evolution. January 29.

———. 2002. School board president reportedly resigns over Harry Potter controversy. January 4.

Association for Library Services to Children. International Relations Committee. 2001. Bilingual books for children. *Journal of Youth Services in Libraries* 14(2): 32–37.

Atkins, S. Beth. 1996. *Voices from the streets. Young former gang members tell their stories.* Boston: Little, Brown.

Attebery, Brian. 1996. Women's coming of age in fantasy. In *Only connect: Readings on children's literature,* 3rd ed., ed. Sheila Egoff, Gordon Stubbs, Ralph Ashley, and Wendy Sutton, 288–300. New York: Oxford University Press.

Axiotis, Vivian M., James R. Harstad, Katharine J. Heintschel, and Bonnie Molnar. 1999. What young adult books have you used successfully to teach the classics? *English Journal* 88(3): 27–29.

Babbitt, Natalie. 1996. Protecting children's literature. In *Only connect. Readings on children's literature,* 3rd ed., ed. Sheila Egoff, Gordon Stubbs, Ralph Ashley, and Wendy Sutton, 32–38. New York: Oxford University Press.

Baker, Colin. 1993. *Foundations of bilingual education and bilingualism.* Bristol, PA: Multilingual Matters, Ltd.

Banks, James A. 1993. The canon debate, knowledge construction, and multicultural education. *Educational Researcher* (June–July): 4–14.

Barber, Karen. 1995. Letter from Boston. *Lambda Book Report* 4(9): 9. http://www.lambdalit. org/lbr_intro.html.

Barrera, Rosalinda B., Ruth E. Quiroa, and Rebecca Valdivia. 2003. Spanish in Latino picture storybooks in English: Its use and textual effects. In *Multicultural issues in literacy research and practice,* ed. Arlette Ingram Willis, Georgia Earnest Garcia, Rosalinda B. Barrera, and Violet J. Harris, 145–165. Mahwah, NJ: L. Erlbaum Associates.

Barton, D. 1998. Schools pushed to have more works by minority writers on reading lists. *Rocky Mountain News,* April 5.

Barton, Stan. 2002. Good and bad books. *Washington Post,* July 13.

Baskin, Barbara H., and Karen H. Harris. 1984. *More notes from a different drummer: A guide to juvenile fiction portraying the disabled.* New York: R.R. Bowker.

———. 1977. *Notes from a different drummer: A guide to juvenile fiction portraying the handicapped.* New York: R.R. Bowker.

Bauer, Carolyn J. 1985. Books can break attitudinal barriers toward the handicapped. *School Counselor* 32: 302–306.

Bauer, Eurydice Bouchereau. 2003. Finding Esmerelda's shoes: A case study of a young bilingual child's response to literature. In *Multicultural issues in literacy research and practice,* ed. Arlette Ingram Willis, Georgia Earnest Garcia, Rosalinda B. Barrera, and Violet J. Harris, 11–27. Mahwah, NJ: L. Erlbaum Associates.

Bauer, Marion Dane. 1994. *Am I Blue?: Coming out from the silence.* New York: HarperCollins.

Beers, G. Kylene, and Teri S. Lesesne, eds. 2001. *Books for you: An annotated booklist for senior high.* 14th ed. Urbana, IL: National Council of Teachers of English.

Benton-Banai, Edward. 1988. *The Mishomis book: Voice of the Ojibway.* Saint Paul, MN: Red School House.

Birnbaum, June, Janet Emig, and Douglas Fisher. 2003. Case studies: Placing literacy phenomena within their actual context. In *Handbook of research on teaching the English language arts,* 2nd ed., ed. James Flood, Diane Lapp, James R. Squire, and Julie M. Jensen, 192–200. Mahwah, NJ: L. Erlbaum Associates.

Blaska, Joan Kay. 2003. *Using children's literature to learn about disabilities and illness.* 2nd ed. Troy, NY: Educator's International Press.

———. 1996. *Using children's literature to learn about disabilities and illness.* Moorehead, MN: Practical Press.

Blaska, J. K., and E. C. Lynch. 1998. Is everyone included? Using children's literature to facilitate the understanding of disabilities. *Young Children* 53(2): 36–37.

Block, Francesca Lia. 1992. *Cherokee bat and the goat guys.* New York: HarperCollins.

———. 1991. *Witch baby.* New York: HarperCollins.

———. 1989. *Weetzie bat.* New York: HarperCollins.

Boston, Rob. 2002. Witch hunt. *Church & State* 55(3): 8–10.

Bottigheimer, Ruth B., ed. 1986. *Fairy tales and society: Illusion, allusion, and paradigm.* Philadelphia: University of Pennsylvania Press.

Bowers, Keith. 2002. Creeping out the kids. Will the real Lemony Snicket please stand up? *Berkeley Express,* December 25.

Brancato, R. F. 2001. In defense of: *Are you there God? It's me! Margaret,* Deannie, and Blubber—Three novels by Judy Blume. In *Censored books: Critical viewpoints,* ed. N. J. Karolides, L. Burress, and J. M. Kean, 87–97. Lanham, MD: Scarecrow Press.

Brass, Perry. 2002. Family: The new gay and lesbian culture meets the new family. *Lambda Book Report* 11(3): 44.

Braxton, B. 2003. Bait the boys and hook them into reading. *Teacher Librarian* 30(3): 43–44.

Bridgers, Sue Ellen. 2000. Learning a language of nonviolence. *English Journal* 89(5): 71–73.

———. 1996. *All we know of heaven.* Wilmington, NC: Banks Channel Books.

Briggs, John V. 1977. *School employees homosexuality initiative statute.* State of California. Los Angeles County Law Library. California Ballot Initiatives. http://www.lalaw.lib.ca.us/ballots.html.

Briggs, Julia. 1996. Critical opinion: Reading children's books. In *Only connect: Readings on children's literature*, 3rd ed., ed. Sheila Egoff, Gordon Stubbs, Ralph Ashley, and Wendy Sutton, 18–31. New York: Oxford University Press.

Brimner, Larry Dane. 1995. *Being different. Lambda youths speak out.* New York: F. Watts.

Brinkley, Ellen Henson. 1999. *Caught off guard: Teachers rethinking censorship and controversy.* Boston: Allyn and Bacon.

Brown, Jean E., and Elaine C. Stephens, eds. 2003. *Your reading: An annotated booklist for middle school and junior high.* 11th ed. Urbana, IL: National Council of Teachers of English.

Broz, William J. 2001. Hope and irony: Annie on my mind. *English Journal* 90(6): 47–53.

Bryan, L., D. Owens, and Linda Walker. 2004. Y-RAP (Young Readers Art Project). A pragmatic solution for reluctant readers. *Reading Improvement* 41(4): 235–240.

Bryson, Joseph E., and Elizabeth W. Detty. 1982. *Censorship of public school library and instructional material.* Charlottesville, VA: Michie Company.

Buckley, Arabella B. c. 1800–1899? *The fairyland of science.* Philadelphia: Henry Altemus Co.

Bulfinch, Thomas. 1979. *Bulfinch's mythology.* New York: Viking Penguin.

Bunch, Gary Owen. 1996. *Kids, disabilities and regular classrooms: An annotated bibliography of selected children's literature on disability.* Toronto: Inclusion Press.

Burgess, Sue. 1999. Professional reading. *School Library Journal* 45(12): 168.

Burress, Lee. 1989. *Battle of the books: Literary censorship in the public schools, 1950–1985.* Metuchen, NJ: Scarecrow Press.

Byars, Betsy. 2000. Byars, Betsy, 1928– , Autobiography feature. In *Something about the author*, vol. 108, ed. Alan Hedblad, 23–39. Detroit, MI: Gale Group.

———. 1970. *The summer of the swans.* New York: Viking Press.

California Department of Education. 2002– . *Recommended literature: Kindergarten through grade twelve.* Sacramento, CA: California Department of Education. http://www.cde.ca.gov/ci/rl/ll.

Campbell, Patty. 1993. The sand in the oyster. *Horn Book Magazine* 69(5): 568–573.

Canada, Geoffrey. 1998. Foreword. In *Things get hectic: Teens write about violence that surrounds them, Youth Communication,* ed. Philip Kay, Andrea Estepa, and Al Desetta. New York: Simon and Schuster.

Cart, Michael. 2004. What a wonderful world: Notes on the evolution of GLBTQ literature for young adults. *Alan Review* 31(2): 46–52.

———, ed. 2002. *911: The book of help.* Chicago: Cricket Books.

———. 1999. Saying no to stereotypes. *Booklist* 95(19–20): 1810–1811.

———. 1996. *From romance to realism: 50 years of growth and change in young adult literature.* New York: HarperCollins Children's Books.

Cassidy, L. 2002. Challenge to a summer reading list. *SLATE Support for the Learning and Teaching of English Newsletter* 27(3): 3–4.

Castro, April. 2003. Board votes to keep evolution in Texas textbooks. *Columbian* (Vancouver, WA), November 8, sec. A.

Caywood, Carolyn. 1993. Reaching out to gay teens. *School Library Journal* 39(4): 50.

Censorship roundup. 2005. *School Library Journal* 39(4): 50.

Chambers, Aidan. 1999. *Postcards from no man's land*. London: Bodley Head.

———. 1982. *Dance on my grave*. New York: Harper & Row.

Chick, Kay A. 2002. Challenging gender stereotypes through literature: Picture books with strong female characters. *Journal of Children's Literature* 28(2): 19–24.

Chiles, Nick. 1998. Talk of success with Ebonics: Class posts higher test scores. *Austin American-Statesman* (TX), June 14, sec. Insight.

Cho, David. 2001. Fairfax school board limits access to book. Parents want *Druids* banned. *Washington Post*, February 14.

Christian-Smith, Linda K. 2000. More than crime on her mind: Nancy Drew as woman hero. In *A necessary fantasy?: The heroic figure in children's popular culture*, ed. Dudley Jones and Tony Watkins, 87–110. New York: Garland.

Christopher, Kevin. 2003. Evolution battle in Texas textbooks. *Skeptical Inquirer* 27(6): 7.

Clark, Beverly Lyon. 1996. *Regendering the school story: Sassy sissies and tattling tomboys*. New York: Routledge.

Clark, Beverly Lyon, and M. R. Higonnet, eds. 1999. *Girls, boys, books, toys: Gender in children's literature and culture*. Baltimore, MD: Johns Hopkins University Press.

Clark, J. Elizabeth, Erica Rand, and Leonard Vogt. 2003. Climate control. Teaching about gender and sexuality in 2003. *Radical Teacher* 66: 2–5.

———. 2003a. Climate control. Teaching about gender and sexuality in 2003—Part 2. *Radical Teacher* 67: 2–3.

Clark, Roger, Heidi Kulkin, and Liam Clancy. 1999. The liberal bias in feminist social science research on children's books. In *Girls, boys, books, toys: Gender in children's literature and culture,* ed. Beverly Lyon Clark and M. R. Higonnet, 71–82. Baltimore, MD: Johns Hopkins University Press.

Clothier, M. 1999. TechReport: Site encourages kids to read. *Atlanta Journal and Constitution*, May 16.

Coats, Karen. 2002. Dangerous intersections: Feminists at work. *Children's literature* 30: 205–210.

———. 2001. Fish stories: Teaching children's literature in a postmodern world. *Pedagogy: Critical Approaches to Teaching Literature, Language, Composition and Culture* 1(2): 401–409.

Cockett, Lynn. 1995. Entering the mainstream: Fiction about gay and lesbian teens. *School Library Journal* 41(2): 32–33.

Coelho, Elizabeth. 1998. *Teaching and learning in multicultural schools: An integrated approach*. Bilingual Education and Bilingualism. Philadelphia, PA: Multilingual Matters, Ltd.

Coerr, Eleanor. 1993. *Sadako*. New York: Putnam.

———. 1977. *Sadako and the thousand paper cranes.* New York: Putnam.

Coghlan, Rosemarie. 2000. The teaching of anti-violence strategies within the English curriculum. *English Journal* 89(5): 84–89.

Cole, Babette. 1987. *Prince Cinders.* New York: Putnam.

Coles, Robert. 1987. The child's understanding of tragedy. In *Children's literature*, vol. 15, ed. Margaret Higgonet and Barbara Rosen, 1–6. New Haven, CT: Yale University Press.

Collins, Carol Jones. 1998. The way we do the things we do: Required reading lists and girls. *Knowledge Quest* 26(4): 34–37.

Connor, Steve. 1997. World's languages dying at alarming rate: Shrinking linguistic diversity mourned; state's native tongues especially hard hit. In *The New Press guide to multicultural resources for young readers,* ed. Daphne Muse, 464. New York: New Press.

Consiglio, Anthony. 1999. Gender identity and narrative truth: An autobiographical approach to bias. *English Journal* 88(3): 71–77.

Cooper, Michael. 2000. Influential and gay. Editor Roger Sutton shapes opinions on kid lit. *Lambda Book Report* 8(8): 9–10.

Crabb, P. B., and D. Bielawski. 1994. The social representation of material culture and gender in children's books. *Sex Roles* 30: 69–79.

Crawford, James. 2003. A few things Ron Unz would prefer you didn't know about English learners in California. http://ourworld.compuserve.com/homepages/JWCRAWFORD/castats.htm.

———. 2002. The bilingual education act, 1968–2002. Obituary. *Rethinking Schools Online* 16(4). http://www.rethinkingschools.org/archive/16_04/Bil164.shtml.

Cruikshank, Margaret. 2003. Reflection. *Radical Teacher* 67: 15.

Cummins, Jim. 1994. Primary language instruction and the education of language minority students. In *Schooling and language minority students: A theoretical framework*, 2nd ed., 3–46. Los Angeles: Evaluation, Dissemination and Assessment Center, California State University.

Curry, A. 2001. Where is Judy Blume? Controversial fiction for older children and young adults. *Journal of Youth Services* 14 (Spring): 24–33.

Dancy, Shelvia. 2001. Finding the spiritual power of Harry Potter. *Washington Post*, June 30, sec. B.

Davis, Derek. 1999. Kansas schools challenge Darwinism: The history and future of the creationism-evolution controversy in American public education. *Journal of Church & State* 41(4): 661–676.

Dawson, Jim. 2003. Antievolutionists lose critical fight in Texas textbook decision. *Physics Today* 56(12): 36–38.

Day, B. 1993. State refuses to take book off school reading list. *Los Angeles Times*, April 16.

Day, Francis Ann. 2000. *Lesbian and gay voices: An annotated bibliography and guide to literature for children and young adults.* Westport, CT: Greenwood Press.

Demers, Patricia. 1993. *Heaven upon earth: The form of moral and religious children's literature, to 1850.* Knoxville: University of Tennessee Press.

Demetrulias, Diana Mayer. 2000. The depiction in juvenile literature of children with attention deficit disorder. *Journal of Youth Services in Libraries* 13(2): 36–42.

de Paola, Tomie. 1979. *Oliver Button is a sissy.* New York: Harcourt Brace Jovanovich.

Desai, Christina M. 2001. Picture book soldiers: Men and messages. *Reading Horizons* 42(2): 77–98.

Dicker, Susan J. 2000. Official English and bilingual education. In *Sociopolitics of English teaching*, ed. Joan Kelly Hall and William G. Eggington, 45–66. Tonawanda, NY: Multilingual Matters, Ltd.

Diekman, Amanda B., and Sara K. Murnen. 2004. Learning to be little women and little men: The inequitable gender equality of nonsexist children's literature. *Sex Roles* 50(5–6): 373–385.

Dodson, Shireen. 1998. *100 books for girls to grow on: Lively descriptions of the most inspiring books for girls, terrific discussion questions to spark conversation, great ideas for book-inspired activities, crafts, and field trips.* New York: HarperCollins.

Doiron, Ray. 2003. Boys books, girls books. Should we re-organize our school library collections? *Teacher Librarian* 30(3): 14–16.

Dole, Patricia Pearl. 1999. *Children's books about religion.* Englewood, CO: Libraries Unlimited.

Donoghue, Emma. 1997. *Kissing the witch. Old tales in new skins.* New York: HarperCollins.

Donovan, John. 1969. *I'll get there, it better be worth the trip; a novel.* New York: Harper & Row.

Durell, Ann, and Marilyn Sachs. 1990. *The big book for peace.* New York: E. P. Dutton Children's Books.

Elizabeth, Jane. 2001. Like magic, Harry Potter draws a record number of complaints. *Pittsburgh Post-Gazette*, November 17.

Engel et al. v. Vitale et al. 1962. 370 U.S. 421.

English, Hugh. 2003. Learning and unlearning historical sexual identities. *Radical Teacher* 66: 5–9.

Ernst, S. B. 1995. Gender issues in books for children and young adults. In *Battling dragons: Issues and controversy in children's literature,* ed. Susan Lehr, 66–78. Portsmouth, NH: Heinemann.

Evaluating the treatment of gay themes in books for children and younger adults. What to do until utopia arrives. http://www.niulib.niu.edu/lgbt/bibthemeslit.htm.

Evans, Carol. 1994. *Monstruos, pesadillas,* and other frights: A thematic unit. *Reading Teacher* 47 (February): 428–430.

Fader, Ellen. 1994. Booklist: Nonfiction. *Horn Book Magazine* 70(4): 472.

———. 1991. *Understanding sexual identity: A book for gay teens and their friends* (book). *Horn Book Magazine* 67(2): 220.

Feinberg, Leslie. 1993. *Stone butch blues. A novel.* Ithaca, NY: Firebrand Books.

Fine, Anne. 1992. *Flour babies.* New York: Little, Brown.

Flinn, Alex. 2002. *Breaking point.* New York: HarperTempest.

Flood, Craig P., and Susan Shaffer. 2000. Safe boys, safe schools. *WEEA Digest* (Newton, MA) (November): 3–11.

Ford, Elizabeth A. 1998. H/Z: Why Leslea Newman makes Heather into Zoe. *Children's Literature Association Quarterly* 23(3): 128–133.

Ford, Paul Leicester, ed. 1962. *The New England primer: A history of its origin and development.* New York City: Teachers College, Columbia University.

Forecasts: Children's books. 1998. *Publisher's Weekly* 245(25): 43.

Fox, Mem. 2001. Author profile. In *Beauty, brains, and brawn: The construction of gender in children's literature*, ed. Susan Lehr, 67–69. Portsmouth, NH: Heinemann.

———. 2001. Have we lost our way? *Language Arts* 79(2): 105–113.

———. 1993. Men who weep, boys who dance: The gender agenda between the lines in children's literature. *Language Arts* 70(2): 84–88.

Fractor, Jann Sorrell, Marjorie Ciruti Woodruff, Miriam G. Martinez, and William H. Teale. 1993. Let's not miss opportunities to promote voluntary reading: Classroom libraries in the elementary school. *Reading Teacher* 46(6): 476–484.

Frangedis, Helen. 1988. Dealing with the controversial elements in *The catcher in the rye. English Journal* 77(7): 72–75.

Fraser, James W. 1999. *Between church and state: Religion and public education in a multicultural America.* New York: St. Martin's Press.

Frazier, Matt. 2000. Book to remain in Arlington school libraries. Parents had complained of content, but trustees say they're legally tied. *Fort Worth Star-Telegram*, September 29.

Fredrickson, Elaine. 2000. Muted colors: Gender and classroom silence. *Language Arts* 77(4): 301–308

Freeman, Yvonne S. 1998. Providing quality children's literature in Spanish. *New Advocate* 11 (Winter): 23–38.

Freymann-Weyr, Garret. 2002. *My heartbeat.* Boston: Houghton Mifflin.

Friedberg, Joan Brest, June B. Mullins, and Adelaide Weir Sukiennik. 1985. *Accept me as I am: Best books of junvenile nonfiction on impairments and disabilities.* New York: Bowker.

Fuoss, Kirk. 1994. A portrait of the adolescent as a young gay: The politics of male homosexuality in young adult fiction. In *Queer words, queer images: Communication and the construction of homosexuality*, ed. Jeffrey R. Ringer, 159–174. New York: New York University Press.

Future classics. Books. 1993–1994. *American Visions* 8(6): 35.

Galda, Lee, and Bernice E. Cullinan. 2003. Literature for literacy: What research says about the benefits of using trade books in the classroom. In *Handbook of research on teaching the English language arts*, 2nd ed., ed. James Flood, Diane Lapp, James R. Squire, and Julie M. Jensen, 640–647. Mahwah, NJ: Lawrence Erlbaum Associates.

Galley, Michelle. 2003. Texas adopts biology texts, evolution included. *Education Week* 23(12): 5.

Gallo, Don. 2004. The boldest books. *English Journal* 94(1): 126–130.

Gamallo, Isabel C. Anievas. 1998. Subversive storytelling. The construction of lesbian girlhood through fantasy and fairy tale in Jeanette Winterson's *Oranges are not the only fruit.* In *The girl: Con-*

structions of the girl in contemporary fiction by women, ed. Ruth O. Saxton, 119–134. New York: St. Martin's Press.

Garden, Nancy. 2001. Gay books for teens & kids: Coming into their own? *Lambda Book Report* 9(7): 22.

———. 1997. Gay fiction for kids: Is anyone out there publishing it? *Lambda Book Report* 6(4): 25.

———. 1994. Banned: Lesbian and gay books under fire. *Lambda Book Report* 4(7): 11–16.

———. 1992. Dick and Jane grow up gay: The importance of (gay) young adult fiction. *Lambda Book Report* 3(6): 7.

———. 1982. *Annie on my mind*. New York: Farrar, Straus, Groux.

Gardner, Richard A. 1980. *Dr. Gardner's fairy tales for today's children*. Cresskill, NJ: Creative Thera-peutics.

Gates, Gary J., and Jason Ost. 2004. *The gay and lesbian atlas*. Washington, DC: Urban Institute Press.

Gay and Lesbian Educators of British Columbia (GALE-BC). 2001. Challenging homophobia in schools. *Teacher Librarian* 28(3): 27–30.

Giblin, James Cross. 1995. Violence, children, and children's books. *School Library Journal* 41(11): 30–31.

Gill, Carol. 1987. A new social perspective on disability and its implications for rehabilitation. *Occupational Therapy and Health Care* 7(1): 49–55.

GLBTRT Newsletter (A publication of the Gay, Lesbian, Bisexual, Transgendered Round Table of the American Library Association). 2003. 15(2): 1–7.

Gold, Janet T. 1983. "THAT'S ME!" The LD child in literature. *Academic Therapy* 18: 609–617.

Goldberg, Beverly. 2000. Fallen angels resurrected. *American Libraries* 31(10): 17.

Goldsborough, James O. 2004. Another attempt to deny evolution. *Copley News Service*, February 12.

Goodenough, Elizabeth. 2000a. Introduction to Violence and children's literature. Special issue, *Lion and the Unicorn* 24(3): v–ix.

———, ed. 2000b. Violence and children's literature. Special issue, *Lion and the Unicorn* 24(3).

Goodman, Michelle. 2003. A warning, not titillation. *Modesto Bee*, November 27.

Greenbaum, Vicky. 1994. Literature out of the closet: bringing gay and lesbian texts and subtexts out in high school English. *English Journal* 83(5): 71–74.

Greever, Ellen A., Patricia Austin, and Karyn Welhousen. 2000. *William's doll* revisited. *Language Arts* 7(4): 324–329.

Grizzle, Darrell. 2002. Fear & trembling at an ex-gay confab. *Gay & Lesbian Review* 9(1): 27–29.

Groves, Martha. 2001. The state education department vastly widens best books list. *Los Angeles Times*, June 29.

Gutierrez, Rochelle. 2002. Beyond essentialism: The complexity of language in teaching mathematics to Latina/o students. *American Educational Research Journal* 39(4): 1047–1088.

Hamilton, Greg. 2004. Teaching the difficult. *English Journal* 94(2): 106–109.

Hamilton, R. J. 1995. *Who framed Lorenzo Garcia?* Los Angeles: Alyson Books.

Hamilton, Virginia. 2001. Author profile. In *Beauty, brains, and brawn: The construction of gender in children's literature*, ed. Susan Lehr, 21–23. Portsmouth, NH: Heinemann.

Hanckel, Frances, and John Cunningham. 1979. *A way of love, a way of life: A young person's introduction to what it means to be gay.* New York: Lothrop, Lee & Shepard Books.

Hannan, Dennis J. 1967. *Meeting censorship in the school: A series of case studies.* Champaign, IL: National Council of Teachers of English.

Hansen-Krening, Nancy, ed. 2003. *Kaleidoscope: A multicultural booklist for grades K–8.* Urbana, IL: National Council of Teachers of English.

Happermann, Christine. 1998. Book reviews. *Horn Book Magazine* 74(3): 358–360.

Harris, Karen H., and Barbara H. Baskin. 1988. Treatment of disabilities in young adult fiction. *Education Digest* 53(7): 56–59.

———. 1987. Evolution of disability characterization in young adult fiction. *Educational Horizons* 65 (Summer): 188–191.

Harris, Violet J. 1995. "May I read this book?" Controversies, dilemmas, and delights in children's literature. In *Battling dragons: Issues and controversy in children's literature*, ed. Susan Lehr, 275–283. Portsmouth, NH: Heinemann.

Hearing us out: Voices from the gay and lesbian community. 1996. *English Journal* 85(1): 90.

Heine, Pat, and Christine Inkster. 1999. Strong female characters in recent children's literature. *Language Arts* 76(5): 427–434.

Herald, Diana. 2000. Bibliography for gay teens. Gay Teens in the 21st Century: Access to the Future Preconference to the 2000 Annual Conference of the American Library Association, July 7. Gay, Lesbian, Bisexual & Transgendered Round Table of the American Library Association. http://www.niulib.niu.edu/lgbt/bibteens.htm.

Herendeen, Susan. 2003a. Panel supports book list selection: "Always running," pulled for review, is reinstated. *Modesto Bee*, November 19.

———. 2003b. District removes book after parent's objection. Author says raw tale of gangs not for everyone. *Modesto Bee*, November 1.

Herren, Greg. 2001a. ACLU battles school district over gay books. *Lambda Book Report* 9(7): 6.

———. 2001b. Hearts and minds. *Lambda Book Report* 9(9): 26.

Herron, Ann. 1994. *Two teenagers in twenty: Writings by gay and lesbian youth.* Boston: Alyson Publications.

Higgonet, Margaret, and Barbara Rosen, eds. 1987. *Children's literature.* Vol. 15. New Haven, CT: Yale University Press.

Hill, Mary Jo. 2005. Cormier still stirs dissent; Chocolate war controversy roles. *Telegram & Gazette* (Worcester, MA), February 27.

Hindu. 1998. The sweet serenity of books. September 6.

Hinton, S. E. 1967. *The outsiders*. New York: Viking Press.

Holden, Constance. 2003. Texas resolves war over biology texts. *Science* 302(5648): 1130.

Homes, A. M. 1989. *Jack*. New York: Vintage Books.

Honawar, Vaishali. 2002. Parents to debate "appropriate books in schools." *Washington Times*, April 21.

———. 2001a. Book decency rules weak, parents say. *Washington Times*, October 22.

———. 2001b. Fairfax board OKs keeping explicit book. *Washington Times*, February 14.

———. 2001c. Is it vital reading or vile reading? Fairfax parents want veto power over additions to class book lists. *Washington Times*, February 12.

Hood, Lucy. 2002. Textbooks await nod from the state this week: Chairwoman thinks board will OK list. *San Antonio Express-News* (Metro/South Texas ed.), November 14.

Horning, K. T. 2001. *From cover to cover. Evaluating and reviewing children's books*. New York: Harper-Collins.

Houston Chronicle. 2002. Book banning spans the globe. October 3.

Hove, John, and NCTE. 1967. *Meeting censorship in the schools: A series of case studies*. Champaign, IL: National Council of Teachers of English.

Hudelson, Sarah, Julia Fournier, Cecilia Espinosa, and Renee Bachman. 1994. Chasing windmills: Confronting the obstacles to literature-based programs in Spanish. *Language Arts* 71 (March): 164–171.

Hudelson, Sarah, and Pat Rigg. 1994–1995. *My abuela can fly:* Children's books about old people in English and Spanish. *TESOL Journal* 3 (Winter): 5–10.

Hunt, Peter. 1996. Defining children's literature. In *Only connect: Readings on children's literature*, 3rd ed., ed. Sheila Egoff, Gordon Stubbs, Ralph Ashley, and Wendy Sutton, 3–17. New York: Oxford University Press.

Inness, Sherrie A., ed. 1997. Introduction. In *Nancy Drew® and company: Culture, gender, and girls' series*, 1–13. Bowling Green, OH: Bowling Green University Popular Press.

International Board on Books for Young People. 2005. Help the children hit by the tsunami disaster. http://www.ibby.org/index.php?id=257.

———. 1998. *26th Congress of the International Board on Books for Young People. Peace through Children's Books. Proceedings*. New Delhi, India: Indian BBY, Association of Writers and Illustrators for Children.

International Relations Committees 1998–99 and 1999–2000. 2001. Bilingual books for children. *Journal of Youth Services* 14 (Winter): 32–37.

Isaacs, K. T. 2003. Reality check: A look at the disturbing growth of violence in books for teens. *School Library Journal* 49(10): 50–51.

Ishizuka, Kathy. 2002. Harry Potter book burning draws fire. *School Library Journal* 48(2): 27.

Iskander, Sylvia Patterson. 1987. Readers, realism and Robert Cormier. In *Children's literature*, vol. 15, ed. Margaret R. Higgonet and Barbara Rosen, 7–18. New Haven, CT: Yale University Press.

Jago, Carol. 2000. *With rigor for all: Teaching the classics to contemporary students*. Portland, ME: Calendar Island Publishers.

Janeczko, P. 1977. Interview with Robert Cormier. *English Journal* 66: 10–11.

Jenkins, Christine A. 2003. Annie on her mind. *School Library Journal* 49(6): 48–50.

———. 1998a. From queer to gay and back again: Young adult novels with gay/lesbian/queer content, 1969–1997. *Library Quarterly* 68(3): 298–334.

———. 1998b. Heartthrobs and heartbreaks: A guide to young adult books with gay themes. *Outlook* 1(3): 82–92.

———. 1993. Young adult novels with gay/lesbian characters and themes 1969–92: A historical reading of content, gender and narrative distance. *Journal of Youth Services in Libraries* 7: 43–55.

Johnson, Elizabeth. 2003. Trustees vote 4–3 for book. It shouldn't be on reading list, critics of "Always running" claim. *Modesto Bee*, December 16.

Johnston, Robert C. 2002. State journal: Politics and prose. *Education Week* 22(2): 18.

Jones, Dudley, and Tony Watkins. 2000. *A necessary fantasy? The heroic figure in children's popular culture*. New York: Garland.

Jones, Patrick, and Dawn Cartwright Fiorelli. 2003. Overcoming the obstacle course: Teenage boys and reading. *Teacher Librarian* 30(3): 9–13.

Jordan, June. 1973. Young people: Victims of realism in books & life. *Wilson Library Bulletin* 48: 140–145.

Karolides, Nicholas J. 2002. *Censored books II: Critical viewpoints, 1985–2000*. Lanham, MD: Scarecrow Press.

Karolides, Nicholas J., and Lee Burress. 1985. Celebrating censored books. Racine, WI: Wisconsin Council of Teachers of English. (120)

Karolides, Nicholas J., Lee Burress, and John M. Kean, eds. 1993a. *Censored books: Critical viewpoints*. Lanham, MD: Scarecrow Press.

———. 1993b. Introduction. In *Censored books: Critical viewpoints*, ed. Nicholas J. Karolides, Lee Burress, and John M. Kean, xiii–xxii. Lanham, MD: Scarecrow Press.

Kay, Philip, Andrea Estepa, and Al Desetta, eds. 1998. *Things get hectic: Teens write about violence that surrounds them/Youth Communication*. New York: Simon and Schuster.

Keith, Lois. 2001. *Take up thy bed and walk: Death, disability and cure in classic fiction for girls*. New York: Routledge.

Kerr, M. E. 1994. *Deliver us from Evie*. New York: HarperCollins.

———. 1986. *Night kites*. New York: Harper & Row.

———. 1977. *I'll love you when you're more like me*. New York: Harper & Row.

Keyser, Elizabeth. 1989. Feminist revisions: Frauds on the fairies? In *Children's literature*, vol. 17, ed. Francelia Butler, Margaret Higonnet, and Barbara Rosen, 156–170. New Haven, CT: Yale University Press.

Khan, Noor Inayat. 1985. *Twenty Jakata tales*. New York: Inner Traditions International.

Khan, Rukhsana, and Patty Gallinger. 2002. *Muslim child: Understanding Islam through stories and poems*. Morton Grove, IL: Albert Whitman.

Kidd, Kenneth. 2000. Material girls and boys. *Michigan Quarterly Review* 39(3): 674–678.

————. 1998. Introduction: Lesbian/gay literature for children and young adults. Special Issue: Lesbian/Gay Literature for Children and Young Adults. *Children's Literature Association Quarterly* 23(3): 114–119.

Kindlon, Daniel J., and Michale Thompson. 1999. *Raising cain. Protecting the emotional life of boys*. New York: Ballantine Books.

Kingsley, Charles. 1863. *The water-babies: A fairytale for a land-baby*. New York: T. Nelson.

Knowles, Elizabeth, and Martha Smith. 1999. *More reading connections: Bringing parents, teachers, and librarians together*. Englewood, CO: Libraries Unlimited.

Koertge, Ron. 2001. *The brimstone journals*. Cambridge, MA: Candlewick Press.

Krishnaswami, Uma. 1996. *The broken tusk: Stories of the Hindu god Ganesha*. North Haven, CT: Linnet Books.

Kronick, Doreen. 1986. Children's books and games. Books about handicaps. *Academic Therapy* 21 (January): 373–376.

Kulkarni, Suneeta, and Prasanna Hulikavi. 1998. Books for traumatized children. Content analysis of peace and violence in children's books. In *26th Congress of the International Board on Books for Young People. Peace through Children's Books. Proceedings*. New Delhi, India: Indian BBY, Association of Writers and Illustrators for Children.

Kupper, Lisa, ed. 1994. *A guide to children's literature and disability: 1989–1994*. Washington, DC: National Information Center for Children and Youth with Disabilities. ED389 114.

Landrum, Judith. 2001. Selecting intermediate novels that feature characters with disabilities. *Reading Teacher* 55(3): 252–258.

Larson, Edward J. 1997. *Summer for the gods: The Scopes trial and America's continuing debate over science and religion*. New York: Basic Books.

Larson, Richard L. 1974. To the readers of CCC: Resolution on language. Students' right to their own language. *College Composition and Communication* 25(3): i.

Learning the Lonestar way. 2002. *Ecologist* 32(9): 6.

Lehr, Susan. 2001. The hidden curriculum: Are we teaching young girls to wait for the prince? In *Beauty, brains, and brawn: The construction of gender in children's literature*, ed. Susan Lehr, 1–18. Portsmouth, NH: Heinemann.

Leistyna, Pepi, Magaly Lavadenz, and Thomas Nelson. 2004. Introduction—Critical pedagogy: Revitalizing and democratizing teacher education. *Teacher Education Quarterly* 31 (Winter): 3–15.

Leslie, Roger. 2001. *Lesbian and gay voices: Annotated bibliography and guide to literature for children and young adults* (book review). *Booklist* 97(14): 1406.

Lessow-Hurley, Judith. 2000. *The foundations of dual language instruction*. 3rd ed. New York: Addison Wesley Longman.

Levithan, David. 2003. *Boy meets boy*. New York: Knopf.

Levy, P. 1992. Reading lists diversify, but complaints continue. *Minneapolis Star Tribune*, September 21.

Lewison, Mitzi, Amy Seely Flint, Katie Van Sluys, and Roxanne Henkin. 2002. Taking on critical literacy: The journey of newcomers and novices. *Language Arts* 79(5): 382–392.

Lindberg, Stanley W. 1976. Introduction. In *The annotated McGuffey: Selections from the McGuffey eclectic readers 1936–1920*. New York: Van Nostrand Reinhold.

Llywelyn, Morgan. 1991. *Druids*. New York: William Morrow.

Lockman, Darcy. 2002. Meet the author: Lemony Snicket. *Instructor* 112(3): 50–51.

Lorbiecki, Marybeth. 1996. *Just one flick of a finger*. New York: Dial Books.

Lord, Mary. 2002. Remaking history: The latest skirmish in the Texas textbooks wars could decide what kids will read across the nation. *U.S. News and World Report* 133(20): 46.

Los Angeles Times. 2001. A reading list must appeal to students to be teachable. July 23.

———. 2001b. State education department vastly widens best books list. June 29.

———. 1988. "Caged bird": Let it sing. November 13.

Louie, Belinda Y. 2001. Why gender stereotypes still persist in contemporary children's literature. In *Beauty, brains, and brawn: The construction of gender in children's literature,* ed. Susan Lehr, 142–151. Portsmouth, NH: Heinemann.

Mabin, Connie. 2002. Groups spar over what goes in social studies books. *Abiline Reporter News Online*, November 12. http://www.texnews.com/1998/2002/texas/texas_Groups_sp1112.html.

Manzo, Kathleen Kennedy. 2002a. History repeats itself in Texas for textbook-review process. *Education Week* 21(43): 11.

———. 2002b. Texas board adopts scores of new textbooks. *Education Week* 22(13): 17.

———. 2001. Charmed and challenged. *Education Week* 21(11): 1–4.

Margolis, Howard, and Arther Shapiro. 1987. Countering negative images of disability in classical literature. *English Journal* 76(3): 18–22.

Marlowe, Mike, and George Maycock. 2001. Using literary texts in teacher education to promote positive attitudes toward children with disabilities. *Teacher Education and Special Education* 24(2): 75–83.

Marsalek, Kevin. 1995. Humanism, science fiction, and fairy tales. *Free Inquiry* 15(3): 39–44.

Marshall, Elizabeth. 2004. Stripping for the wolf: Rethinking representations of gender in children's literature. *Reading Research Quarterly* 39(3): 256–270.

May, Jill P. 1995. *Children's literature and critical theory: Reading and writing for understanding.* New York: Oxford University Press.

McDonell, Nick. 2002. *Twelve.* New York: Grove Press.

McGovern, Edythe. 1995. Secular humanism in literature. *Free Inquiry* 15(3): 49–55.

McKay, Sandra Lee. 1992. Stories to tell our children. *TESOL Journal* 1 (Spring): 35–36.

McRuer, Robert. 1998. Reading and writing "immunity": Children and the anti-body. *Children's Literature Association Quarterly* 23(3): 134–142.

Mead, Alice. 2001. Author profile. In *Beauty, brains, and brawn: The construction of gender in children's literature,* ed. Susan Lehr, 152–155. Portsmouth, NH: Heinemann.

Mellon, Constance A. 1989. Exceptionality in children's books: Combining apples and oranges. *School Library Journal* 35(14): 46–47.

Mercier, Cathryn M. 2001. Professional reading 2000–2001. *Horn Book Magazine* 77(3): 289–299.

Milner, Joseph O'Beirne, and Lucy Floyd Moorcock Milner. 1987. *Webs and wardrobes: Humanist and religious world views in children's literature.* Lanham, MD: University Press of America.

Modesto Bee. 2004. Achievement gap. September 15.

———. 2003a. Book ban, reinstatement offers valuable lessons. November 21.

———. 2003b. Book ban reinstatement offers valuable lessons. November 11.

———. 2003c. Curriculum censored. Important book wrongly pulled from classrooms on 1 complaint. November 9.

Moffett, James. 1988. *Storm in the mountains: A case study of censorship, conflict, and consciousness.* Carbondale: Southern Illinois University Press.

Mora, Pat. 2001. Author profile. In *Beauty, brains, and brawn: The construction of gender in children's literature,* ed. Susan Lehr, 157–161. Portsmouth, NH: Heinemann.

Morales, Candace A. 2001. Our own voice: The necessity of Chicano literature in mainstream curriculum. *Multicultural Education* 9 (Winter): 16–20.

Moran, Carol E., and Kenji Hakuta. 2001. Bilingual education: Broadening research perspectives. In *Handbook of research on multicultural education,* ed. James A. Banks, and Cherry McGee Banks, 445–462. San Francisco: Jossey-Bass.

Morrison, William F., and Harvey A. Rude. 2002. Beyond textbooks: A rationale for a more inclusive user of literature in preservice special education teacher programs. *Teacher Education and Special Education* 25(2): 114–123.

Moss, Anita. 1987. Sacred and secular visions of imagination and reality in nineteenth century British fantasy for children. In *Webs and Wardrobes: Humanist and religious worldviews in children's literature,* ed. Joseph O'Beirne Milner, and Lucy Floyd Moorcock Milner. Lanham, MD: University Press of America.

Movers & Shakers. 2002. The people who are shaping the future of libraries. *Library Journal*, suppl., 127(5): 15.

Muggles for Harry Potter. 2000. *SLATE Support for the Learning and Teaching of English Newsletter* 25(3): 4.

"Muggles for Harry Potter" coalition fights censorship. 2000. *Journal of Adolescent & Adult Literacy* 44(1): 81.

Mumford Jurding, Christy, ed. 2003. *State of the First Amendment*. Nashville, TN: First Amendment Center.

Murphy, Bernadette. 2004. A taste for blood taints Hinton's new venture (book review). *Los Angeles Times*, September 14.

M.V.K. booklist: Nonfiction. 1995. *Horn Book Magazine* 71(1): 71.

Myers, Mitzi. 2000a. Storying war: a capsule overview. *Lion and the Unicorn* 24(3): 327–336.

———. 2000b. "No safe place to run to": An interview with Robert Cormier. *Lion and the Unicorn* 24(3): 445–464.

Myers, Walter Dean. 1988. *Scorpions*. New York: Harper & Row.

Naidoo, Beverly. 1995. Undesirable publication: A journey to Jo'burg. In *Battling dragons: Issues and controversy in children's literature,* ed. Susan Lehr, 31–38. Portsmouth, NH: Heinemann.

National Council of Teachers of English. 2003. NCTE members approve resolutions on composing with nonprint media and students' right to their own language. News release, December 1. http://www.ncte.org/about/over/positions/level/gen/107502.htm.

———. 2002. *Adventuring with books: A booklist for pre-K–grade-6.* Urbana, IL: National Council of Teachers of English.

———. 2000. NCTE pledges anti-censorship support to "Muggles for Harry Potter" coalition. http://www.ncte.org/news/muggles2000March13.shtml.

National Information Center for Children and Youth with Disabilities. 2001. *Children's literature and disability. Resources you can use.* 2nd ed. Washington, DC: National Information Center for Children and Youth with Disabilities. ED389114.

Neal, Connie. 2001. *What's a Christian to do with Harry Potter?* Colorado Springs: Waterbrook Press.

Nelson, Theresa. 1994. *Earthshine. A novel.* New York: Orchard Books.

Newman, Leslea. 2000. *Heather has two mommies.* 2nd ed., 10th anniversary ed. Los Angeles: Alyson Wonderland.

———. 1997. *Heather* and her critics. *Horn Book Magazine* 73(2): 149–153.

———. 1991. *Gloria goes to gay pride.* Boston: Alyson Wonderland.

———. 1989. *Heather has two mommies.* Boston: Alyson Wonderland.

New York City Board of Education. 1993. *Pan American educational resources & cultural materials.* Brooklyn: Office of Bilingual Education, New York City Board of Education.

New York Times. 1989. Education. School reading lists shun women and black authors. June 21.

Nilsen, Alleen Pace. 1991. Speaking loudly for good books: Promoting the wheat & winnowing the chaff. *School Library Journal* 37(9): 180–183.

Noddings, Nel. 1993. Humanism and unbelief. In *Educating for intelligent belief or unbelief.* New York: Teachers College Press.

Nodelman, Perry. 1985. *Touchstones: Reflections on the best in children's literature.* 3 vols. West Lafayette, IN: Children's Literature Association.

———, ed. 1981. Children's literature & literary theory. *Children's Literature Association Quarterly* (Spring): 9–40.

———. 1980. Grand canon suite. *Children's Literature Association Quarterly* (Summer): 1, 3–8.

Norton, Terry L., and Jonatha W. Vare. 2004. Literature for today's gay and lesbian teens: Subverting the culture of silence. *English Journal* 94(2): 65–69.

Noz, Kristen. 1999. 7th graders have message about violence. *Richmond Times,* May 18.

Odean, Kathleen. 2002. *Great books for girls: More than 600 recommended books for girls, ages 3–14.* New York: Ballantine Books.

———. 1998. *Great books for boys: More than 600 books for boys from 2 to 14.* New York: Ballantine Books.

Office for Intellectual Freedom. 2005. *Intellectual freedom and censorship Q & A.* Chicago: American Library Association. http://www.ala.org/ala/oif/basics/intellectual.htm.

———. 1998. *Workbook for selection policy writing.* Chicago: American Library Association. http://www.ala.org/Template.cfm?Section=dealing&Template=/ContentManagement/ContentDisplay.cfm&ContentID=77103.

Office of Special Education and Rehabilitative Services. 2003. Archived information. An overview of the bill to provide a broad understanding of some of the changes in IDEA '97. http://www.ed.gov/offices/OSERS/Policy/IDEA/overview.html.

O'Keefe, Deborah. 2000. *Good girl messages: How young women were misled by their favorite books.* New York: Continuum International Publishing Group.

Olsen, Laurie. 1998. The Unz/Tuchman "English for Children" initiative: A new attack on immigrant children and the schools. *Multicultural Education* 5 (Spring): 11–13.

Oran, Sally M. 2003. From the mountain to the mesa: Scaffolding preservice teachers' knowledge about the cultural contexts of literacy. In *Multicultural issues in literacy research and practice,* ed. Arlette Ingram Willis, Georgia Earnest Garcia, Rosalinda B. Barrera, and Violet J. Harris, 167–184. Mahwah, NJ: L. Erlbaum Associates.

Orr, Tamara. 2003. *Violence in the schools. Halls of hope, halls of fear.* New York: Scholastic.

Parille, Ken. 2001. "Wake up and be a man": *Little women,* Laurie and the ethic of submission. In *Children's literature,* vol. 29, ed. Elizabeth Lennox, Keyser, and Julie Pfeiffer, 34–51. New Haven, CT: Yale University Press.

Parker, Hershel. 1991. The price of diversity: An ambivalent minority report on the American literary canon. *College Literature* 18(3): 15–30.

Parker, Jessica. 2001. Language: A pernicious and powerful tool. *English Journal* 91(2): 74–78.

Paterson, Katherine. 1996. Cultural politics from a writer's point of view. In *Only connect: Readings on children's literature*, 3rd ed., ed. Sheila Egoff, Gordon Stubbs, Ralph Ashley, and Wendy Sutton, 343–349. New York: Oxford University Press.

Paterson, Sheryl Bender, and Mary Alyce Lach. 1990. Gender stereotypes in children's books: Their prevalance and influence on cognitive and affective development. Gender and Education 2(2): 185–197.

Paull, Laura. 2003. Letter to the editor. *Modesto Bee*, November 19, sec. B.

Peace begins with you. 1990. Children's Literature Reviews. *Children's Literature Comprehensive Database.* http://clcd.odyssi.com.

Peregoy, Suzanne F., and Owen F. Boyle. 1993. *Reading, writing, and learning in ESL: A resource book for K–8 teachers.* Tempe, AZ: Bilingual Press.

Perry, Theresa, and Lisa Delpit, eds. 1998. *The real Ebonics debate: Power, language, and the education of African-American children.* Boston: Beacon Press.

Peterson, Carolyn. 1975. A study of censorship affecting the secondary school English literature teachers. Ed.D. diss., Temple University.

Phelps, Ethel Johnston. 1981. *The maid of the North: Feminist folktales from around the world.* New York: Holt, Rinehart and Winston.

———. 1978. *Tatterhood and other tales: Stories of magic and adventure.* Old Westbury, NY: Feminist Press.

Phifer, Nan. 1994. Homophobia: The theme of the novel, *Jack. Alan Review* 20(2): 10. http://scholar.lib.vt.edu/ejournals/ALAN/winter94.

Pinsent, Pat. 1997. *Children's literature and the politics of equality.* New York: Teachers College Press.

Poarch, Renae, and Elizabeth Monk-Turner. 2001. Gender roles in children's literature: A review of non-award-winning "Easy-to-Read" books. *Journal of Research in Childhood Education* 16(1): 70–76.

Pollack, William. 1999. *Real boys. Rescuing our sons from the myths of boyhood.* New York: Henry Holt and Company.

Prater, Mary Anne. 2003. Learning disabilities in children's and adolescent literature: How are characters portrayed? *Learning Disability Quarterly* 26(1): 47–62.

———. 2000. Using juvenile literature with portrayals of disabilities in your classroom. *Intervention in School and Clinic* 35(3): 167–176.

Queer resource list. 2003. *Radical Teacher* 67: 30–31.

Quicke, John. 1985. *Disability in modern children's fiction.* Cambridge, MA: Brookline Books.

Quinn, Mary Ellen. 2000. *Lesbian and gay voices: An annotated bibliography and guide to literature. Booklist* 97(6): 668–669.

Radencich, Marguerite C. 1986. Literature for minority handicapped students. *Reading Research Instruction* 25 (Summer): 288–294.

Rainbow boys. 2005. *Book Links* 14(3): 34.

Rainbow boys (book review). 2001. *Publisher's Weekly*, November 26.

Rasinski, Timothy V., and Cindy Gillespie. 1992. *Sensitive issues: An annotated guide to children's literature K–6.* Phoenix, AZ: Oryx Press.

Rauch, Alan. 1989. A world of faith on a foundation of science: Science and religion in British children's literature: 1761–1878. *Children's Literature Association Quarterly* 14(1): 13–19.

Recommendations. 1998. *26th Congress of the International Board on Books for Young People. Peace through Children's Books. Proceedings.* New Delhi, India: Indian BBY, Association of Writers and Illustrators for Children.

Reichman, H. 2001. *Censorship and selection: Issues and answers for schools.* Chicago: American Library Association.

Reinstadler, Kym 2002. Potter book fight brews discord. *Grand Rapids Press*, January 4.

———. 2000a. Harry Potter backers push to get rid of ban. *Grand Rapids Press*, February 18.

———. 2000b. Harry Potter backers will confront school board over ban. *Grand Rapids Press*, February 18.

Religious Right groups join forces to select Texas textbooks. 2000. *Church & State* 55(9): 17–19.

Rice, Peggy S. 2002. Creating spaces for boys and girls to expand their definitions of masculinity and femininity through children's literature. *Journal of Children's Literature* 28(2): 33–42.

———. 2000. Gendered readings of a traditional "feminist" folktale by sixth-grade boys and girls. Special Issue: Reader Response. *Journal of Literacy Research* 32(2): 211–236.

Roberts, Patricia L., Nancy L. Cecil, and Sharon Alexander. 1993. *Gender positive!: A teachers' and librarians' guide to nonstereotyped children's literature, K–8.* Jefferson, NC: McFarland.

Robertson, Debra. 1992. *Portraying persons with disabilities: An annotated bibliography of fiction for children and teenagers.* 3rd ed. New Providence, NJ: Reed Publishing (USA).

Rochman, Hazel. 2003. Top 10 youth romances. *Booklist* 100(2): 235.

———. 1996. Just one flick of a finger. *Booklist* 92 (19–20).

Rodriguez, Luis J. 1999. *It doesn't have to be this way. A barrio story.* San Francisco: Children's Book Press.

———. 1993. *Always running: La vida loca, gang days in L.A.* Willimantic, CT: Curbstone Press.

Rosberg, Merilee. 1995. *Exploring language through multicultural literature.* ERIC Report. Cedar Rapids, IA. ED 389 175.

Rosenblatt, Louise M. 2003. Literary theory. In *Handbook of research on teaching the English language arts*, 2nd ed., ed. James Flood, Diane Lapp, James R. Squire, and Julie M. Jensen, 67–73. Mahwah, NJ: Lawrence Erlbaum.

———. 1991. Literary theory. In *Handbook of research on teaching the English language arts,* ed. James, Flood, Julie M. Jensen, Diane Lapp, and James R. Squire, 57–62. New York: Macmillan.

Rosendo, Miriam. 2000. Book browse: A creative approach to meaningful language learning. *Multicultural Teaching* 19 (Autumn): 33–38.

Rowling, J. K. 1998. *Harry Potter and the sorcerer's stone.* New York: A. A. Levine Books.

Rudin, Ernst. 1996. *Tender accents of sound: Spanish in the Chicano novel in English.* Tempe, AZ: Bilingual Press/Editorial Bilingue.

Rudman, Masha Kabakow. 1995. *Children's literature.* 3rd ed. New York: Longman Publishers.

Rutten, Tim. 2001. Weighing the classics. Whitman and Cervantes are out, but educators say California's new reading list is a serious blueprint for compromise in the culture war. *Los Angeles Times,* July 15.

Sachar, Louis. *Marvin Redpost: Is he a girl?* New York: Random House.

Salvadore, M. B. 1988. Review of *Fallen angels* by Walter Dean Myers. *School Library Journal* (June–July): 118.

Salwi, Dilip M. 1998. Peace through science fiction? In *26th Congress of the International Board on Books for Young People. Peace through Children's Books.* Proceedings. New Dehli, India: Indian BBY Association of Writers and Illustrators for Children.

Sanchez, Alex. 2005a. Open eyes and change lives. Narrative resources addressing gay-straight themes. *English Journal* 94(3): 46–48.

———. 2005b. *Rainbow Road.* New York: Simon and Schuster.

———. 2005c. *Rainbow High.* New York: Simon and Schuster.

———. 2001. *Rainbow Boys.* New York: Simon and Schuster.

———. 2004. Beheading images seen in classrooms. School district puts two on paid leave after complaints from students, parents. *San Diego Union Tribune,* May 15.

Saunders, Kathy. 2000. *Happy ever afters. A storybook guide to teaching children about disability.* Staffordshire, England: Trentham Books Limited.

Saxena, Ira. 1999. Indian children's stories through the centuries. *Bookbird* 37(2): 56–61.

———. 1998. A Ghandian way for children. In *26th Congress of the International Board on Books for Young People. Peace through Children's Books.* Proceedings. New Delhi, India: Indian BBY, Association of Writers and Illustrators for Children.

Saxton, Ruth O., ed. 1998. *The girl: Constructions of the girl in contemporary fiction by women.* New York: St. Martin's Press.

Schall, Janine, and Gloria Kauffmann. 2003. Exploring literature with gay and lesbian characters in the elementary school. *Journal of Children's Literature* 29(1): 36–45.

Scholes, Katherine. 1990. *Peace begins with you.* San Francisco: Sierra Club Books.

———. 1989. *Peacetimes.* Melbourne, Australia: Hill of Content Publishers.

Schon, I. 2005. *El gato garabato (The cat in the hat).* *Booklist* 101(13):1208.

———. 2004a. Libros de ciencias en Español. A selection of recent science trade books in Spanish. *Science and Children* (March): 43–47.

———. 2004b. Board books, supernatural tales and more: Children's books in Spanish. *Language* (February): 39.

———. 2004c. Latinos, Hispanics, and Latin Americans. *Book Links* (January): 44–48.

———. 2004d. Bilingual books: Celebration vs. confusion. *Booklist* 101(1): 136–138.

———. 2004e. *Recommended books in Spanish for children and young adults: 2000–2004.* Lanham, MD: Scarecrow Press.

———. 2003a. From the U.S. and abroad: Books in Spanish for children and adolescents. *Multicultural Review* (December): 43–46.

———. 2003b. Huicholes to Monstruos: Books in Spanish from Spanish-speaking countries. *Language* (November): 37–39.

———. 2003c. Noteworthy books in Spanish for adolescents. *VOYA* (August): 190–192.

———. 2003d. From Newbery winners to Islam. Books in Spanish for adolescents. *CR* 37(2): 40–43.

———. 2000a. From *Cinco lobitos to Los tres cerditos*: Children's books in Spanish from around the world. *Childhood Education*, 93–95.

———. 2000b. *Recommended books in Spanish for children and young adults, 1996 through 1999.* Lanham, MD: Scarecrow Press.

———. 1993. *Books in Spanish for children and young adults: An annotated guide.* Metuchen, NJ: Scarecrow Press.

School Law News. 2003. Court orders Harry Potter books back in Arkansas schools. May 31(5): 3.

Scieszka, Jon. 2003. Guys and reading. *Teacher Librarian* 30(3): 17–18.

———. 1989. *The true story of the 3 little pigs.* New York: Viking.

Sedgewick, Eve Kosofsky. 1998. How to bring your kids up gay. In *The children's culture reader*, ed. Henry Jenkins, 231–240. New York: New York University Press.

Senick, Gerard J., ed. 1978. Donovan, John 1928– . *Children's Literature Review* 3.

Seymour, Liz. 2002. Couple asks schools to get rid of nine books. *Washington Post*, December 1.

———. 2002a. Fairfax couple challenges schools' books; district to reconsider multi-layered system after examining list of 23 works. *Washington Post*, December 1.

———. 2002b. Graphic war novel to stay on school shelves despite protest. *Washington Post*, April 25, sec. 6.

———. 2001. A novel effort to ban books in Va.; Fairfax parents' group uses Web to push for school standards. *Washington Post*, June 17.

Short, Kathy G. 2001. Why do educators need a political agenda on gender? In *Beauty, brains, and brawn: The construction of gender in children's literature*, ed. Susan Lehr, 186–192. Portsmouth, NH: Heinemann.

Singh, Majari, and Lu Mei-Yu. 2003. Exploring the function of heroes and heroines in children's literature from around the world. ERIC Digest. Bloomington, IN: ERIC Clearinghouse on Reading English and Communication, 1–3. ED47709.

SLATE Support for the learning and teaching of English Newsletter. 1980. The attack on humanism (5): 9: np. http://www.ncte.org/about/issues/slate/sheets/108544.htm (accessed August 26, 2005).

Smallwood, Betty Ansin. 2002. Thematic literature and curriculum for English language learners in early childhood education. ERIC Digest. Washington, DC: ERIC Clearinghouse on Languages and Linguistics. ED470 980.

————. 1991. *The literature connection: A read-aloud guide for multicultural classrooms.* Reading, MA: Addison Wesley.

Smallwood, Betty Ansin, Wendy McDonell, Rob Clement, and Ruth Lambach. 1993. Ask the TJ. *TESOL Journal* 2(4): 45–47.

Smallwood, Betty Ansin, et al. 2002. *Integrating the ESL standards into classroom practice. Grades pre-K–2.* Washington, DC: Teachers of English to Speakers of Other Languages.

Smith, M. W., and J. D. Wilhelm. 2002. *"Reading don't fix no chevys": Literacy in the lives of young men.* Portsmouth, NH: Heinemann.

Smith-D'Arezzo, Wendy M. 2003. Diversity in children's literature: Not just black and white issue. *Children's Literature in Education* 34(1): 75–94.

Snicket, Lemony. 2001. *The ersatz elevator. A series of unfortunate events. Book six.* New York: Harper-Collins.

————. 1999. *The bad beginning. A series of unfortunate events. Book one.* New York: HarperCollins.

Stamps, Lisa. 2003. Bibliotherapy: How books can help students cope with concerns and conflicts. *Delta Kappa Gamma Bulletin* 70(1): 25–29.

St. Clair, Nancy. 1995. Outside looking in: Representations of gay and lesbian experiences in the young adult novel. *Alan Review* 23(1). http://scholar.lib.vt.edu/ejournals/ALAN.

Stelle, Lucinda C. H. 1999. Review of children's literature: Children with disabilities as main characters. *Intervention in School and Clinic* 35(2): 123–128.

Stott, John C. 1981. Literary criticism and teaching children. *Children's Literature Association Quarterly* 1: 39–40.

Strasser, Todd. 2000. *Give a boy a gun.* NY: Simon and Schuster Books for Young Readers.

Suhor, Charles. 2002. From the front line. Fewer calls, more book bannings—Why? *SLATE Support for the Learning and Teaching of English Newsletter* 27(3): 1, 6.

————. 2001. From the front line. No shortage of censorship calls. *SLATE Support for the Learning and Teaching of English Newsletter* 27(1): 1, 8.

————. 2000a. From the front line. Censorship cases up, way up. *SLATE Support for the Learning and Teaching of English Newsletter* 25(3): 1–3.

————. 2000b. From the front line. Recent *SLATE* anti-censorship actions. *SLATE Support for the Learning and Teaching of English Newsletter* 26(1): 1–3.

———. 1999. From the front line. Recent *SLATE* anti-censorship actions. *SLATE Support for the Learning and Teaching of English Newsletter* 25(1): 1–4.

Summer, Bob. 1995. Lambda Rising expands on AOL. *Publishers Weekly* 242(36): 24.

Susswein, Gary. 2002. Conservatives want to strip textbooks of facts, critics say. *Austin American Statesman*, November 13.

Sutton, 1994. *Hearing us out. Voices from the gay and lesbian community.* Boston: Little, Brown.

Swartz, Patti Capel. 2003. Bridging multicultural education: Bringing sexual orientation into the children's and young adult literature classrooms. *Radical Teacher* 66: 11.

Tamayo, Lincoln, Rosalie Porter, and Christine Rossell. 2001. The text of the Massachusetts initiative. An initiative petition for law: An act related to the teaching of English in public schools. http://onenation.org/matext.html.

Tatar, Maria. 1998. "Violent delights" in children's literature. In *Why we watch: The attractions of violent entertainment,* ed. Jeffery Goldstein, 69–86. New York: Oxford University Press.

Taxel, Joel. 1995. Cultural politics and writing for young people. In *Battling dragons: Issues and controversy in children's literature*, ed. Susan Lehr, 155–169. Portsmouth, NH: Heinemann.

Telescope, Tom, Oliver Goldsmith, and John Newbery. 1761. *The Newtonian system of philosophy: Adapted to the capacities of young gentlemen and ladies, and familiarized and made entertaining by objects with which they are intimately acquainted: Being the substance of six lectures read to the Lilliputian Society.* London: John Newbery.

Temple, Charles. 1993. "What if beauty had been ugly?" Reading against the grain of gender bias in children's books. *Language Arts* 70(2): 89–93.

Torres-Zayas, Adalin. 2004. *Current issues: Books in Spanish for young readers.* Workshop. Barahona Center for the Study of Books in Spanish for Children and Adolescents, California State University, San Marcos.

Torrey, Ruben Archer, and Amzi Clarence Dixon. 1910. *The fundamentals: A testimony to the truth.* Chicago: Testimony Publishing Company.

Town, Caren J. 2004. *The new southern girl.* Jefferson, NC: McFarland.

Tremmel, M. 2002. Censoring ourselves: Another side to book challenges. *SLATE Support for the Learning and Teaching of English Newsletter* 27(3): 1, 6.

Trites, Roberta Seelinger. 1997. *Waking Sleeping Beauty: Feminist voices in children's novels.* Iowa City: University of Iowa Press.

Truscott, Diane M., and Susan Watts-Taffe. 2003. English as a second language, literacy development in mainstream classrooms: Application of a model for effective practice. In *Multicultural issues in literacy research and practice,* ed. Arlette Ingram Willis, Georgia Earnest Garcia, Rosalinda B. Barrera, and Violet J. Harris, 185–202. Mahwah, NJ: L. Erlbaum Associates.

Valpy, Michael. 1996. Fathers fare poorly in children's books. In *Only connect: Readings on children's literature*, 3rd ed., Sheila Egoff, Gordon Stubbs, Ralph Ashley, and Wendy Sutton, 300–302. New York: Oxford University Press.

Vandergrift, Kay E. 1995. Female protagonists and beyond: Picture books for future feminists. *Feminist Teacher* 9(2): 61–70.

Von Drasek, Lisa. 2002. Boy, oh, boy—books! *Teaching PreK–8* 33(2): 72–73.

Wagner, Erica. 2000. Divinely inspired. *The Times* (London), October 19.

Walker, Carole, and Martha M. Foote. 1999–2000. Emergent inquiry: Using children's literature to ask hard questions about gender bias. *Childhood Education* 76(2): 89–91.

Walsh, D. 1998. San Francisco proposal is more extreme than others. *San Francisco Examiner*, March 13.

Walter, Virginia. 1998. *Making Up Megaboy*. New York: DK, Ink.

Ward, Cheryl Karp. 2001. It's a girl thing. *Voices from the Middle* 9(2): 64–66.

Wariner, Marina. 1996. The absent mother: Women against women in old wives' tales. In *Only connect: Readings on children's literature*, 3rd ed., Sheila Egoff, Gordon Stubbs, Ralph Ashley, and Wendy Sutton, 278–287. New York: Oxford University Press.

———. 1995. *From the beast to the blonde: On fairy tales and their tellers*. New York: Farrar, Straus, Giroux.

Washington Post. 1995. Deciding what to read. April 28.

Webb, C. Anne. 1995. Taboo curriculum. *English Journal* 84(1): 120.

Weinstein-Shr, Gail. 1992. *Stories to tell our children*. Boston: Heinle & Heinle.

Welsh, Patrick. 2002a. Why I teach "bad books." *Pittsburgh Post Gazette*, September 1.

———. 2002b. Not on the same page; some fear "bad books." I worry about unread ones. *Outlook*, June 30.

West, M. 1997. *Trust your children. Voices against censorship in children's literature*. New York: Neal-Schuman Publishers.

What is the best thing a teacher-librarian can do to encourage boys to read? 2003. *Teacher Librarian* 30(3): 32–33.

What to do until utopia arrives. 1976. *Wilson Library Bulletin* 50(7): 532–533.

Wilder Gish, Kimbra. 2000. Hunting down Harry Potter: An exploration of religious concerns about children's literature. *Horn Book Magazine* 76(3): 262–272.

Wilhouite, Michael. 1990. *Daddy's roommate*. Boston: Alyson Wonderland.

Williams, Stanley "Tookie." 1996. *Gangs and violence. Stanley "Tookie" Williams, with Barbara Collman Becnel*. New York: Rosen/Powerkids Press.

Witeck, Bob. 2001. Their only mysteries themselves. *Lambda Book Report* 10(2): 21.

Wittlinger, Ellen. 1999. *Hard love*. New York: Simon and Schuster Books for Young Readers.

Wolf, Shelby Anne. 2004. *Interpreting literature with children*. Mahwah, NJ: Lawrence Erlbaum Associates.

Woodson, Jacqueline. 1995. *From the notebooks of Melanin Sun*. New York: Blue Sky Press.

———. 1991. *The dear one*. New York: Delacorte Press.

Wullshlager, J. 1991. Twilight of the enchanters. *London Financial Times*, March 30.

Yampell, Cat. 1999. Alyson Wonderland publishing. *Bookbird* 37(3): 31–33.

Yasuda, Gene. 1988a. Teacher panel resists censorship call, wants book to stay on required reading list. *Los Angeles Times*, December 18.

———. 1988b. Controversial autobiography book is cut from list at Vista schools. *Los Angeles Times*, November 18.

———. 1988c. Angelou book's listing in curriculum attacked. *Los Angeles Times*, October 17.

Yolen, Jane, et al. 2002. How books tell the world's bad news to children. *Lilith* 27(3): 32–39.

Zaleski, Jeff. 2001. Religion notes. *Publisher's Weekly* 248(15): 72.

Zipes, Jack. 1996. Taking political stock: New theoretical and critical approaches to Anglo-American children's literature in the 1980s. In *Only connect: Readings on children's literature*, 3rd ed., ed. Sheila Egoff, Gordon Stubbs, Ralph Ashley, and Wendy Sutton, 365–376. New York: Oxford University Press.

———, ed. 1986. *Don't bet on the prince: Contemporary feminist fairy tales in North America and England*. New York: Methuen.

Zvirin, Stephanie. 2001. Top 10 gay and lesbian books for youth. *Booklist* 97(19–20): 1863.

Index

academic freedom, 17

ADHD (attention deficit hyperactivity disorder) in literature, 72, 79, 80

adventure stories, 85

African American speech, 41, 42, 46–47

age appropriateness, 19, 54

Alice's Adventures in Wonderland (Carroll), 24

All We Know of Heaven (Bridgers), 54

Always Running: La Vida Loca, Gang Days in L.A. (Rodriguez), 58, 62–64

American Civil Liberties Union (ACLU), 17

American Library Association (ALA), 5, 14, 17, 29, 34

Americans United for Separation of Church and State, 29, 32

Angelou, Maya, 18

Annie on My Mind (Garden), 105

anti-gay stereotypes, 103

antisexist books, 89

Association for Library Services to Children, 5

autism in literature, 72

Baskin, Barbara, 70, 71, 76, 77

bibliotherapy, 54, 61, 73

bilingual education, 39, 40–41

bilingual literacy, 45

bilingual literature, 39, 41, 44, 58

Bin Laden, Osama, 32

Blaska, Joan, 73, 79–80

blindness in literature, 70, 72, 75

Block, Francesca Lia, 88, 108–109

book challenges
    background and history of, 13–15
    case studies, 16–19, 34–35, 62–64, 114
    gay literature, 105, 106–107, 114
    handling, 15–16
    on religious grounds, 25, 26, 27–28, 34–35

book databases, 6, 7

booklists, 4–5, 6–8, 95–96

book reviews and reviewing sources, 5–6, 16

Boston Globe-Horn Book Awards, 5

Boy Meets Boy (Levithan), 109

boys and sexism, 91–92

boys' literature and reading habits, 85, 92–93, 96–97

Bridgers, Sue Ellen, 54

Bridge to Terabithia (Paterson), 27

bullying in literature, 53, 54, 61

Bunch, Gary Owen, 72, 73
Byars, Betsy, 81, 82

Caldecott Medal, 5
California Department of Education, 6, 7–8
canon, classic literary, 1, 4
Canterbury Tales (Chaucer), 6
Carroll, Lewis, 24
Catcher in the Rye (Salinger), 27–28
censorship, defining, 14, 16
Charlie (fictional character), 81, 82
Children's Literature Association, 4
Chocolate War (Cormier), 27, 55, 59–60
Christian Coalition, 30
Christian fundamentalism, 26, 29, 34
Columbine High School killings, 58
coming of age, literary treatment of, 94
conflict resolution, 58, 60, 92
    See also peace in literature
contemporary classics vs. historical fiction, 94–95
content analysis, 79–81
Coretta Scott King Award, 5
Cormier, Robert, 27, 55, 59–60
creationism, 28, 29
critical literacy, 2

Daddy's Roommate (Willhoite), 106, 107
Dana, Mary, 34–35
Darwin, Charles, 28
Day, Francis Ann, 112, 113
deafness in literature, 72
democratic values in literature, 13–14
Dewey, John, 25
dialects, 41, 42
DICSEY Code, 78–79
disability, fear of, 78
disability as symbolism, 75, 76
disabled people
    discrimination against, 74, 75
    mainstreaming of, 69, 70, 73
    stereotyping of, 69–70, 74, 75, 76, 78, 80
disabled people in literature
    awareness raising, literature role in, 73–74
    bibliographies, 70–72
    discussion and analysis of, 75–76
    evaluating and selecting titles, 72–73, 76–81

history of, 69–70
    sociopolitical contexts, 74–75
divorce in literature, 104
domestic violence in literature, 54
Donovan, John, 104
Drew, Nancy (fictional character), 94
Druids (Llewelyn), 17
dual-language books, 39, 44, 58

Eagle Forum, 30, 32
East of Eden (Steinbeck), 28
East Side Dreams (Rodriguez), 63
Ebonics, 41, 42, 46–47
Elementary and Secondary Education Act
    (ESEA), 39, 40
emancipatory fiction, 89
English-only laws, 39
equality in literature, 13–14
ethnic diversity in literature, 1, 6–8
evolution theory, 28–29, 33

fairy tales, 75, 93–94, 108
fantasy, 24, 26–27, 34–35, 61, 77, 94
fathers in literature, 92
female characters in literature, 86, 89–90, 93
feminism and literature, 86, 87, 88–90, 93–94
fiction, 2, 24, 55, 89, 104
    See also historical fiction; science fiction
Firestarter (King), 27
folktales, 93–94
Fox, Mem, 2, 86, 87, 97
Frankenstein (Shelley), 25
freedom to read, 14–15
Freedom to Read Foundation, 29, 34
fundamentalism, 26, 29, 34

gangs in literature, 53, 57, 58, 62–64
Garden, Nancy, 105, 108, 109, 113
Gay, Lesbian, Bisexual, Transgendered Round
    Table (GLBTRT), 111–112, 113
gay and lesbian presses, 106
gay students, school environment of, 109–111
gender-fair teaching, 86, 87–88, 91
gender identity, 85, 90–91, 94
gender issues in literature
    analysis and title selection, 86–87, 88, 95

bibliographies, 95–96
history, 85–86, 89, 94–95
gender stereotypes, 85, 86, 88, 93
See also sexism in literature
girls
and feminism, 89–90
literature and reading habits, 85, 90, 93, 94, 96
GLBTQ literature
evaluating and selecting, 109, 111–113
history of, 103–109
nonfiction, 108–109, 111
teacher use of, 110–111
good and evil in literature, 26, 34, 60
Grapes of Wrath (Steinbeck), 27
gun violence, 58–59

Hamilton, Virginia, 2, 86–87, 88, 94
Handler, Daniel (a.k.a. Lemony Snicket), xx
Happy Ever Afters. A Storybook Guide to Teaching Children about Disability (Saunders), 76
Harris, Karen, 70, 71, 76, 77
Harry Potter series, 26–27, 34–35
Heather Has Two Mommies (Newman), 95–96, 106–107, 112–113
heterosexism, 109
Hinton, S. E., 54, 55
His Dark Materials series, 27
historical fiction, 61, 77, 94–95
history textbooks, 30–33
HIV/AIDS in literature, 53, 58, 72, 105, 108
Homes, A. M., 105, 111
home schooling, 29
homophobia, 103, 104, 109–110, 111
Horn Book, 5, 112
horror novels, 55
Huckleberry Finn (Twain), 6
humanism, 24, 25
humor in literature, 61

I Am the Cheese (Cormier), 59–60
IDEA (Individuals with Disabilities Act), 69, 70
I Know Why the Caged Bird Sings (Angelou), 18–19
I'll Get There, It Better Be Worth the Trip (Donovan), 104

I'll Love You When You're More Like Me (Kerr), 104
independent reading, 45
intellectual freedom, 14, 17
International Board on Books for Young People (http://www.ibby.org), 53, 57, 60
International Children's Digital Library (http://www.icdlbooks.org), 6, 30, 45, 47, 48
Islam in literature, 30, 32
It Doesn't Have to Be This Way. A Barrio Story (Rodriguez), 58

Jack (Homes), 105, 111
Jenkins, Christine, 112, 113
Jewish literature, 61, 77
Justice and Her Brothers (Hamilton), 94

Kerr, M. E., 26, 104, 105
Kids, Disabilities and Regular Classrooms: An Annotated Bibliography of Selected Children's Literature on Disability (Bunch), 72
King, Stephen, 27, 55

language skills, 44
learning disabilities in literature, 72, 79, 81–82
LeGuin, Ursula, 26, 88–89
L'Engle, Madeleine, 26
Lesbian and Gay Voices: An Annotated Bibliography and Guide to Literature for Children and Young Adults (Day), 113
Levithan, David, 109
Lewis, C. S., 26, 27
linguistic transfer, 40, 41, 43
Lion, the Witch and the Wardrobe (Lewis), 26
literary analysis and criticism, 3
literary awards, 5, 81, 82, 105, 108, 111, 113
literary bilingualism, 41
literary quality
determining, 1
disabled, works on, 82
in gay literature, 108, 112, 113
and language, 43
vs. political correctness, 2
Llewelyn, Morgan, 17

Macbeth (Shakespeare), 27
MacDonald, George, 24
male characters in literature, 91–92
Mann, Horace, 28
Margaret A. Edwards Award, 105, 108
McDonnell, Nick, 55
McGuffey Eclectic Readers, 28
Mellon, Constance, 77–78
mental retardation in literature, 72, 80
Merchant of Venice (Shakespeare), 27
Michael L. Printz Award for Excellence in
        Young Adult Literature, 5, 108
Milton, John, 25, 27
minority representation in literature, 1, 6–8, 77
Muggles for Harry Potter, 34
multicultural education, 30, 39, 44, 77
Muslims in literature, 30, 32

National Book Award for Children's Books, 5
National Council of Teachers of English
        (NCTE), 5, 14, 16, 25, 34, 41
natural disasters, 57
Newbery, John, 28
Newbery Medal, 5, 81, 82
Newman, Leslea, 106, 107, 112–113
Newtonian System of Philosophy (Newbery), 28
Night Kites (Kerr), 105
No Child Left Behind Act (NCLB), 40
non-English language books, 39, 40–41, 42–43,
        45–46
nonfiction, 57–58, 107–108, 111
nonsexist books, 89
nonviolence in literature, 56
        See also peace in literature
Notes from a Different Drummer (Baskin and
        Harris), 71, 75, 76

Office for Intellectual Freedom (OIF), 14
Outsiders (Hinton), 54–55

Paradise Lost (Milton), 25, 27
Parents against Bad Books (PABBIS), 16–18
Paterson, Katherine, 2–3, 26, 27
peace in literature, 53, 54, 56, 60
        See also conflict resolution
PEN American Center, 30, 34

People for the American Way, 14, 30
picture books, 43, 58, 59, 81, 106–107
polio in literature, 70
political correctness, 2–3
political elements in literature, 87, 112–113
Prater, Mary Anne, 79, 80, 81
ProFamily Forum, 30
Pullman, Philip, 27
purpose of literature, 1–3

racism in literature, 3
Rainbow Books (series), 114–115
rape in literature, 17, 18
reading lists, 4–5, 6–8, 95–96
realism in literature, 53, 54–55, 56, 57–60, 61
        See also gender issues in literature; GLBTQ
                literature; violence in literature
religion
    and fantasy, 24, 26–27, 34, 35
    fiction, influence on, 24
    textbooks, influence on, 24, 28, 29, 32–33
religious characters in literature, 71
religious freedom, 23–24, 29
religious literature, 24, 25, 26, 30
Religious Right, 26–27, 31–32
Robertson, Pat, 26–27
Rodriguez, Art, 63
Rodriguez, Luis, 58, 62, 63, 64
Romeo and Juliet (Shakespeare), 6
Rowling, J. K., 26, 34
Rylant, Cynthia, 26

Sadako and the Thousand Paper Cranes (Coerr),
        56
Salinger, J. D., 27–28
Sanchez, Alex, 114–115
Saunders, Kathy, 76, 79
Schon, Isabel, 42–43, 44, 45–46
school shootings, 58
science, 24
science fiction, 25–26, 55–56, 77
science textbooks, 28–29
Scieszka, Jon, 96
Scopes, John Thomas, 29
Scott O'Dell Award for Historical Fiction, 5
second-language development, 42

secular humanism, 24, 25

selection policies, 15

self-censorship, 14, 33

self-confidence and language, 45

self-reliance in literature, 13–14

September 11, 2001, 23, 53

Series of Unfortunate Events (Snicket), 60, 61

sexism in literature, 88, 89, 91–92, 97

　　See also gender stereotypes

sexual content in literature, 17, 18, 63

sexual orientation, 7

Shakespeare, William, 6, 27

Shelley, Mary, 25

SLATE Support for the Learning and Teaching of English (newsletter), 16, 25

Snicket, Lemony, 60, 61

social issues in literature, 53–54

　　See also gender issues in literature; GLBTQ literature; peace in literature; realism in literature; violence in literature

social responsibility, teaching, 2

Social Responsibilities Round Table, Gay Task Force (GLBTRT), 111–112, 113

social sciences textbooks, 30–33

Spanish-language books, 40, 42–43, 45–46, 47–48

Steinbeck, John, 27, 28

stereotyping, 2, 41

　　See also anti-gay stereotypes; disabled people, stereotyping of; gender stereotypes

Stinky Cheese Man and Other Stupid Fairy Tales (Scieszka), 96

Stonewall Book Award, 113

subtractive bilingualism, 40

Summer of the Swans (Byars), 81–82

Sutton, Roger, 112

symbolism, disability as, 75, 76

Texas, 30–33

Texas Education Agency (TEA), 31

textbooks, 24, 28–29, 30–33

thematic book grouping, 44

Tomas Rivera Mexican-American Children's Book Award, 5

Tom Telescope (fictional character), 28

translation, literature in, 39, 42–43

True Story of the 3 Little Pigs (Scieszka), 96

Twain, Mark, 6

Twelve (McDonnell), 55

unhappy endings, 54–55, 59–60

violence in literature, 14, 34, 53–54, 55, 57, 60–61

　　See also gangs in literature; gun violence; rape in literature

war stories, 53, 54, 56, 61, 92

Wicca and witchcraft, 26, 27, 34

Willhoite, John, 106

world religions, 30

Young Adult Library Services Association (YALSA), 5

young adult problem novels, 104

young people as authors, 44, 55, 57–58

Zeeland, Michigan, 34–35

About the Author

LINDA SALEM is the children's literature subject bibliographer at San Diego State University, location of the National Center for the Study of Children's Literature. She has been an education librarian for many years and teaches education courses. She began developing the essays and cases for this book while teaching children's literature at University of Redlands. These materials provide instructors with subject coverage and activities not found in standard children's literature texts.